THE CITY GARDEN BIBLE MATT JAMES

THE CITY GARDEN BIBLE

SIMPLE SOLUTIONS FOR SMALL SPACES

MATT JAMES

TRANSWORLD PUBLISHERS
61-63 Uxbridge Road, London W5 5SA
a division of The Random House Group Ltd

RANDOM HOUSE AUSTRALIA (PTY) LTD
20 Alfred Street, Milsons Point, Sydney,
New South Wales 2061, Australia

RANDOM HOUSE NEW ZEALAND LTD
18 Poland Road, Glenfield, Auckland 10, New Zealand

RANDOM HOUSE SOUTH AFRICA (PTY) LTD
Isle of Houghton, Corner of Boundary Road and Carse
O'Gowrie, Houghton 2198, South Africa

Published 2005 by Channel 4 Books
a division of Transworld Publishers

A catalogue record for this book is available from the British Library.
ISBN 1905 026048/9781905 026043

Designed and typeset by Smith & Gilmour, London

Printed in Germany

1 3 5 7 9 10 8 6 4 2

Papers used by Transworld Publishers are natural, recyclable products made from wood grown in sustainable forests. The manufacturing processes conform to the environmental regulations of the country of origin.

CONTENTS

CHAPTER ONE
REFLECTIONS OF A CITY GARDENER

OPPOSITE A 'garden' is where you make it!

OVERLEAF Stand out from the crowd.

People garden everywhere, in places you'd least expect. It's sad that so many, like my friends, think a garden proper is merely a piece of land out the back and feel short-changed about what they have. All you have to do to get yourself out of this mind-set is sit up and look around you. Your strip of soil absolutely doesn't have to be at ground level. On my travels I've seen incredible gardens growing on Thames houseboats, pavements in Vauxhall (south London), atop converted churches, up on the highest windowsills and balconies and down in the lowest basements. Gardening is for everyone – no matter where you live.

This little chapter is all about some of the city spaces and places I've been 'wowed' by on my travels and some of the favourite spots where I like to hang out. Admittedly, it's only a small slice and much of it is London-based, but please don't feel excluded if you live outside the capital – you might have the very garden that'll wow my socks off, but it's just that I haven't seen it yet! I make no apologies for mentioning London nurseries either, simply because I actually use them and, hey, I'm a Londoner!

NOSY NEIGHBOURS

For many of us who have tiny gardens, the huge country park or grand National Trust estate can offer little when it comes to inspiration and ideas for our own city spaces. So why not go and see your neighbours' gardens instead? Combining gardening with good deeds, the National Gardens Scheme encourages ordinary gardeners to open their gardens to the public on special days throughout the year, and do it all for charity. The scheme has been going for seventy-five years and now has over 3,500 different gardens signed up. Look by the till at your local garden centre for a copy of 'The Yellow Book' (or as it's officially entitled, *The Gardens of England and Wales Open for Charity*). This is their annual publication which lists what's open and when, countrywide.

Go on, forget lying in bed all weekend, go and have a nosy round other people's gardens. Not only will you see how people like yourself have tackled their spaces, but what could be more delightful in summer than to pay these wonderful gardens a visit, and have afternoon tea (and perhaps buy a few plants raised by the owner) into the bargain! Most of these gardens haven't been created by designers or professionals, but people like you and me. A lot of them are in cities and the owners are really proud to show off what they've achieved, often in the most inhospitable of places.

Talking to anyone who cares passionately about their garden is the best way to get the creative juices flowing, plus glean some useful tips. Gardeners are often only too happy to share their successes and talk about their failures because gardening is, of course, a social 'sport'. For little more than £2 entrance money you'll learn so much you'll become an addict.

MARINER

GROW YOUR OWN

OPPOSITE No garden? No problem! How about an allotment?

Having your own little patch of land to grow your food on goes back to medieval times. Around 1000AD the local community cleared areas of woodland and the land was shared out between them, but it wasn't until 1887 that the Allotment Act came into force, and as a result, local authorities are now obliged to provide allotments for the communities they serve.

Of course, allotments really came into their own during World War Two, when every bit of available land was used to grow food; even football pitches and parks were requisitioned for the 'Dig for Victory' campaign that supported the war effort. For a while their popularity declined, perhaps because of the unjustified stigma attached to them. But now they're back with a vengeance and there are long waiting lists for city allotments as I write. So get your name down quick, but be patient! You do need to be dedicated to your allotment and prepared to give it time on a very regular basis. To be honest, when I first started mine I just couldn't give it enough but, fortunately my girlfriend's taken over now, and boy, does she run the show! Don't be daunted at the prospect of lots of work, allotments are fantastic places packed with people with incredible gardening know-how that's not in any book, and most are more than willing to help any newcomer find their gardening feet.

One place everybody's talking about is the Coriander Club in Islington. On a patch of land in north London a group of Bangladeshi women are growing their own Asian and English veggies and working together with terrific community spirit. Apparently they started humbly by growing foodstuffs in window boxes at their flats, but they wanted to expand and now they have polytunnels full of veggies. They are also running workshops on all things gardening. I haven't been there yet because I've been flat out this year – but I shall.

TREE-HUGGERS UNITE!

Trees have always been my particular passion. I can't give you a ream of reasons why they grab me more than anything else in the world of plant species out there, because ultimately I don't know why they do! I guess I noticed their size, shape and variety at an early age and they affected me in some profound way that I just can't ignore – much like the enthusiast who grows nothing but auriculas or sweet peas.

Trees are so vital in cities. In the countryside, like in Somerset where my mum lives, they are almost taken for granted. Huge willows line all the roads down in that part of the West Country, and no-one gets worked up about them simply because there are so many. In the heart of the city, though, a tree is that much more precious because there are so few set amongst the dominant concrete cityscape. And these trees aren't poor relations either; many are magnificent mature specimens worthy of space in an arboretum.

THE ULTIMATE AIR FRESHENERS

So, the facts first. Trees purify the air, cleaning it of harmful carbon dioxide and carbon monoxide. They hide unpleasant eyesores, they soothe with all that wonderful green and they create an aura of stability and permanence around them. In Ashcombe Road next to Carshalton Park, near where I grew up, have a look at the sweet chestnut trees. You won't find better – even in the countryside. These monsters are ancient, with their gnarled, contorted trunks and twisted limbs, but fortunately the local council have allowed them to age with all their dignity intact. The shapes they have made in their dotage are incredible; so see them while you can. Sights such as this are rare to find in a suburban landscape where everything seems to be municipally managed. Again in Carshalton, see if you can spot the giant plane tree by the ponds. It's the biggest I've ever seen! Just how many people have sat underneath its shade and taken it for granted? If you want to find this favourite of mine, it's opposite the back entrance to the ecology centre, you can't miss it. Go on – give it a hug!

Plane trees are synonymous with London. They just 'fit' all the requirements of city living. Tolerant of airborne pollution, they actually exfoliate in order to cope with the clogged air; they cast off not only their leaves but the bark, too, so they can breathe through unclogged pores. I love the big lime-green, maple-shaped leaves, the bark that looks like a soldier's camouflage and the sheer generosity of size. Planes are statuesque giants, and I'm forever in awe of them for the fact that they still survive, indeed positively thrive, in the most polluted areas of London, with such grace.

MY FAVOURITE THINGS

If you are standing on Putney Bridge, look to the west for the rows of plane trees lining the River Thames. Have you noticed them? Every year on 5 November I go there to watch the fireworks. My girlfriend and I take comfort in a pint while the focus of our attention on this cold, and often rainy, night is the fireworks bursting forth from Bishops Park. Admittedly, we can't see the Catherine wheels, but large mortars punch into the air above a row of ginormous plane trees and the shadows cast by the light on these hulks are eerily beautiful. The trees are perfectly backlit by the illuminated sky and I spend more time looking at the trees themselves than the bursts of red, orange, yellow and blue. During the day it's a lovely place to walk, too. Start by Putney Bridge and walk down to Fulham football stadium, on either side of the river.

If the tree bug has bitten you, visit the Chelsea Physic Garden next time you're in the centre of London. This walled garden was founded in 1673 and is second only to the one in Oxford, which is the oldest botanical garden in England. However, it boasts the oldest olive tree in the country and many other early introductions, too. A visit in July is recommended for the Indian bean trees alone. In this 3.5 acre site (tiny for a garden crammed so full with trees and plants), you'll find an oasis of horticulture that, in my opinion, is unsurpassed in London. What excites me is that you just stumble across it if you've not been there before. The high brick walls give no indication as to the treasures within, and all you can see from the outside is the tantalising glimpse of the tallest trees above the walls.

One of my favourite trees is *Parottia persica*, commonly known as the Persian Ironwood. This broad-spreading tree (which belongs to the witch hazel family) could almost be a huge shrub as it fans out so much wider than it is high. In autumn it colours brilliant reds and yellows, and mature trees have flaking bark similar to the London plane. There's a huge specimen at RHS Wisley, in Surrey, but none have excited me more than the one I found at Dublin Botanical Gardens, purely by chance. A group of us had arrived in preparation to see in the millennium in style but found that most of the city, including the pubs, was shut (in Ireland?!) due to some silly overtime dispute.

ABOVE One of our most precious native trees, beech has an other-worldly presence in our landscape like no other tree.

Stuck with nothing to do on a rainy New Year's Day I dragged my mates to the botanical gardens. There, in front of a large ornate glasshouse was a huge parottia (which almost made me forgive Dublin its mean opening hours). I've a picture up in the bathroom at home of me standing in front, wet through, but grinning like a Cheshire Cat. If you don't mind missing a Guinness (or three), you know where to go, and if you do visit, look for the dramatic stand of silver birch, too.

Beech is another favourite tree of mine. If oak is the 'King' of trees, beech is undoubtedly the 'Queen'. An oak always looks slightly grumpy in comparison to a magnificent beech tree alive with autumn colour. Like oak, beech takes an age to mature but does so in a truly regal manner. I love the fresh, early spring leaves. They have to be the purest green ever as they emerge from the buds beautifully translucent, a little down on their surface and looking almost too delicate to survive spring gales and rain. Snoozing under a beech tree in early spring is magical!

Richmond Park is my local chill-out zone. Because of that, it's probably my favourite place in London. I love its sheer size (over 2,500 acres) and silence – yes, silence! If you cycle into the middle you'll think you are in the country. A curious sight are the trees, all neatly levelled off underneath. Not the work of a team of gardeners with shears, but rather the nibbling of countless deer. I always head straight to the wooded Isabella Plantation and usually to my favourite beech, which is hidden from the main paths by oaks, Lawson cypress, elderly silver birches and overgrown *Rhododendron ponticum*. It's a true hulkster, and one with the most perfect shape imaginable. I used to collect the beech mast as soon as it fell and sow the seeds wherever I could find space at my dad's. The Isabella Plantation has a lot of fine specimen trees too, among them *Nyssa sylvatica* – the tupelo tree, *Liquidambar*, a wonderful *Prunus serrula* with its unbelievable polished red-brown bark, and a collection of snake bark maples to die for. Do go along in February for the witch hazels in full flower, or for its famous rhododendrons and azalea collection. A woodland oasis amongst the oaks and bracken, the Isabella Plantation is an incredibly tranquil place, even when packed with Sunday walkers. Go and recharge your batteries there – just stay away from my beech!

THE OLD ONES ARE THE BEST

It sounds a little morbid, but old graveyards are brilliant places for tree-spotting as most are generally left alone to do their own thing. This is the place to seek out mature yews. I can never quite work out whether I'm soothed by these trees or a little frightened by their sombre, heavy presence.

BELOW *Parottia persica*, commonly known as the Persian Ironwood, isn't a tree for a small garden which is a shame as the autumn colour is exquisite.

ABOVE Sweet chestnut is a real spiky customer, but at least you can eat the fruit.

Southampton has some superb ones. Next to Southampton Common, and not too far from the Cowherds pub, you'll come to a cemetery that is full of enormous catalpas, sweet chestnuts and monster yews. Mortlake Cemetery, near Kew Gardens, is worth a visit if you're on a tree pilgrimage too – look for the giant redwoods if nothing else. Although thats a contradiction in terms, because you can't miss 'em!

Quercus ilex, or the Holm oak, is a tree steeped in history. There's a huge one in Valance Park, East London, but it's not the oldest I've seen. The one in Fulham Palace Park is 320 years old. For the oldest gingko I've ever seen, go to West End Park in East London; it's described as being over 240 years old. West End Park also has two very rare oaks – *Quercus* 'Fulhamensis' and a very old *Koelreuteria paniculata*, or 'golden rain tree'. In April and May the cherry blossom is breathtaking. The Corporation of London also holds the national collection of *Liquidambar* there, too. If you go during early autumn you'll witness one of the most spectacular displays of seasonal colour you could wish to see. The vibrant red and purples of the dying leaves is just, well, gob-smacking. The liquidambar cultivar 'Worplesdon' was actually found at Merrist Wood College where I was once a student, although unfortunately I'm not responsible for its introduction. West End Park is a bit of an underexposed, not-so-popular-as-it-should-be park; something that should change.

If you're a fan of the elm, go to The Meadows in Edinburgh. Huge, beautiful billowing specimens surround this park near the hospital. Some have fallen victim to the dreaded Dutch elm disease, but the ones which remain are just so redolent of the countryside as it used to be years ago that you must see them before they go. In London, look for the 'Wembley Elm' in front of The Greyhound pub in Wembley. What a whopper, and so lovely to see a tree which has almost died out throughout the country thriving in such an inhospitable location.

I must bring in 'Trees for Cities' here. They are an independent charity devoted (and I mean devoted) to planting up our cities with as many trees as the urban landscape can support. Every year they campaign strenuously for a green renaissance in cities throughout the country, and more recently throughout the world, too. In June 2002 they launched a campaign to plant another 1 million trees by 2010. As part of this they're planning a yearly 'tree-athlon' a 5km run in Battersea Park. As I write in 2005, I have been roped in for this. Hey, I'm a horticulturalist, not a marathon runner, so don't expect too much in the way of a result!

SHOPAHOLIC?

C'mon, retail therapy is how many of us relax, so don't knock it, and what better to spend your readies on than plants that'll benefit not just you, but your neighbours, the local community and the environment as well.

ABOVE **Make plant shopping a real experience, head down to a street market like this one at Columbia Road in east London.**

ROLL UP, ROLL UP!

The definitive place to buy plants in London has to be at Columbia Road street market. It is to be found between Gosset Street and The Royal Oak pub in E2, and if you get there at 8am on a Sunday morning you'll find yourself pushing and shoving with all the other plantaholics that London is home to. Do arrive early, or get there late-morning and be prepared to miss the best bargains, because at 10-11am it's often so rammed its almost impossible to get through the crowds. It is literally packed – and I do mean packed – every week. Why? Look no further for cheap bedding plants, exotics, grasses, orchids, cut flowers, cacti, houseplants, perennials, herbs. You name it, it's probably there. Add in the odd live band and the pubs opening early for bacon sarnies and you have a bo-ho treat. In addition, all the shops lining the main and side streets are mini horticultural paradises and will tempt you despite all your resolve. This is real impulse-buy territory – I've been seduced there

so many times. Once I fell in love with a bright purple metal watering can and when I went back to buy it I found it had disappeared. Fortunately, one of my friends had bagged it for me already!

Columbia Road is just like a traditional market, with some East-End voices still shouting bargain prices above the hubbub, but it serves a contemporary buying public. It's got to be one of the coolest weekend places to shop – and then stop at a nearby pub.

Early risers only, please, at the New Covent Garden flower market on Nine Elms Lane. This is the place for the freshest cut flowers at wholesale prices. Sample the atmosphere, listen to the stallholder's cheeky talk, and look up a bargain. For competitive prices in topiary, climbers established on frames and manicured evergreens, look no further. The market opens at 5am, and this is the time to arrive.

URBAN NURSERIES

Unlike large out-of-town 'department' stores, urban garden centres are *the* place for those with an investigative nature. The benefit of going to a city-based garden centre is that the people who run them also garden in the city and therefore they understand the pitfalls of this type of gardening better than anyone. I'm close to the Fulham Palace Road Garden Centre, which supports a charity called Fairbridge for disadvantaged children. This little goldmine is just down from Bishops Park, so take a walk through the park, and while you're there, have a look at the superb allotments opposite the tennis courts. Beautiful pots, especially terracotta, feature strongly at this garden centre, but they're not cheap. What also stands out for me is the quality and variety of roses, climbers and houseplants. If you like your plantaholic's paradise to be densely packed and feel like a treasure trove, this is the place for you.

In nearby Richmond you'll find the wonderful Petersham Nurseries which, despite having been recently refurbished, still remain delightfully old-fashioned. This nursery also has one particular ethic: all plastic is banned! There are no plastic pots or plastic twine tying plants into supports here, it's all clay, metal, raffia and hairy string. The place has a definite image and is conscious of promoting it – sort of back-to-nature but ultra-chic at the same time. They also do reclamation yard stuff and antiques in the main glasshouse. Here, the big overhead fans remind me of those TV programmes about the Raj in India. (One feels one should be wearing khaki whenever one comes for tea!) The cafe sells fabulous award-winning food and delicious juices as well. I like the casual-chic, non-uniform tables and chairs, the gravel floors, and the overhead shade created by 'opaque' bamboo screens. Close by the nurseries is the Palm Centre in Ham – a wow of a place for all things exotic, including bananas, bamboos, tree ferns and, of course, palms. If you want something a bit different, pay them a visit.

ABOVE ***Buddleja*** **is a real urban toughie and a favourite with butterflies.**

Sheen Garden Centre is another local haunt for me, and for a city garden centre it has a superb plant collection. It's a place for the serious gardener who's done their research and knows what they want.

But the very best one of the bunch for me has got to be Clifton Nurseries in Little Venice, W9. They have got everything, I can't remember a single time that I've been there and come away empty-handed. The staff are fantastically knowledgeable and genuinely enthusiastic. This is a gem: no big roadside frontage, instead you have to walk down a little alley lined with potted olives and *Hydrangea anomala* subsp. *petiolaris* until you come upon it, tucked away, like a gardeners' dining table spread with plant goodies. Great for big plants to give your garden an instant feeling of maturity, but keep a tight grip on your wallet!

Out of London, gardeners in Leicester have the wonderful 'Outer Eden', a contemporary garden store in Stonygate owned by Matt Sellicks, who sources rare stuff from abroad as well as this country. Great modern furniture is his speciality – everything from plastic bubble chairs to ultra-contemporary sleek metal or aluminium ones, and he's hot on lighting, pots and modern objects d'art too. If you can't get to Leicester, you'll catch him at the Grand Design Show in London.

CLOSE ENCOUNTERS OF THE UNEXPECTED KIND!

As you travel to work on the train, wherever you are in the country, look at the railway sidings as you go. In July and August the buddleia will be in flower everywhere – what a sight. These huge drooping mauve panicles seem to attract all the insect life around. If I was a butterfly I'd go by train! This is a tough plant, often the first to colonize derelict land, and therefore a good plant for city gardens simply because of that built-in toughness and drought resistance. All it needs is some vicious pruning in early spring and then it just romps away.

If you're up at Waterloo or the South Bank in London, take a closer look at the Imax theatre, and in particular around the base of the tower. The cinema itself pops out of the middle of a roundabout and you can drive round the top and also walk underneath it. Honeysuckle, ivies, jasmine and Virginia creeper grow partway up the tower on wire supports which splay down like the ribbons on a maypole. The shade underneath this canopy is welcome and if you look up it feels like you're in a jungle – not what you would expect to see in this particularly gloomy part of town. Even the avenue leading up to the London Eye, next to Jubilee Gardens, is worthy of a second glance. From the Waterloo end there's an avenue of pleached hornbeams to keep you company as you approach.

The Embankment is one of my favourite places to walk, especially on the Chelsea side. Instead of walking along the pavement, I often go on the opposite side of the road to look at the gardens. Here you'll see ornate railings and balconies smothered with wisteria, tiny parterres and wonderful bedding displays against a notable backdrop of good old London planes.

'PARK' OF THE SOLUTION

British municipal gardening must be the most heckled horticulture on the planet! Those displays of brilliant scarlet salvias and blue ageratums in lurid borders in parks or on roundabouts are, for the most part, taken for granted or even sneered at. But municipal gardening has a difficult, if not impossible, task – to please all of us all the time, and to provide displays that last for ages. Roundabouts and roadside verges are great places for plant inspiration because the plants are chosen specifically with neglect and extreme pollution in mind. Pleasing everyone is a tall order, so perhaps we should be less condemnatory.

No longer is municipal gardening stuck in the dark ages, either; gone are the flat displays of monochromatic pelargoniums in soulless lines. It's a sweeping generalization, I know, but park flower beds used to be pretty dire and predictable and nobody paid much attention to those boring bedding displays. You can still find them, of course, but now things are so much more exciting. Parks departments seem to be experimenting, which is great news.

Most local authorities used to have their own 'in-house' nursery where all the seasonal bedding throughout the borough was grown. Unfortunately, these nurseries have all but disappeared and now big contractors are used instead. It is, sadly, another example of centralization killing passion and inspiration. Nevertheless, don't knock the parks departments, because they are still champions of city horticulture.

Britain in Bloom is a yearly competition run by the Royal Horticultural Society where parks departments, private individuals and local groups alike are involved in the regeneration of their local environment. The aim is to contribute imaginative planting of trees, shrubs, flowers and landscaping in each village, town or city.

ABOVE **A stone's throw from the River Thames is one of the capital's most treasured gardens; The Chelsea Physic Garden. Go there and it's easy to see why.**

Bath city centre is renowned for its bedding displays, as are Cheltenham and Gloucester – the latter has had fabulous tulips in recent years. Glastonbury, where my mum lives, used to be pretty dull, but now you notice the hanging baskets and lamp-post baskets throughout the town more than you do the not-so-nice areas. In fact, the towns in the West Country are renowned for their community displays. But, for me, the best bedding display to date has to be in Swanley, in Kent.

I go there three times a month on business to visit a nursery, so I see what's going on throughout the year. And it's impressive. Wherever you look you'll see something floriferous: baskets, wall baskets, huge troughs on top of railings and bus stops, planted up verges and roundabouts. Even shops have big tubs bursting with bedding outside – the best way to jazz up a dour shopping precinct. There's colour everywhere. Recently, I drove through the town for two and half miles and couldn't spot a single lamp-post *without* a vibrant hanging basket wrapped around the middle.

ABOVE **Urban regeneration at its best. Amazingly, the 'waves' in the centre are the original level of the park, and to the left and right is the new level.**

PARKLIFE

Syon Park is a beautiful old country-house-style park in Brentford. It's opposite Kew, but it's definitely not as busy. From here you can see the magnificent Palm House in Kew Gardens it's one of the best viewing places. The gardens at Syon were designed by 'Capability' Brown and include lakes, fine trees and wonderful vistas over 55 acres. The conservatory, with its domed roof, houses a dreamy collection of scented plants and exotics. Avoid the adjacent garden centre if you want to stay solvent!

Mile End Park in the East End's Stepney is well worth a visit. Designed in 2000 as a Millennium Commission lottery project, it's essentially a series of smaller parks that lead the eye to Canary Wharf. It actually spans the Mile End Road and a special bridge designed by Piers Gough takes you from one side to the other. This bridge, called the 'green bridge', sports grasses, silver birch and numerous wild flowers – I barely realized I was walking over a bridge until I looked down! There's an ecology centre, an arts area, terraced gardens with weirs and a children's park, so devote a whole day to exploring the lot, if you can.

Thames Barrier Park is also a relatively new park. It grew out of the huge flood barrier that was begun in 1982. The area – a pretty grim industrial wasteland and disused dockyard – was demolished and instead of carting

MY FAVOURITE GARDEN

I couldn't write about urban horticulture without mentioning my favourite small garden: York Gate, near Leeds. It's owned by a horticultural charity called Perennial, the new name for the Royal Gardeners' Benevolent Society. Apart from the quality of the planting or the clever use of both common and unusual materials, there's a wonderful feel to this place which, in my opinion, is exactly what a garden is all about. That said, it's well planned, with different parts cleverly divided into rooms. For city gardeners, it's an ideal place to go and get inspiration: especially on the correct positioning of focal points, how to inspire movement, and how to successfully create all-important tension and surprise in a small space. Living in London I haven't been back for a while, something I must remedy soon.

away all the old building materials to a landfill site outside the capital, the whole lot was dumped on top of the construction site where the barrier was assembled. The park was created on top of this – think of how much topsoil was needed. Literally tons and tons! The most dramatic part of the park is the green dock with its hedges clipped to resemble the waves of the sea. Here, you'll actually be standing at the original level of the whole park. The rest of the park above you is created from infill with rubble and brick.

If you want to see some of the largest nursery-grown, containerized trees to be planted in an urban regeneration project, come to Jubilee Park, part of the Canary Wharf complex. One hundred and fifty odd dawn redwoods have been planted here, although admittedly some are struggling. However, it's a bold project and it needs to be: the buildings all compete for dominance, so the gardens beneath have to possess a feisty, bold modernity to complement them. The planting is sparse, but well thought out: grasses and reeds sway alongside the watercourse and modern drifts of tough shrubs grow elsewhere. The twenty-two natural-limestone, interconnecting pools invigorate the air and serve to break up the space.

You can't miss Ron Arad's sculpture 'The Big Blue' in Cabot Square, which is just round the corner from Canary Wharf. The remit for this site is well met, in that it provides somewhere for office workers to relax and take time out from their toils. Most of the day the place is quiet, but at lunchtime in summer it's heaving as people pour out of the surrounding office blocks, like one big human tide.

CHAPTER TWO
CONCRETE JUNGLE?

WILLIAMSON

If you think about it, the words 'city' and 'gardening' seem to be a bit of a contradiction in terms. In the rush to create the dense housing developments where the majority of us live, the idea of garden spaces appears to be way down the list of priorities. Contemporary city living seems to be more about flats than ever before. For the past thirty years these have been going up at a terrific rate throughout the country; some have balconies, some don't even have those.

But this new style of city living increases our need for green spaces to act as a balance to all the concrete surrounding us. These outside areas should be considered a necessity, not offered as a token gesture. Planners, architects and all those involved in building our cities should weave gardens into their designs as an absolute, not as an afterthought.

BRING ON THE GOOD LIFE

According to research done in 2004 by the soup folks, Heinz, 71% of people would like to grow vegetables if they had access to more garden space. Among 16–24-year-olds this figure rises to 78%, proving that younger people are getting a taste for gardening and that it's even becoming, dare I say it, 'trendy'. What's even more interesting is that 56% of city people say they'd like to grow vegetables more than they would like to have barbecues and entertain friends. Bring back Tom and Barbara!

URBAN EDEN

So, will we see this happening? The good news is, yes, we will. There are already many exciting developments and regeneration schemes springing up which take full account of the fact that our mental, physical and spiritual well-being depends on contact with nature, no matter how small our allotted parcel of land. City gardening is on the move, and it's changing. Those grim high-risers of the 60s, when developers thought vertical cramming was the way to house people, are being replaced with developments where aesthetics are a defining factor. Back in the 60s gardening was seen as unnecessary hard work, not as a life-enhancing or trendy thing to be doing – apart from, of course, meditating on orange flowers and zoning out to Jefferson Airplane. So, what's changed?

RURAL HEAVEN?

As the pace of life increases, so too does the desire for areas in which to relax. It's often not an option any more to jump in the car and drive out into the country for a fix of green. Increasingly, city people want to have a slice of quality outdoor-living on their doorstep. And those people, like you and me, have a voice now – and a very powerful one at that.

A lot of city people feel they're missing out on country life. They dream of being self-sufficient and living off the land, keeping chickens and bees and growing their own vegetables and fruit. This siren call makes us feel wistful but, in reality, the 'good life' is extremely hard work and not for everyone. If you're going to be infected by the call to the wild, I'll bet it's strongest in spring and summer when nature is at its best. I also bet a muddy, damp autumn and winter don't figure much in your thinking!

Apparently, one in four people think their garden is 'too small'. But, whatever size your garden, the city is blooming and I hope this book will show you more ways you can improve your outdoor space, large or small.

ABOVE City dwellers have the best of both worlds: unique garden spaces and the hustle and bustle of the city on your doorstep.

I LOVE THE CITY AND I LOVE GARDENING

I live in the centre of London in a flat with a small shady balcony and a stairwell for a garden and an allotment – but I don't feel restricted. I still grow loads of my favourites: box topiary, hostas, bleeding heart, brunnera, grasses, ferns, lily-of-the-valley, *Daphne odora* 'Aureomarginata', lemon verbena and *Pittosporum tobira*, to name but a few. I'm also a lily freak and love to grow them in pots – even though they don't seem to do too well for me, I still persist. I have some exciting houseplants, too: *Gomphrena globosa*, with its lurid purple drumstick flowers, *Cyrtanthus elatus* (the Scarborough lily), and good old *Tradescantia* 'Purple Heart' are today's favourites. And whilst I'm boosting my ego, I have two clivia to die for!

Admittedly, sometimes my ambitions to grow something get frustrated because of lack of space but, on balance, I don't feel short-changed. Far from it, I love city living – where else can you be spoilt for choice when you want to eat out? I have at least 20 restaurants to sample, all virtually on my doorstep. I can go clubbing if I want to, and walk there and home again afterwards; the local pub really is just around the corner, and there are loads of places to have coffee and meet up with friends. I'm five minutes from the Thames and a morning's meander along the river, and I'm 20 minutes from the centre of town. Yes, the city really speaks to me: it's my kind of place.

But what about gardening – I love that too – and the one complaint of city people everywhere, that they don't have enough space? It might seem that the issue would be a simple one: if I like gardening and growing plants then I should move to the country, whereas if I'm a city dweller I should think of the culture instead and forget about the plants. This is so much rubbish! I think it comes from the erroneous idea that big is always better. It isn't.

SMALL IS DEFINITELY BEAUTIFUL

In one sense, the tinier your garden space the luckier you are, because you have the opportunity to make *all* of it top-notch without too much effort. It's a bit like decorating: a small room is manageable and so all the little bits that come under the umbrella of 'finishing off' get done, whereas with a larger project we often run out of steam before it's finished and the details get skimped. When a task is too big, a kind of tunnel vision creeps in, and tatty areas can stay like that for years because we neatly edit them out and just don't see them any more. Having little space to play with also helps knock down your wish list – that impractical Jacuzzi might have to be shelved, likewise the 50-foot-high concrete rocket! Small spaces help you to carefully

critique any decision and ultimately make the whole process more manageable. But not only are small gardens easier to manage, they're cheaper too. Our money goes a lot further; that expensive terracotta pot or mature 6-foot tree fern is often well within the reach of those with a small garden, whereas those with larger spaces have to stop and think because they need so much other stuff.

ABOVE Whilst tiny gardens mean you can go to town design-wise, sometimes nothing beats the quiet restraint of something a little more traditional.

Small city gardens also enable you to be radical. Come again? Well, actually most innovative or cutting-edge garden designs are born in the city. Many materials which are often too expensive to use on a large scale were first used experimentally in city gardens, and often with stunning results. Contemporary hardware like steel, aluminium, glass and plastic are now familiar to us all, due to innovative urban-garden designers. This desire to be different helps us to break convention which, arguably, isn't so easy to do in the country. A Moorish garden may well look out of place in the country, but in the city and the 'burbs it's fine, because by their very nature cities are eclectic and cosmopolitan; they are made up of so many different cultures and styles that anything goes. Therefore a myriad design styles and garden themes happily live out there in city-garden land: Mediterranean, Japanese, Italian,

Baroque, cottage, naturalistic, Modernist, Minimalist, Deconstructivist, formal, informal, Victorian, Edwardian, classic, neo-classic – the choice is bewildering.

I'm not knocking country gardens in the least, but I do sometimes feel that city folk appreciate the green they've got rather more than those who are surrounded by acres of it. In a shortage economy you tend to be aware of your blessings and not take the little you have for granted. It's very uplifting to have your attention caught by a tiny slit of green jazzed up with splashes of colour on the side of a tower block – somebody's really made an effort there and we admire them for it. Take this further and you'll be amazed at how and where people garden in cities: on roofs, at the kerbside, along narrow passageways and up ladders! Discovering a successful garden where it seems impossible for anything to grow is sheer delight.

City gardening *is* more challenging, but I'm going to stick my neck out and say that, because of that, it's more rewarding: it makes you think long and hard about how to use your space effectively, rather than being blasé about it, and thinking gets your creative juices going. You need ingenuity, sleight of hand and eye, and a whole host of other skills; things we all have but sometimes don't bother to use. The sense of achievement you can get from gardening in the city is one of the most positive feelings I know. I certainly don't want to move away; I'd miss the buzz and the enormous variety that London gives me. And I can have my garden and eat it, too.

NATURE'S SPIRIT

Contact with nature is very important to our well-being. Nature on your doorstep, nature which you have a hand in encouraging, will give you a regular buzz, recharge your batteries and make you feel spiritually in touch with forms other than concrete ones. The garden is your doorstep sanctuary. Gardening s l o w s . . . y o u . . . d o w n . . . That's vital if we're not going to keel over from overwork and stress. Align yourself to The Slow Movement – stop focusing on your goals and what's to come and, rather, enjoy the process of getting there.

The garden is always changing, is never static; following the pace of the seasons is the sensible way to live if we want to stay healthy. If we went along with nature – coming to life in spring, slobbing out and enjoying summer and being less active in winter – we'd be more balanced. A garden lets you plug into all that and, because it's your own space, you get to know it well. Appreciating the intimacy of Mother Nature will become second nature to you.

SLOW UP, SLOW DOWN – WHAT GARDENING WILL DO FOR YOU

Gardening can have a very positive effect on your life – as long as you take it slowly. Everything, but everything, is just moving so fast these days it's hard to keep up. Doing the garden should be a time when you let your hair down, go at your own pace and have no-one to measure up to. Quite a few people have said to me that television makeover programmes – mine included – make them feel they've got to get out there and do up their gardens double quick! I'll admit that the emphasis does seem to be on getting the job done as quickly as possible, often with the clock ticking away, but do recognize that that's simply 'TV' – where entertainment and the over-used media trick of 'jeopardy' (what I call the 'will-they/won't-they like it' syndrome) is perceived to be more important than the gardening. But, while some programmes are, admittedly, a bit OTT and others over-simplify the whole thing, they've also had an important effect: they've made the public realise what *can* be done in the average garden, the small garden, the city garden. Just remember: you don't have to go at the speed of the average makeover crew!

'If we went along with nature – coming to life in spring, slobbing out and enjoying summer and being less active in winter – we'd be more balanced.'

My mum complains that gardening has become too hasty, too commercial, but not just as a result of television. 'There used to be nice little nurseries selling nothing but plants,' she says, 'and now all they sell is soft toys, Christmas decorations and pet food.' This might be true, but there are still scores of specialist nurseries around which are well worth hunting out. I suppose, too, that a lot of people want to make a day out of buying plants, and a coffee and a cake can be a welcome break from deciphering Latin names. Whilst somewhat damaging to the traditional nurseryman and women, however, these new gardening 'superstores' do illustrate one thing: gardening has never been more popular.

OPPOSITE Picture returning home from work after a stressful day and kicking back in your own urban oasis.

GARDENING AS THERAPY

Don't underestimate the importance of your city garden. Honestly, it might sound like a cliché, but making a garden and looking after it will change your life. In the first series of *The City Gardener*, Brum-living Rob just wanted a decent outdoor space to entertain in and pretty much nothing more. Easy come, easy go, easy maintenance. But then the mysterious gardening bug bit him and now he's collecting fuchsias – what happened there?

Gardens shouldn't always be perfect places, like the kind of house where you feel you have to take your shoes off on the doorstep, or are frightened to sit down because it's so tidy. Instead, the garden should be a space where you can relax your grip. After all, nature will have its own way whether you want it to or not. The best way to enjoy gardening is to have a relaxed attitude towards it, not treat it as a race to get to some non-existent finish-line as fast as you can. A lot of people have told me that they find gardening to be a spiritual activity. Well, monks and nuns have gardened for centuries, and their gardens have a particularly calm atmosphere which must be a joy to work in. But, whatever your definition of spiritual, there's no doubt that the garden can be a place to let your worries return to the earth where, as my mum says, they're 'harmlessly neutralized'.

Pottering is the best therapy for a stressed mind that I know. You get so immersed in the activity and so caught up with the insects and birds going about their lives around you, that time seems to slow down. I predict that gardening will be seen more and more as therapy in the years to come – perhaps doctors will even write the odd prescription for getting your hands dirty!

THE GARDEN IS A NECESSITY

For city people, the garden is more than just an oasis. In recent years, having any size of outdoor space has become important. Why? Housing prices have rocketed and many people have found that, although they want to move, they can't. This is why you see skips and scaffolding on every back street in London

or Manchester: people are extending their properties up, down and sideways – and out – outdoor space is definitely 'in'.

Years ago, if you had what was designated 'the garden', you kind of stared at it and felt that at some time you'd have a go and turn it into something 'garden-y' and nice. I've seen a lot of gardens like that, where the owners have fallen into the trap of thinking that they must simply conform. Usually these places just end up as a store for the bins and other rubbish and might sport a couple of dusty shrubs and a few sad-looking pansies in pots. I've got friends who often want to blot out the space altogether; they don't know what to do with it and, as time goes by, they find themselves apologizing and saying the same old things: 'I must get round to the garden', 'it's too much work', 'it's too overgrown', 'it's too big', 'there's too much shade', 'nothing grows', 'it's basically a loo for the neighbours' cats', 'the kids constantly mess it up kicking a ball around', 'there's nowhere for the kids to play', 'there's nowhere to sit'. Sounds familiar? In the minds of so many people, the word 'garden' has become synonymous with chore and burden. I hope you'll get inspired to change that.

You don't need to feel guilty if all you want to do is use your outdoor space for socialising or catching a tan. On my travels I've seen gardeners get just as much enjoyment from a terraced sun-trap as they do from the adjacent planting. And that's just fine – at the very least they're outside and using the space.

GARDENS ARE 'OUT', OUTDOOR ROOMS ARE 'IN'

In recent years there has been a revolution in how city gardens are approached. Think of it like this: if you cut out the word 'garden'and substitute 'outdoor room' instead, it's immensely freeing and just leaps with potential. Wow. Maybe now you can actually do something with that little piece of Britain you previously felt guilty about; not only have you found a real use for it, but it can actually add value to your home.

The idea of the outdoor room is, of course, nothing new – people in hotter climates have 'lived' outside for years – but it's a helpful way to look at your own garden space. So, move up, move down and now move out – but stay in the same place. In short: expand. The outdoor room is simply an extension of the house where you can carry on activities you might do in your kitchen or living room; like cooking, entertaining, reading the papers and, in some cases, even watching television. By echoing the interior décor outside, the boundary between house and garden gets blurred, making both spaces seem bigger.

City gardens are no longer about a few plants and the garden shed: there's so much more you can do with an outdoor room. Keep the weather out by covering it completely with glass: many back garden areas sport modern purpose-built conservatories where people and plants share the same environment. Pergolas and overhead trellis can define space both vertically and horizontally while also giving privacy and shade when smothered with climbing plants. Many gardens have been entirely paved or decked, removing the lawn-mowing chore for ever and giving a safe, clean surface to walk on barefoot or to use to display an arrangement of pots, or simply somewhere to while away hot summer evenings with a barbecue, a few beers, and a group of friends. Simple lighting will encourage you to spend time outside well into the evening, and add a heater or a fire pit and on cold days you can still eat alfresco.

A typical garden only gets used for five, maybe six, months of year when the sun's out; an outdoor room can be used for double that amount of time. From March to October the family can spread out and enjoy a lot more freedom. Even in winter the space becomes a 'picture' made up of bulbs, winter perennials and flowering shrubs that will cheer up grey days immensely and remind us that spring is just around the corner.

ABOVE Gardens are for living, and in this entertaining space plants play a supporting role.

ABOVE Grasses and architectural plants need little maintenance and this garden goes to show that low maintenance doesn't mean boring.

NOT INTERESTED IN GARDENING? JOIN THE CLUB

Not everybody who has an outdoor space wants to be a gardener. That may be an unusual thing to say in a book about city gardening, but I do acknowledge the fact that a lot of people simply have no interest in gardening at all. It's not a crime. The last thing I want is for you to feel guilty about *not* wanting to be a garden-freak – it just isn't everyone's cup of tea. *But*, I defy anyone to say they don't want or won't enjoy an attractive, versatile, functional green space outdoors. If you are put off by doing-it-yourself or the planning stage seems daunting, you could employ a garden designer and builder to construct and plant up the outdoor room. You won't have to lift a finger until it's all done, and even then you can reduce the amount of maintenance work by automating the watering systems. Even if you've had no hand in making it, or know absolutely nothing about plants, you and your friends and neighbours will definitely still enjoy it. And maybe, like Rob, the bug will bite and nobody will be more amazed than yourself. I'll make a bet with the most disinterested gardeners on the planet: you won't regret making your backyard into a city oasis.

TO DESIGN OR NOT TO DESIGN?

When I ask people what they most want from their outdoor space, one answer crops up more than any other: they want somewhere to entertain. Within this brief, they also want somewhere to feel proud of and, dare I say it, somewhere which will impress. Nothing wrong with that! Then, in the next breath, their faces drop, they go all serious and they say, 'but I don't know what to do with my garden. I'm hopeless at design.' Then they add, 'I want something that's easy to maintain.' And why not? I'm all for that.

Why are so many people fazed when it comes to design? Design seems to be the subtitle to so many television programmes and books, all showing how wonderful gardens can be achieved if only you've got an artistic 'vision' or you're good with a sketch book. Don't be daunted; you don't need to know how to draw or how to run up detailed, scaled diagrams to be able to design a garden.

Start by demystifying the design process and think about how you decided to decorate your house: you probably chose the paint, bought some matching cushions and curtains, made the fireplace into a focal point and pulled the whole look together as harmoniously as you could. You know when something isn't right, you just do. Trial and error mean that eventually you'll end up with something pleasing and something that reflects your taste. So it is with the garden – just apply the same principles you used when designing your interior.

BELOW It's so easy to over-design, feeling that you should put in a wealth of plants and features, but sometimes less is most definitely more.

'ORGANIC DESIGN'

Whilst I believe that small gardens need careful forethought, some of the best gardens I've seen have been those that 'sort of grew' of their own accord – rather like old cottage gardens fifty years ago. These gardens were simply created with gravel or ash paths and were packed with plants. Today, we'd say they were organic in their development: they just happened naturally, without the gardener working out where to plant his annuals or vegetables. Plenty of mistakes were made – with plants put in places they didn't like – but there was no disaster; they were just hoiked out and moved. Trial and error was the traditional, relaxed way of our gardening forefathers. They grew what they needed to eat, along with plants to treat common ailments, herbs for the cooking pot and flowers just for scent and beauty.

If you can draw, that's great; you can have fun drawing pretty pictures and plans, but even when ideas leave the drawing board for the real world, many of them get altered. Plans always change. Design doodles are useful in that they help you collect your thoughts and ideas together and they can give you the feeling that you're in control of the project. Think of them as an aide-memoire, something which helps you make sense of your needs and wants.

Of course, like I said before, you can use a professional designer – and for those who are too busy, having an expert control the whole thing does take away some of the stress and hassle. But if you've only got a small balcony or tiny courtyard, you really don't need to shell out for a professional; get inspiration from your neighbours, gardening magazines, television programmes and the like. Visit your local library and gen up with gardening books – then you can enjoy the kudos of doing it yourself!

LOW MAINTENANCE – RELAXATION PRIORITY

Today, low-maintenance gardens are a good idea for city dwellers, not a dirty word for work-shy gardeners. We can all do with a break when it comes to taking on extra work. Those who go out to work all day or travel a lot don't want to come home to a garden that makes too many demands on them; they simply don't have the time or the energy. Don't forget that not everybody wants to emulate Gertrude Jekyll's Monet-like perennial borders, although they appreciate what they see in other people's gardens. Even if you have got oodles of spare time there's so much to do in the city that you want to be able to take advantage of it all, not spend every weekend doing the garden. After all, there is absolutely nothing wrong with appreciating your garden from a deckchair.

ABOVE A garden like this needs lots of looking after and, personally, this is just my cup of tea.

HIGH MAINTENANCE – PLANTAHOLIC PRIORITY

Of course, the opposite is also true, some people just love plants; they are addicted to them and spend weekends sourcing rare and unusual varieties. They might design themed gardens based on one colour, become obsessed with growing one particular plant to the exclusion of all others. Or they pore over plant catalogues, buy all their snowdrops 'in the green' and have windowsills you can't see in or out of for plants. Plantaholics don't have a twelve-step programme, though some of them might feel they need it. I'm poking fun here because in reality the plantaholic is a delightful gardener, someone who'll give you advice on when to prune roses and will leave clumps of hearty perennials wrapped in wet newspaper on your doorstep. They actually *need* to have lots to do in the garden and are never happier than when tending to their plants, whatever the weather. My point is that neither approach is wrong. You can do as much or as little as you want, but at least do something.

NOT GARDENING SNOBBERY, SURELY?

OPPOSITE On this balcony large plants add instant impact. Why wait ten years for a *Trachycarpus fortunei* (Chusan palm) to reach this height when you can enjoy it straight away?

I really think it's time we completely clobbered some of the snobby notions around gardening. They do exist, even as a faint echo at the back of the minds of those who live in the heart of the city. This ghost speaks of only country gardens being 'real', and everything else merely a preposterous stab at the proper gardens. But city gardening is not the poor relation of country gardening – it's a different breed altogether.

The truth is that most of us live in cities and very few of us live in stately homes with lots of manpower. In centuries past, gardening was seen as a leisure activity – though how much hands-on gardening the actual owners did is a moot point – and, more importantly to these grand estate owners, was a way of showing off their huge disposable income. The legacy of those times is with us today in the form of National Trust gardens and estates which are maintained by passionate, enthusiastic plants-people, and they are beautiful places to visit. But to think that if you only have a balcony or a couple of windowboxes means you're not a gardener is rubbish. Gardening is about enjoying yourself, whether growing plants, enjoying wildlife, getting some exercise or simply breathing the outdoors, and you can do that anywhere, in almost anything. Size really doesn't matter, it's what you do with it that counts.

Buying semi-mature plants can be a tricky (and costly) business. For complete peace of mind, always go to a specialist nursery as they will be able to give invaluable advice on what plant goes where and how to handle them. Most will deliver, too – transporting whopper plants is difficult to say the least, so take advantage of the professionals!

Snobbery also extends to instant gardens – the sort where semi-mature trees and huge shrubs arrive on a truck and are crane-lifted into a garden. It might be expensive, but the result is a fully mature garden that looks as though it's been there for years. If you're impatient for a lovely garden and willing to spend money on getting one straight away, then go for it. There's no doubt that a garden made this way has 'instant' appeal. The 'wow' factor of using huge specimen maples, palms, bamboo and even ginormous topiary spirals (very expensive!) is immediate, and the effect these monsters give is something to be proud of, not – as some purists would have us believe – something to be ashamed of simply because we haven't done all the work.

Perhaps what drives the snobs to turn up their noses is just this: envy. They really do want a mature-looking garden, but masochistically feel they have to wait years to get there. Purists need to loosen up and let other gardeners do it their way; there's masses of room for us all.

My belief is that whatever you do gardening-wise that gives you pleasure is 100 per cent right. Every small plant nurtured, or every large plant tended adds immeasurably to the greening of our cities, and it doesn't matter at which end of the scale you begin the process.

DO YOUR BIT

Of course, city gardening isn't just about merely enhancing the spiritual well-being of a few people like me; greening the city is for the good of everyone. I'm a firm believer that city dwellers have an obligation to hide the flat, featureless grey of our cityscape. Green spaces, be they public or private, help create a sense of community, give us something in common, help slow us down, and take us back to nature. So, do your bit.

Town planners and developers may grudgingly give new affordable housing the smallest possible outside space, but that doesn't mean we should approach our gardens or balconies with the same mind-set. Meet the challenge with gusto: think big, encourage urban wildlife, mark out a space for the kids to play safely, create somewhere that'll make you smile every time you set foot in it.

Chances are I'll never have a big garden; chances are I'll always live in the city; chances are I'll never get my bloody frangipani to flower! I know one thing, though – the city gives me all I need, and more, and being a part of the great city green-up is definitely where it's at.

'City gardening is more challenging, but because of that, it's more rewarding: it makes you think long and hard about how to use your space effectively, rather than being blasé about it, and thinking gets your creative juices going. You need ingenuity, sleight of hand and eye, and a whole host of other skills; things we all have but sometimes don't bother to use. The sense of achievement you can get from gardening in the city is one of the most positive feelings I know.'

CHAPTER THREE
CHARACTERISTICS OF CITY SPACES

OPPOSITE **Every garden has 'challenges', a tall ash, surrounding buildings and changes of level feature here, but they have become part of the design instead of fighting against it.**

CITY PROBLEM?

I don't like the word 'problem'. Somehow, when you hear it, you feel a slump in energy and a sort of 'uh-oh', 'oh-no' stream of thought kicks in. In short, you think you're going to be faced with something that you just can't do. 'Problem' seems like an insurmountably high brick wall. However, substitute it with the word 'challenge' and suddenly everything seems brighter. 'Challenge' has a hopeful ring, there's room for you to actually do something. That wall now has a door – you just need to find the key.

There's no doubt that city gardens have their fair share of challenges – some of which can make growing plants particularly tricky – but even country gardeners have challenges. Depending on what you want to do, *any* area is a challenge – if you simply must grow tender exotics outdoors in northern Scotland, you're going to find your gardening experience very challenging (or problematical) indeed.

In part, the reason we sometimes perceive the garden as a problem is due to wanting our own way too much, when what we should be doing is working with the characteristics and ecology of our gardens. Whilst plants are amazing in that many will often survive in even the most inhospitable places, we do also need to be realistic. If your garden is a wet and shady site you'd be better off choosing bog plants, and if it's hot and sunny go for drought-tolerant lavenders, Californian lilac or rosemary – plants that originate from hotter climates. It might seem obvious, but if you plant sun-lovers in the shade they are going to sulk mightily, whereas shy shade-lovers faced with blazing sun are just going to curl up and probably die on you. Make gardening easy on yourself: work with nature, not against it.

There's always some clash of interest between how and where to incorporate plants and how you would actually like to use the garden, especially for city people where space is limited. Everyone craves a seating area in a sunny corner, but what happens to that sun-worshipping loquat tree you want, where does that go? A compromise has to be reached, and it might mean sacrificing that tree for one that tolerates the shade in another part of the garden, leaving you free to soak up the sun instead.

OPPOSITE Where else could you grow bananas if you don't live in Costa Rica? Why, in a city garden, of course!

WHAT'S GOING ON IN THE GARDEN?

In addition to your regional climate, every garden has its own complex, thriving miniclimate and, just like a jigsaw puzzle, it's made up of different pieces. Factors like aspect, wind exposure, tree cover, topography, soil type and soil pH all affect this microclimate and they all combine to influence what you can grow in the garden successfully. In city gardens, surrounding buildings and pollution levels also come into the mix. It's the combination of these factors which gives your garden its unique character; learning what that is and understanding how it can work for you is vital to having a glorious garden.

However, for many people, the successful city garden isn't just about healthy, beautiful plants; how much you actually use and appreciate the space is an important element, too. Ask most people who've yet to tackle their city garden what they think their biggest challenge is and one of the first things they'll say is, 'we're overlooked by our neighbours', or, 'everyone can see in', or, 'it's too noisy'. Poor access, security, noise pollution, eyesores and lack of privacy are all issues which many city folk think are more important than those factors that will directly affect their plants. This is, perhaps, understandable, for it's the presence of these challenges that determines whether we even go outside in the first place.

This chapter talks about all the things that make city gardeners groan and that they cite as problems. In the spirit of the garden pioneers, I'm going to refer to them as challenges. In this chapter we'll identify what's on the ground but later on, in Chapter Five, I will offer some solutions for specific city gardens.

GET TO KNOW YOUR GARDEN

Unless you have a dark, sheltered basement or an exposed, sunny balcony, city gardens usually have more than one microclimate. For example, a south-facing garden may have trees on a railway embankment which overhang the bottom of your garden, meaning you'll probably have to contend with dry shade as well as a hot, south-facing house wall. Get to know the complexities of your garden's character and how all the individual features interact, then you will get the very best out of the deal.

GEOGRAPHICAL LOCATION

Where you live in the country has a significant impact on the types of plants that you can grow successfully, as well as on the length of your growing season – i.e., the length of time that your plants are actively growing. If you live in the less clement conditions in the north of the country or on a hilltop, chances are that your growing season will be three or four weeks shorter than if you live down in the south of England or by the sea.

In addition, your geographical location also determines the time of the first and last frosts. Gardeners always want to know an approximate date for the first frost so that they can wrap up tender tree ferns, tuck houseplants back inside and over-winter dahlia tubers. Knowing the time of the last frost in spring is important, too, because it's not until it has passed that half-hardy bedding plants can be planted outside and tender exotics, such as *Brugmansia*, *Cassia*, and *Hibiscus rosa-sinensis*, can be brought out of the greenhouse or conservatory. Again, both these dates vary a great deal from region to region, year after year, so there is no hard-and-fast rule, except to keep an eye on the local weather forecast. As a rough guide, the last frost is usually around the beginning to the middle of May and the first frost usually hits at the beginning of October but, of course, it does depend upon where you are.

TEMPERATURE

Cities are several degrees warmer than the surrounding countryside – good news indeed. It doesn't take a rocket scientist to work out why: buildings all concentrated together act like a very large storage radiator. This heat, combined with the heating used in shops and houses, that from lighting and burnt car fuel and, of course, the heat of the sun, seeps into the concrete and stone and is then slowly released at night. Protected basements and courtyards are generally the warmest city gardens, often two or three degrees higher than other gardens in the surrounding neighbourhood. It's these places that are good for those people who want to nurture tender exotics outside all year round, plants that won't survive in the open country unless they are cosseted over the winter. Walls, especially south- or west-facing ones, are excellent heat reservoirs and, because they give protection (you know how you feel when someone nice and big and safe is standing behind you), tender climbing plants like *Cobaea*, *Ipomoea* and *Cuphea*, which perhaps would shiver at growing in the open garden, usually flourish.

But it's not all plain sailing. As with country gardens, city spaces can be prone to frost pockets; these are typically found at the bottom of slopes or in alleys between tall buildings. Frost, which is heavier than air, collects in these hollows and as a result the temperature is going to be much colder than that of the rest of the garden until it thaws. So it's not a place for your prized canna!

ABOVE **Where does this beautiful city balcony end? It uses the skyline perfectly, plus has a range of grasses, phormiums and alpines which will thrive in such an exposed spot.**

OVER-EXPOSED

It's not just humans who don't like being buffeted by strong winds, exposure to wind can seriously affect the growth of your plants. Think of those growing near the sea. Often they appear stunted or look as if they are being pushed over – they seem to be literally battling the elements. Hawthorns and blackthorn always look particularly gnarled and somewhat witchy as they bend away from the main force of the wind (and the salt-laden air only adds to their problems), but it's the relentless force of the wind that does the most damage.

Balconies and roof terraces are the urban equivalent of a cliff-top garden. A balcony might seem wonderfully sunny, but the wind up there is a force to reckon with and you and your plants are going to feel it, far more so than in a ground-level garden. Roof terraces face the same problem – what appears to be a gentle breeze on the streets below can feel like a roaring gale up there – and because temperature is also affected by wind, roof gardens that are protected will be significantly warmer than those that aren't.

MIND THE GAP!
You might think a wall in your garden equals shelter: it does, but if your garden is in an exposed position running across the direction of the prevailing wind, it can mean more damage than protection. When wind hits a solid boundary, such as a wall, it will rush over the top of it, gathering force, and gust over it like a hurricane, demolishing the plants below in its wake. That's why in this situation it's sometimes better to grow hedges or erect picket fencing, as the gaps in both diffuse the wind gently and lessen its force.

In cities, you might think that gardens both up high and at street level would be protected from the wind by all the surrounding buildings. It's true that some areas are more sheltered and that buildings can act as a buffer to prevailing winds, but narrow gaps between structures can also act as a funnel for the wind, which can howl down between them even on what might be an otherwise relatively calm day. This funnelling effect serves to crank up the force of the wind and plants battered by intense winds like these don't do well, unless they have been selected for their tolerance.

Plants with rigid, brittle, delicate or floppy leaves and branches don't thrive in very exposed gardens. Tender plants with big leaves like nicotianas, bananas and ricinis often look like they've been scissored by a madman if they're planted in a windy spot. Wind batters plants, breaks their branches, shreds their leaves and it also dries them out – think what an afternoon on a windy mountainside does to your skin. Plants that don't have any protection from prevailing winds lose all their moisture, shrivel and die.

NORTH, SOUTH, EAST OR WEST?

The orientation of your garden determines how much light it gets, and therefore the range of plants you can grow. A shady, north-facing slope won't support a vineyard in the same way that you won't be able to grow woodland plants like bluebells, ferns and cyclamen on a south-facing one. To establish your garden aspect, simply go outside with a compass or, if you haven't got a compass, look to the sun at 1pm British Summer Time, which is when it will be directly due south.

But whilst having this information is useful, do take a reading from each of your boundaries, too, because, as city gardens are usually square or rectangular, it's probable that you'll have a north-, south-, east- and west-facing wall; something you'll need to consider when putting together a planting plan.

Make sure you note the position of surrounding trees and buildings, too. In urban environments they can obstruct valuable sunlight, making your wonderfully warm and sunny south-facing wall pretty dark; the benefits of that aspect then go out of the window.

ABOVE On a hot, sunny wall, grape vines are a must.

BRING ME SUNSHINE

Of all city gardens, exposed roof terraces get the most sunshine – perhaps more than twelve hours a day during the summer. Balconies usually face in one direction only and therefore will get sun at a specific time of the day. My balcony is north-east facing – tough indeed. Front gardens and courtyards, on the other hand, get an average amount of sun as long as they're not shaded by trees or buildings. Basements are the darkest city gardens – some only getting two or three hours of sun a day, and only in midsummer when the sun's highest in the sky. However, it's not all doom and gloom – glass used in the construction of our homes and offices helps to reflect some light into even the darkest corner.

Although many gardeners believe 'west is best' when it comes to aspect, north, south and east have positive attributes too. It's the way that you work with what you've got that counts. Don't fight the ecology of your space too hard or you may end up with costly failures.

North

Contrary to popular belief, having a north-facing wall isn't the summons to down tools and retreat. Yes, these walls are in perpetual shade with only a couple of hours of sun in summer, but a north-facing garden gives you the opportunity to grow lush woodland and shade-loving plants such as mahonias, *Garrya*, foxgloves, hostas, epimediums, ferns, regal lilies and skimmias – all of which hate hot sunny sites. You can also grow morello cherries, gooseberries and currants on north-facing walls. Tender, shade-loving plants such as tree ferns (*Dicksonia antarctica*), though, will need some cover over winter, though, because north-facing walls can get extremely cold.

South

South equals sun . . . and lots of it. This might be thought of as an enviable aspect to have, especially if there's been a long dull winter, but south-facing gardens have their problems too. How about too much sun for starters? Can too much sun be a bad thing, I hear you ask? Well, yes, for plants it can mean drought and sun scorch, so true south-facing spots need careful planning. With global warming worsening and less rain predicted, look to plant southerly gardens with real drought-tolerant sun worshippers: plants such as *Ceanothus*, *Campsis*, *Callistemon*, *Leptospermum*, *Abutilon* and *Hoheria* – plants that come from the Mediterranean, Australia, South Africa and South America.

The soil beneath south-facing boundaries also needs careful management as it can dry out very quickly, so incorporate loads of organic matter to soak up and hold on to the water like a sponge. Throwing down a 7–10 cm (3–4 in) layer of mulch on the soil surface after heavy rainfall will help, too.

East

East-facing walls are the trickiest to deal with. In winter they're very cool, sometimes freezing, and in summer they can get very dry. Think of an east-facing wall like open scrubland; early morning sunshine clobbers it, which can lead to 'scorching' of new foliage, especially after recent rainfall. Scorch occurs when droplets of water on the leaves intensify the sun's rays like a magnifying glass, causing the foliage underneath to go brown. It looks like someone's gone mad with a blowtorch.

East-facing sites are not a good position for evergreens with thick waxy leaves, such as camellias, unless you shade them with taller plants so they can slowly get used to that harsh, early- morning sun. All plants that grow in north-facing aspects will do well here, but some protection from winds and early frosts may also be necessary.

ABOVE Many say that west is best, because it allows you to grow the widest range of plants, such as here with *Euphorbia mellifera, Astelia* and *Eriobotrya.*

West

Gardens with a westerly aspect are not hammered by strong sunlight all day, nor desiccated by cold winds, and therefore they have a wonderful temperament for growing almost any plant – except, of course, those which crave deep shade or intense sunshine. It's the ideal place to grow more tender plants like *Eremurus*, *Nicotiana*, *Hibiscus*, *Actinidia* and *Euphorbia mellifera*. Think of a west-facing site as the edge of deciduous woodland; the trees overhead cast dappled shade whilst protecting the plants underneath.

AIR POLLUTION

One of the more obvious challenges in city gardening is the amount of air pollution. There's no getting around this one, it does exist and until governments seriously strive to meet the numerous protocols and legislation it's something that we city gardeners will have to live with, at least for the foreseeable future. Not only do air pollutants give humans and animals respiratory problems, but they also do the same to plants. You gotta be tough to live in the city.

Most pollution is air-borne and the major culprit is exhaust fumes from road traffic. If you have an airport near by, this gives out a colossal amount of

OPPOSITE Not only does a simple spout like this provide a wonderful focal point, but the falling water helps mask the sound of surrounding traffic. (Hopefully!)

harmful gasses into the atmosphere, too – just think about the amount of gunk which is released into the air every time a plane lands and takes off. Many experts believe that the exhaust gasses from planes are the largest contributor to the greenhouse effect and global warming. It's the sad price we pay for the life we lead today.

As well as harmful sulphur dioxide, carbon monoxide and nitrogen dioxide, there are a lot of airborne particles which originate from the combustion process and brake and tyre wear. You'll notice this as a thick layer of dust on leaves that haven't seen rain for a while. In short, plants have to cope with it, and some plants are better at coping than others – it's these we have to select for those city gardens where air pollution is a real problem.

Plants which lose their leaves naturally, i.e. deciduous shrubs and trees such as *Weigela*, *Buddleja*, *Amelanchier*, *Forsythia*, flowering currant and lilac, cope well simply because in autumn they lose all that pollution with the falling leaves. Some really tough trees, such as the London plane, not only lose their leaves but also shed their bark to get rid of the toxic overload.

Plants that have very thick waxy leaves also thrive in heavily polluted sites: *Aucuba*, *Skimmia*, *Mahonia*, *Olearia*, camellias, box, yew and laurel (left-over plants from the Victorians) do particularly well, even next to busy main roads where their leaves can often be greyer than green. If the problem is really dire, keep your eyes open to what the local council are using; chances are if it's thriving in a nearby supermarket car park or on your local roundabout or motorway verge, it'll thrive in your garden.

Plants which have very hairy leaves are more temperamental and need extra pampering, or the occasional shower with clean water to wash off the dust. Remember, though, that apart from in the most highly-polluted situations, it's possible to grow all kinds of plants that might prefer to live out in the country simply by giving them excellent soil and looking after their feeding and watering needs well. If you can lessen the number of stressors on any one plant it will do much better, even if the air is thick with pollutants.

IT'S ALL ABOUT TIMING

Some plants, like chrysanthemums, are called 'short-day plants' because they flower later in the year, when the nights are drawing in and the daylight is less. Others, like sedum, are called 'long-day plants' because they flower in spring and summer, when the amount of daylight is increasing. Many plants are 'day-neutral plants'. Viburnum is one of these and it flowers irrespective of day length.

The Phoenix

PREVIOUS PAGE **Everyone's getting in on the act. This restaurant uses tall bamboos to create privacy for its diners.**

NOISE POLLUTION

I don't know if plants suffer from noise pollution, but we certainly do. Living next to a busy road is common for most city folk and many ask me what they can do about the noise that threatens to spoil their time in the garden. In this situation I sometimes feel like King Canute – it's a pretty oceanic-sized challenge.

Having some kind of barrier between you and the noise-offender is a good idea, and before you start work on your garden, attending to solid boundary noise-defences should be the number-one task. The theory that, 'if you can't see the origin of the noise then it must be quieter' definitely does ring true, and there's no harm in practising a little self-deception here. However, at university I was once told that to get just a one decibel drop in noise levels you'd have to grow a hedge 7 metres thick. Whether that's true or not, I'd be a liar if I said you could get rid of noise altogether – you can't. Rather than try and trounce the noise by making a bigger one yourself (like playing music loudly outdoors and wrecking good relations with all your neighbours), think laterally and go for *distracting* the senses with much better things inside your garden. Dainty wind chimes and grasses or bamboos, that make a swishing sound when caught by a breeze, can work well; so can the gentle trickle of water from a fountain or spout. Do beware of installing a thunderous torrent in your backyard, though, because I've seen a few of these and they bear an uncanny resemblance, ear-wise, to a horse urinating. (Unless, of course, that's the distraction level you want!) Concentrate on tickling the ear rather than creating the sound of the farmyard. Aim to create something the ear has to strain just a bit to hear and in so doing, hopefully, you'll forget about the traffic.

Playing to other senses will also help reduce noise pollution. Water features, stunning planting, amusing objets d'art and well-positioned focal points provide a visual distraction which focuses the attention inwards, and as a result makes the noise outside seem less important. Hey, the good stuff's all going on *in here!*

VISUAL POLLUTION

Visual pollution is a big challenge. When dealing witheyesores, plants are definitely your best allies, and for screening you can't beat them – why build a costly wall or erect a tall fence when you can use a tree? Trees are absolutely vital in cities and we should all become tree defenders and stop them from being cut down unless it's completely necessary. Think of the eyesores that trees take care of: imagine railway embankments without trees – not a pretty thought – or imagine treeless squares in between office blocks and estates with no trees. Hideous.

‘Plants need the dark as much as we do, this is when they chill out and form flower buds. Street lighting stops this process and simply makes plants grow lots of leaves and produce no flowers.’

Big trees do a big job, but trees in small city gardens also screen and bring great eye refreshment. Siting them cunningly means you can cut out the view of that pylon/garage backside/ugly concrete flyover/electricity substation and your neighbours sunbathing in the nude.

Eyesores within the garden, like sheds, the compost heap or the place where all the kids' toys seem to end up in a pile, can all be easily screened off out of sight with a little strategic planting.

LIGHT POLLUTION

Light pollution is something that we've all heard about, mostly in connection with not being able to see the stars as well as we should because of all the street and stadium lighting. So how does this affect the city gardener? As plants need light for photosynthesis to produce food, surely more light is better? Not if you're a plant under a sodium street lamp it's not.

The growth of all plants is affected by day length – it's something tecchies call photoperiodism and is the one factor affecting plant growth that's remained unchanged for millions of years. Photoperiodism is a control system, albeit an entirely natural one, and it helps plants to flower at a time when the right pollinating insects are around, thus making sure the species survives. (In turn, this system also ensures the survival of animals, too, because all natural systems are linked.)

Crafty nurserymen can manipulate this response to produce plants that flower out of season, either by using artificial lights to give longer days or by using blackouts to give the plants less daylight hours. This is why we can buy chrysanthemums in early spring; because they are a 'short-day plant' they can be forced into flower earlier by cutting out hours of light. This works in reverse, too; they can be stopped from flowering by not allowing them to have any darkness.

In cities, many street lamps unintentionally muck about with the natural photoperiodic response of plants in a similar way, often with tragic results. You know how odd you feel if you don't get any sleep. Well, plants that are subjected to continuous 'daylight' are also affected by this and will start behaving very uncharacteristically. Plants need the dark as much as we do, this is when they chill out and form flower buds. Street lighting stops this process and simply makes plants grow lots of leaves and produce no flowers. It happened to me last year; I put some pots of regal lilies outside my flat and couldn't understand why they were growing so strongly without forming any flowers. Then I looked up. Above them was a sodium lamp that came on just as the natural light was fading. Result: no night break, no flowers.

Not only do they affect flowering, but roadside lamps can also cause street trees to come into leaf too early and make shrubs lean grotesquely in their pathetic quest for the light.

The other victims of night-lighting are birds; they get very confused and will sometimes begin their dawn chorus at 2am, instead of hours later. Their breeding is also affected – it's something well documented by *Lighting in the Countryside* on their website:

'The attraction of birds to lights has been known for a long time. A close correlation has been demonstrated between commencement of dawn singing in thrushes and critical light intensity at sunrise, suggesting that artificial lighting may modify the timing of natural behaviour patterns. Reproduction in birds is photoperiodically controlled, and artificial increase of day length can induce hormonal, physiological and behavioural changes, initiating breeding. Around sixty species of wild birds have been brought into breeding condition prematurely by exposure to artificially long days in winter. In addition, bright lights such as those on telecommunication towers, lighthouses and other tall structures may attract and disorientate birds, especially on moonless nights, resulting in mortalities. Nocturnal species, many of which are already under threat, are particularly likely to be disturbed by the presence of bright illumination.'

THE NON-ENVIRONMENTAL STUFF

There are a few other factors to consider, too, which are more practical day-to-day issues and won't actually affect the microclimate of our outdoor spaces as such. But they are common issues none the less and as such they'll also need to be addressed in the planning stage.

PRIVACY

Ok, so privacy definitely doesn't affect the microclimate, but a lack of it is often a characteristic of city gardens. Some people, unless they can create private areas outdoors, see little point in using their garden for recreation. Cunning and ingenuity are needed to deal with privacy issues, and it's always possible to use a combination of screening and plants to create secret areas where the residents of the tower block next door can't get a look-in on what you're up to!

SECURITY

City gardens have specific security needs, especially those at the front of the house. All the usual deterrents and common sense applies, like using crunchy gravel, spiky hedges and discreet lighting (no big spotlights, though, please). Valuable pots and plants can wander from front gardens – see Chapter Five for some ideas for combatting garden thieves.

OPPOSITE The table and chairs might be pretty straightforward, but what about bringing those decking planks and that huge bamboo out into the garden?

ACCESS

The quality of access into a garden can seriously impede those extravagant plans. Access is the factor everybody – even seasoned garden designers – often clean forget about. Perhaps because of the sheer gardening fever which grips everyone when they start making a garden, sometimes nobody really stops to think whether they can actually bring the tiles, or the cement mixer, or the giant bamboos *into* the garden. Tip: when you go to a nursery, garden centre, reclamation yard or builders' merchant's it is well worth taking a measuring tape with you so that you can make sure that you can get your monster purchases through any access or side door. Don't leave it to chance – there's nothing more embarrassing, believe me!

You can hire all manner of weird and wonderful hoists or an enormous crane to lift stuff over your house, but that's hellishly expensive and not always logistically possible. It's a little nerve-racking, too, watching a hot tub teetering precariously above your roof – even though it's a great crowd-puller!

For gardens with no rear access the size of almost everything you can get into your garden will be dictated by the size of the doorways in your house, because that's the route of passage for all your stuff – from building materials to a pot of pansies. Think carefully about this and don't plan on decorating inside until your garden is finished. Cream carpets are a no-no. Take 'em up, for no matter how well you protect them with plastic, it's guaranteed that some mess will get through.

I always clad any thoroughfare with thick plastic sheeting and then place hardboard on top. With duct tape securing the whole top together, it usually protects any floor underneath from taking a battering and is sturdy enough for wheelbarrows or even . . . a micro-digger. Fingers crossed, though.

In the next chapter I'm going to get back to basics and start from the ground up – literally. I'm going to introduce you to some of the soils you might encounter and try to give you a few pointers to help you to understand your own soil so that you can work with it to create the most successful garden you can. Whatever your particular challenge, there's bound to be a creative solution. There's a beautiful outdoor space out there just waiting for you to make it happen. I promise.

'The reason we sometimes perceive the garden as a problem is due to wanting our own way too much, when what we should be doing is working with the characteristics and the ecology of our gardens. Make gardening easy on yourself: work with nature, not against it.'

CHAPTER FOUR
FROM THE GROUND UP – SOIL

BORING SOIL?

Whenever you pick up any book on gardening you'll be faced with a chapter about soils and I bet you'll skim over it. Why? Because it's b-o-r-i-n-g! I agree – it's hard to enthuse about the stuff you use to grow your plants in when all you really want to do is concentrate on the visuals and plant up a fabulous garden.

Every soil is different; and it's a part of your garden's ecology that you need to be aware of because it's one of the biggest factors affecting the success or failure of your plants. Following on from any hard landscaping, it makes sense to deal with the soil first before you make ambitious planting plans.

GET DOWN TO EARTH

Soil is the real backbone of the garden, the real support. A lot of city gardens have what I call 'very tired soil'. That's simply because many people who are new to gardening don't yet know how soil should be treated, and how they can improve it. Many people have showed me dismal spades of their back garden soil and sighed with despair: nothing can be done, only *they* have the worst soil in the country, and it seems like a death sentence. Don't give up heart; *any* soil can be improved until your plants will positively sing in it.

THE GOOD EARTH

First, let's have the ideal model of a good soil. If you take a spade and dig into the 'perfect soil' you'll find the spade slides in easily and the earth it lifts up will be dark and light. In short, it will resemble dark chocolate but have the texture and feel of a sponge cake, and there will be a lot of worms in it, too. If you take some of this soil in your hand it will be moist, but not wet, and it will squeeze into a ball or sausage shape and then break apart easily. It will smell of nothing in particular. This dark soil will form a distinct layer which will vary from 15 cm (6 in) to a wonderful 60cm (2 ft) deep, if you're lucky.

Below this topsoil is the supporting framework, the subsoil, which is lighter in colour. Most plant roots only use the topsoil with just tap roots plunging many feet down through the subsoil to the water table below. Topsoil is nutrient-rich, subsoil isn't. Always keep subsoil and topsoil separate; don't mix the two when you dig.

BAD EGG

Sometimes poor soils aren't so easy to spot, but here are some useful indicators that'll help:

- If the topsoil is greyish-brown, more a gunmetal colour than chocolate, it's a soil which probably suffers from poor drainage. Most likely, it'll smell of bad eggs, too.
- Grey subsoil tells you that it's either an acidic soil or it's very waterlogged.
- Blue/green/grey/brown/red mottling is a sign of seasonal waterlogging.

THE POWER OF HUMUS

What gives good soil its lovely dark colour is humus. Humus is plant material (and animal material) that has rotted down and literally 'gone back to the earth' and it is absolutely teeming with bacteria. These bacteria are the goodies, and any soil without a thriving population is deemed dead and lifeless.

What the bacteria do is make all the foods in the soil useable to the plant – they're the equivalent of the knife and fork, giving the plant what it needs, and enabling it to get the best from the nutrients. Soil without lots of friendly bacteria is hostile to plants because they have to fight to get what little food there is from the earth, and often they haven't got the strength and just give up the ghost.

TYPES OF SOIL

Soils are mainly made up of a mix of minerals (from weathered rock) and organic matter (rotted plants and animals) and the rest is made up of air and water. The proportions of these elements vary according to the type of soil. Most soils in this country fall into one of the following categories:

CLAY

If you go to pottery classes, you'll be very familiar with the stuff, it's the original modelling material and kids love to make sausages and weird animals from it because it holds its shape. It's like mud when it's wet, and can easily bake hard when it's hot.

So many gardeners moan about clay – well, if you decide to double dig your little plot and you have archetypal clay soil you might get my sympathy, but actually clay soil is a pretty good deal and, as always, it's what you do with it that counts. The very worst kind of clay soil is good soil in the making. It might be heavy and back-breaking to dig, but when you add loads of compost it smiles at you and just crumbles under your spade. You'll know if you have thick clay soil – just grab a handful and squeeze it; it'll feel smooth and when it's wet it will leave a smear all across your palm. (How nice!)

Clay soil takes a long time to warm up in the spring, so plants don't get going as fast, and its surface can bake in summer which causes cracks and makes it difficult to re-wet. On the plus side, a clay soil can be very beneficial in summer because in times of drought it holds on to water far better than other soils, so your plants don't wilt so quickly. It also holds on to nutrients well and when it rains hard the excess water doesn't flush or 'leach' them away.

SANDY

This is the opposite of clay. It's loose when you dig it, and while it's not quite like the sand on the beach, it does share a lot of its beachy characteristics. When you take a handful of it, it will feel gritty and won't make any shapes at all, simply breaking apart and falling through your fingers. When it rains hard, the rain quickly drains through it, so it's ideal for plants that don't like to grow in perpetually wet soil.

But the other side of the coin is that it dries out faster because the water rushes straight through the big gaps between each grain of sand; in hot summers, sandy soil can be as dry as the beach above tide level. It doesn't hold onto nutrients well, either, so plants will starve if they're not fed regularly. Sandy soils are, however, really easy to work and whilst plants can suffer from drought the soil warms up quickly in spring, so your plants get going that little bit earlier.

SILT

Silt is a bit of a cross between clay and sand. It's an 'alluvial' soil, which means that it had its origins as soil washed down from mountainous regions by rivers and carried along until it settled. It feels slightly gritty and 'soapy' when you play with it and it doesn't hold its shape – or if it does, it will immediately disintegrate.

Silty soils are often 'thin' and need lashings of compost to bring them up to good heart and to create air spaces so that plant roots can breathe. They're not heavy like their cousin clay, but can grip a spade as if it's become stuck in quicksand when it's wet. If you have silty soil, don't dig it too often as it can compact down easily.

PEAT

Peaty soil is very black indeed because it is almost all organic matter. It's light, easy to dig and familiar to most of us (until we stopped buying it on environmental grounds) sold in bags from the garden centre. Peat is partially decomposed organic matter, usually made from decaying reeds, rushes and mosses – if you live in a peaty area you won't have any trouble digging your garden.

Peat has plenty of air spaces in it and holds on to water well, so plants tend to love it, although it isn't particularly rich in nutrients so you will have to feed it regularly. Peat is very acidic, though, and a lot of plants don't care for it at all. Real acid lovers like rhododendrons, camellias and azaleas, however, can't get enough of it.

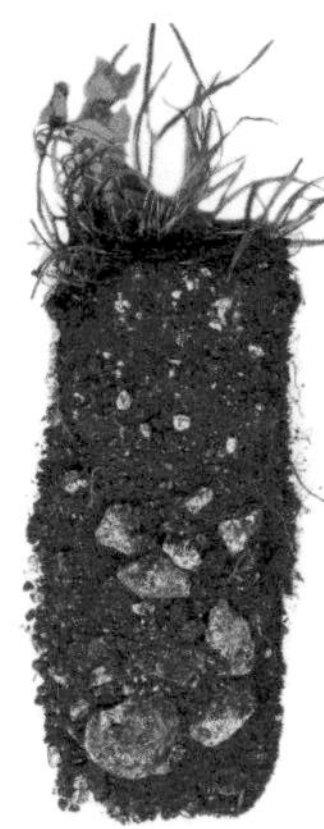

CHALKY

Think of the white cliffs of Dover – they are made of chalk. Soils that have lots of the white stuff in them, sometimes in identifiable chunks, behave in a similar way to sandy soils.

Calcareous soils can be quite fertile but they need lots of organic muck in order to be able to hold on to nutrients and water. Chalky soils are extremely alkaline and plants such as *Clematis*, *Buddleja* and *Dianthus* do well, but acid-loving rhododendrons will just keel over.

Determining your pH is not as complicated as it sounds. The level is measured on a scale from 1 to 14: neutral soil is pH 7, which is neither acid or alkaline, below 7 is acid and above 7 is alkaline. Soils in Britain usually range from 4 to 8.5.

THE MYSTERY OF pH

Having dealt with the texture or feel of your soil, a soil test will determine whether it's acid or alkaline. The pH level is important because it affects soil organisms, soil structure and, most importantly, nutrient availability. This in turn will determine the range of plants you can grow, as some nutrients become 'locked' at certain values. Take samples of soil from various points all over your plot and mix them together to get a proper picture. pH testing kits are available from garden centres, and they're cheap and fun to use.

Whilst adding lime makes soil more alkaline and adding sulphur makes it more acid, they're only short-term solutions; you can't permanently change your soil pH, so you will have to work with what you've got. If you must grow acid-loving rhododendrons but you have chalky soil, the only way to do it successfully is to grow them in containers of ericaceous (lime-free) compost.

SOIL ABUSE

If you have just moved into a recently built small city house you might find a new kind of soil: builders' rubble. This travesty of a garden soil is unfortunately more common than ever and is a rotten start to anyone's gardening aspirations. The builders depart and all you see is a newly laid lawn so you think everything's fine, until the grass browns and dies no matter how carefully you water it. The reason? Below a meagre layer of topsoil (if you're lucky), is all the rubble the builders didn't know what to do with when they built your house. On closer inspection, you'll find it's a junkyard of concrete, cement, sawn-off breeze blocks, sundry ironmongery and anything else that needs to be hidden from sight, double-quick.

While, technically, this isn't fit to be called a garden, this is all too often the reality of what new-home owners in the city face. Before you get too despondent, assess just how extensive the problem actually is by digging holes all over the area – you might be lucky and find that some are rubble-free. Then you can decide whether to dig out all the rubble and buy in skiploads of fresh topsoil, or opt for container gardening instead, where you can tailor the growing medium to suit the plant.

The only soil which should be regarded as a hopeless case is one that is heavily polluted with oil or chemicals, and in most residential areas that degree of pollution is quite rare. The very worst soil can always be shovelled into skips and taken away to be replaced by lovely new topsoil. This also applies to soil that has been buried under concrete for years because it will have no worms, no organic matter and few micro-organisms or friendly bacteria in it. I call this 'dead soil' and it should be renewed if possible. Just dig it out to about a foot and a half deep, and cart it away in a skip.

COMPOST GOLDMINE

A few decades ago it was thought that all you needed to do was sprinkle fertilizer on the soil or spray on some liquid feed and that was good enough. People carted their weeds, garden plant rubbish and grass clippings to the local municipal tip, glad to get rid of the 'mess'. Now, thank goodness, we're realizing that it's vital to use all the garden refuse – recycling it in our own gardens – and that it's actually gold dust, not rubbish. Compost is simply another word for humus, and this surplus garden material can provide all the necessary humus for soil, so it would be stupid to get rid of it. It doesn't matter what type of soil you have, adding as much compost as you have to it (and you can never have too much) will make it better and better.

ABOVE **In an unassuming corner the lowly compost heap yields its weight in gold.**

SOIL MAKEOVER

Bulky organic matter improves the structure of soil and feeds it, too by helping drainage in clay and silty soil and holding on to water and nutrients in those soils which drain too freely. Although homemade compost is considered to be the perfect soil ameliorant and plant food, there's never enough of it to go round in the average garden, so substitutes often have to be bought in.

You can buy bags of well-rotted horse manure, spent hops, mushroom compost, chicken poo, leaf mould, or composts made by the local authority composting scheme. But why not make your own compost if you've got the space? And even in a tiny backyard a worm bin is possible.

COMPOST TO THE RESCUE

Composting isn't a mysterious science or a difficult art – nature composts everything, so to understand the process, take note of what goes on around you. When leaves fall or a plant dies back, the mass of growth rots on the ground and is pulled into the soil by worms and micro-organisms, before feeding the plants again. Go to a beech wood and as you walk you'll almost bounce on the thick, spongy layer of rotted leaves. Nature's cycle wastes nothing; she's the ultimate recycler.

Making compost is easy because we like to be tidy and not leave rotting material lying about. You will need a fair-sized container to store all the dying plant remains in as they rot. You can buy very convenient plastic compost bins from your local garden centre, or check with your local council who often subsidize them, so that a big bin about 127cm (4 ft6in) high will cost you around £15. These bins are made of recycled plastic and look like a bottomless dustbin with a broader base; they also have a lid and a little door low down near the base which opens to allow you to shovel out the compost when it's ready.

ABOVE The compost heap needn't always be considered an ugly eyesore! This one is cleverly designed to look like a beehive.

If you want something a little more rustic, and perhaps a little more aesthetically pleasing, you can make a compost container from wood – by hand or from a kit – but you will need a cover. If you really don't want to advertise the fact that you're making compost, look for cunning bins disguised as beehives.

The best place for your composting activities is a quiet corner of the garden, but if you can, position a bin near the kitchen. If it's closer to hand you'll be more likely to use it and it'll be less of a temptation in winter to shove your potato peelings in the kitchen bin.

WHAT CAN I PUT ON THE COMPOST HEAP?

Everything that once lived can be chucked on the compost heap.
That includes:

- All vegetable and fruit peelings
- All above-ground plant material that's soft: big leaves, prunings, bedding plants, grass clippings, weeds (with the exception of perennial nasties like couch grass, bindweed, horsetail and ground elder which will do better in the wheelie bin).
- All harder plant remains that have been shredded or chopped up into fairly small bits.
- Whole plants, including the earth on their roots.
- Animal manures – but not cat and dog excrement.
- The contents of the vacuum cleaner.

Don't put cooked food on your compost heap; it might encourage pests like rats.

Getting your soil into good heart is one of the first steps to a healthy garden, so it's worth putting in as much effort as you would into any grand designs – this work is vital to ensure good results in the long term.

HOW TO MAKE COMPOST

Site the bin with its open base on the earth, then add a layer about 6 inches deep of dryish, stemmy material, breaking it up loosely. Make sure it's fairly level and then add whatever you've got to hand – perhaps a layer of peelings – and then add a layer of the top-growth of perennials that are cut down in autumn, for instance. Try to keep the layers level and avoid ending up with a volcano in the middle. If you have a heavy load of grass clippings, don't add them in a huge thick layer; instead put a couple of sheets of newspaper every 2 inches to avoid the clippings congealing into a nasty wet mass.
It's best to have a mix of dry and wet material – if there are too many dry ingredients, little rotting will take place; too many wet ingredients and the whole mixture goes sour and smells. If, however, you do get smelly compost it's easy to remedy; just add something dry like hay or dry stems and mix it in. If you like, add some seaweed powder, sprinkling a little every so often between the layers; seaweed is fabulous for adding micronutrients or trace elements to the soil.

It's a good idea to cover your bin because the composting process works best when it's warm – which is why compost made in the summer will be ready to use sooner than compost made during the winter months. The actual process of decomposition also generates heat and this helps to kill any lurking weed seeds and pathogens. If you're an impatient gardener and want to see the results quickly, adding fresh animal manure in small quantities makes the process zip along.

When the bin is full, turn the whole lot over once or twice and then just leave it. (You can buy bins that revolve as you turn a handle, and although these take up a lot of room, they do make compost faster and more easily.) If your bin is sited on the ground (not on concrete, please), special composting worms called brandlings (small reddish-looking creatures) will appear in staggering numbers (where *do* they come from?) and munch through the contents of the bin. Armies of bacteria will digest and heat it all up and when the activity ceases, there will be a layer on the bottom of the bin that looks just like good earth – which is exactly what it is. It's surprising how a huge binful of material will rot down to so little. This is precious stuff; a handful of homemade compost added to ordinary bought compost will bring beneficial lively bacteria to the whole lot – it's a bit like eating live yoghurt.

When you add compost to the garden, spread it on the surface about an inch thick and gently fork it in to the top layer of soil. If you're lazy you can just leave it sitting on the surface and the resident worm population will pull it down, thus doing the work for you.

CHAPTER FIVE
CITY SPACES, GARDEN PLACES

FRONT GARDENS

Front gardens have an identity problem; they don't feel like prime spaces in which to practise being creative, and their potential is much underestimated. It seems that the poor front garden is generally regarded as little more than a sad no-man's land between the house and the street, needing only to be kept tidy and to allow easy access.

The problem lies in the fact that front gardens are spaces shared with all and sundry: the whole street looks in as it passes by and fag ends and litter are often lobbed over the front wall. Nobody respects the fact that the space actually belongs to someone, nor that the owner is responsible for looking after it. But it is our territory – we own it. The challenge, therefore, is how to claim it and how to fashion it into that psychological cushion between ourselves and the outside world.

Of course, front gardens aren't exactly blessed with privacy, are they? We might want to make them more secluded, but that's not always a good idea. Unobstructed access has to be maintained to the front door; not only for us, but also for anyone delivering papers, post, milk or occasional larger items. There's also the uneasy feeling that, if we do break the rules and create a jungle or dark and sheltered space, all we're doing is providing some much appreciated cover for burglars.

Front gardens in the city don't invite the leisurely pottering that a back garden allows – instead they get a quick tidy-up now and then before the owners rush indoors as fast as they can. How often do you see gardeners diligently weeding or digging out there, or lingering with a hosepipe or watering can? Not often. And as a result, front gardens nearly always have the same 'stuck-in-a-rut' look – as if the owner is too frightened to experiment. Front gardeners might be reluctant to commit themselves to being really creative, but these gardens are vital to the greening of the city. Remember how you feel when you walk down a street where the gardens are not just spaces for bins or a parking spot for the car, but where the lawns are manicured, baskets are blooming and giant ornamental cherries are in full flower? The experience brightens up your day.

Making an effort to turn a front garden into something beautiful and eye-catching has a terrific effect upon city neighbourhoods: it only needs one or two people in the street to take the plunge and then the rest of the street follows. Properties sell faster if front gardens have a cared-for appearance, too. It's something that estate agents call 'kerb appeal'; apparently prospective buyers often make up their mind about whether to go inside within a few seconds of pulling up outside. The suggestion is that they're not just looking at the house, they're taking in the complete picture – including the front garden.

ABOVE **What to do with the rubbish/compost heap? Use a frame that will allow access and cover it with plants that'll help smother a multitude of sins.**

PRACTICAL NECESSITIES

Gardening out front is tricky; it's all about making sacrifices because (with a few exceptions) you simply can't do everything you'd like to.

Access has to be the number-one priority. Your path should be wider than you imagine you'll need – think of those removal men struggling with your wardrobe or piano – and it should also lead by a fairly direct route to the front door, one that's obvious to callers. Although it's nice to have a kink in the path to slow visitors down and make them appreciate the plants on either side, it must be easy to use or anyone in a hurry will make their own path, flattening your plants in the process.

Cars parked in the front garden can confuse the issue: is this a garden or a car park? However, if you do decide to use the front garden as off-street parking, you'll need sufficient space to manoeuvre the vehicle and to open its doors. In addition, you'll need to leave enough room beside it to allow visitors to get to your front door without difficulty.

Giving over your front garden entirely to parking isn't an attractive option, but many city people have gone for it simply out of necessity, since they can't park on the street. The key to overcoming the front-garden-car-park syndrome is to provide cunning distractions: make your planting as abundant and striking as possible and fill every available space with bountiful perennials to draw attention away from the accompanying car.

Dustbins are another familiar eyesore, but there are some simple and effective ways round this, too. Camouflage bins behind trellis panels or paint them green if you haven't got room for trickery – you can even buy cellophane camouflage to stick on the wheelie bin. It's kitsch, I know, but it's just whimsical enough to get away with. Alternatively, you can make a 'bin house' using shingles or reclaimed planks of wood and then sit a terracotta dish on top, filled with all kinds of plants. Most importantly, though, when you are deciding where to site bins, make sure you position them where you can wheel them easily to the street on collection days.

UNITY

Unity between house and garden is important in any design, but even more so when it comes to the front garden. Visually, the eye travels from the street, sweeps over the garden and then up the front of the house, so it's crucial to have house and garden linked in some way.

Unity can always be achieved by working with the character of the house: a grand Victorian terrace needs a garden that echoes the period feel, and a simple tiled path bounded by rope-top tiles or saw-toothed brick edging would do the trick. But that doesn't mean that the materials used in construction should be restricted to those of the age when the house was built. On the contrary, when used sympathetically, modern materials like glass and copper can help bring period buildings bang up to date, if that's the effect you want. Most in-keeping with a strong architectural new-build would be uniform modular paving laid at a 45-degree angle, with three or four big bold terrazzo pots overflowing with sun-loving *Phormium tenax*, *Stipa tenuissima*, *Verbena bonariensis*, *Convolvulus cneorum* and *Knautia* Melton pastels.

So what wouldn't work? A contemporary glasshouse, with lots of stainless steel and western red cedar framed by a rambling, overflowing cottage garden? The two wouldn't appear to marry, yet sometimes opposites work surprisingly well. I've seen a wild garden, complete with a pond lined by massed bulrushes, sitting in front of a house that looked like a sophisticated glass sandwich – and the effect was fabulous.

It's often a good idea to consider the character of the whole street when developing your design. This will give your garden a quiet, refined look and will enhance the character of your own plot, simply because it's amongst others of similar ilk. This is one of those occasions when standing out from the crowd is not always a good thing. For example, an imitation Mediterranean garden, complete with ochre-coloured walls, terracotta tiles and rows of lemon trees might look, well, slightly self-conscious situated right in the middle of a road of substantial Edwardian terraces.

So, just how far can you go? It seems to be a commonly felt notion that front gardens should show some restraint, whereas the back garden is the place reserved for your artist's ego. I can't explain all the reasons for this, except to say that this seems to be a typically English cultural thing. We seem to think that front gardens are neutral territory and so, almost out of politeness, should be designed with other people's sensitivities in mind. The rule for designing front gardens, if there is one, is to treat everything you read or watch on television as suggestions only. These ideas should act as a guide, and as something to inspire your creativity. Nothing is set in stone, so if you feel like it, and have the courage, then why not break out of the mould?

One simple way of creating a sense of harmony is to make sure that the size of any hard landscaping is the same, or in multiples of, the width of the windows, the porch, the garden gate, or the front door. You might think you wouldn't notice, but the eye does and the effect makes the composition feel right and pleasing.

'Front gardens nearly always have the same 'stuck-in-a-rut' look – as if the owner is too frightened to experiment. Front gardeners might be reluctant to commit themselves to being really creative, but these gardens are vital to the greening of the city'

ABOVE The car parking space is much maligned in small gardens, but not here where plants help to tie it in to the garden-proper.

FRONT-GARDEN STYLE

A formal design often works best in a city front garden as formal gardens have an air of stability about them and make good use of space; they also say something definite without being over the top, and help to keep things simple. Creating an ordered space by using a formal structure builds a calm bridge between the busy street and the quiet interior of the home.

When the front gate and the front door line up directly in a straight line, then a symmetrical design is often the best way to go, because free-form curves rarely work in small spaces that are bounded by such strict regularity. Creating a balanced layout is relatively simple, especially when you're working with the hard-nosed symmetry of many houses. Rows of standard bay balls rising through a sea of lavender either side of a straightforward brick path, for example, looks stylish and helps pull you to the main focus of any front garden – the front door.

In many front gardens the path tends to run down one side, especially if it doubles up as a place to park the car. Here, the garden-proper will be offset and so viewed from three sides: the path, the house and the pavement. Features and the arrangement of plants in beds and borders must be placed accordingly. In many cases, a simple circular or square layout with a tree or collection of pots positioned in the middle forms the focus of the garden. It's often nice to actually move a path, if it runs down one side, to the middle, perhaps at an angle, so that you're forced to walk through the planting on either side. However, if off-street parking is a must then this is often impractical, as the car will dominate the entire composition.

An informal front garden is what we typically associate with a cottage in the country: random gravel paths with plants spilling over the edges and perennials like lady's mantle popping up between cracks in the paving. But can informal front gardens work in cities? The short answer is 'yes and no'. It all depends on the house and the size of the garden area. Greater care than you might think is required to design informal elements into a front garden. In larger gardens a good layout or skeleton of hard landscaping is needed, otherwise it runs the real risk of looking like a dog's dinner. In tiny front gardens (those no bigger than a shoe-box), a few informal clumps of low-maintenance evergreen grasses such as *Pennisetum alopecuroides* 'Cassian's Choice', *Uncinia rubra* and *Sesleria nitida* work well and would contrast perfectly with the familiar rounded shapes of evergreen shrubs such as *Lonicera nitida* 'Maigrün', *Daphne laureola* and Christmas box – just resist the temptation to go mad.

I must admit I tend to plump for formal when I think about small city front gardens; they just seem to lend themselves better to formal touches. Modern houses in particular are straight and boxy and don't look right with meandering paths, whereas something linear usually works.

BELOW **Boundary blues? Why not pick something a little different?**

NO FRONT GARDEN?

So, what if you have no front garden at all? Well, you do have a front door and an entrance to your house, so you can treat that doorway like an embellished picture frame and grow plants such as clematis or golden hops around it. Or, if you've got a sunny entrance, why not opt for fragrant beauties such as *Trachelospermum asiaticum* or *Jasminum beesianum* to welcome you home after a hard day at the office?

CONTAINERS

Of course, if you're not allowed to put a hefty pot on the pavement, you do have a problem, but a couple of luxuriant hanging-baskets, one on either side of the door, will more than compensate. Nowadays you don't even have to make these baskets up yourself as many nurseries offer a hanging basket service: you pick the plants and then just rely on their expertise and labour. They'll grow them under cover, and once the danger of frost has passed you can put them up for instant impact. You can opt for subtlety in your design, or you can go all out for an eye-socking profusion of colour.

If you can plant some troughs tumbling with *Diascia*, trailing fuchsia, *Lagurus ovatus* and variegated helichrysum or, on a more restrained note,

72

If you really have no outside space to decorate with plants, why not make a 'Brighton statement'? Picture a row of houses, each one painted a different colour. If this sounds too ambitious or too flashy, paint the front door pillar-box red or azure blue, then put up hanging baskets filled with plants that either match or contrast. Even with no garden at all you can still do your bit to inject some colour into a grey cityscape.

planted up with ivies, white lobelia and busy lizzies and perhaps a small conifer, you have effectively decorated the front of your house and made it subtly stand out from the rest. Don't underestimate the power of small things – a whole street decked out with nothing but hanging baskets flowering their hearts out in summer looks absolutely stunning, even if there's not a front garden to be seen.

Similarly, window boxes on windowsills are a nice touch, but do make sure they are really firmly fixed (especially if they are on sills above ground-floor level), and keep the planting simple for best effect. Ideally, repeat certain colours or plants to get a rhythm to the planting which runs through each container. The world's your oyster, but as with the trough idea, combinations of trailing and bushier plants work well, just remember that you are working on a much smaller scale and choose your plants accordingly (see Chapter Six).

If you do have room on the pavement, large tough concrete tubs or troughs are ideal, especially filled with grasses such as *Miscanthus*, *Pennisetum*, *Elymus*, or *Spartina* – plants that won't mind being stroked occasionally by passers-by. But do make sure all troughs and pots aren't too wide, or there'll be no room to walk past them. Down near Vauxhall, in south London, residents have taken over the street and planted dustbins full of colourful annuals mixed with eucalyptus and other architectural plants, as well as topiary and cottage-garden flowers. It looks fabulous: an eclectic slice of city horticulture. And why not?

OPPOSITE Every front door needs a real wow – if only to welcome you home after a hard day's slog at the office.

WALLS

So what else is gardenable at the front of your house? What about the walls? The perfect space for trying your hand at vertical gardening! Climbers can be used to define the front door, or to smother the whole facade. They make fantastic camouflage for pebbledash, render and concrete. *Wisteria floribunda*, with its long tassels of scented purple or white pea-flowers, is a classic here, as are fragrant climbing roses like 'Aloha', 'Constance Spry' and 'New Dawn'.

ON THE SURFACE

Fundamentally, hard landscaping needs to marry well with the house and should also add 'weight', or tie the house into its surroundings. Having said that, it doesn't pay to use the same material as the walls as that's just overkill. Instead what's used should complement them in some way to ensure a sense of harmony between house and garden.

ABOVE Perhaps a little ostentatious for some, but then there's nothing like making an entrance!

Rectangular Blue Lias cobbles and Welsh Pennant flagstones are excellent heavyweights, providing an air of solidity and permanence, and go well with all houses – even those with unattractive orange pebbledashed walls. If you do have orange pebbledashing, don't use orange paving – far better to choose darker, neutral materials which will complement almost anything. Brick houses with slate roofs, like those you find in Liverpool or Manchester, go well with blue-black slate paving, or sandstone of a similar colour. Dark grey granite setts suit brick houses as if they were made for each other. Do restrict yourself on the number of surface materials you use, though: too many and your design will look chaotic and awkward on the eye. I tend to err on the side of caution and stick to one, or maybe two, different materials in a front garden – depending on its size, of course. Personally, I'm a big fan of natural materials; nothing looks more depressing than concrete. Think carefully; do you really want your garden to look like a continuation of the pavement?

It goes without saying that hard landscaping must be solid, feel safe, and be safe – no wobbly stones or prominent leading edges for toes to trip over. Whatever type of surface you choose, it must be safe to walk on in all weathers, especially if it's a damp north-facing garden where moss and algae thrive. This safety caveat doesn't mean you have to go for a surface that's like designer stubble, but the last thing you want is for visitors to injure themselves. You really do have to be public-spirited when it comes to front-garden access, so choose materials with riven or picked finishes.

Subtly changing surface materials, perhaps by their pattern or colour, can help to delineate spaces for different functions. For example, it's easy for cars to creep round and park right outside the front door, but if the space reserved for parking is finished with gravel, and the rest of the garden laid with sandstone pavers, your doorway is much more likely to stay clear. Even a simple strip of gravel to drive over, interplanted with tough ground cover like ivy, *Ajuga reptans*, *Potentilla neumanniana* and *Duchesnea indica* will help determine where you want cars to be parked. Gravel will also catch any oil spills, which you can simply rake out, thus sparing your expensive paving.

Crunchy gravel laid en masse is an excellent low-cost surface for a front garden, and is also a built-in burglar deterrent. But laying a gravel driveway is far removed from putting down a simple gravel path in the garden. If you're going to park your car on top of it, get a professional to do the work and lay a proper sub base; you can't just wheelbarrow a load of gravel in, dump it, and forget it! Bredon gravel is the most solid variety (the National Trust is a big fan of the stuff): it's designed to be compacted, and cats won't want to use it as a toilet either. Unfortunately the downside is that, unlike with pea gravel, for example, self-seeding annuals and perennials like *Phacelia campanularia* and forget-me-nots can never get a proper foothold.

If your front garden is large enough, you can turf much of it and still have room for a sweeping driveway. In small gardens, though, grass is a burden because it needs so much maintenance, and you're hardly going to sit out on the front lawn in a deckchair, are you? (Especially if it's an all-over suntan you're after.) And, of course, front gardens aren't likely to be used for outside entertaining, so ripping up that front lawn gives more space to create a dramatic composition with plants.

SECURITY

Everybody worries about security. It's a fact of city life, but there's no need to become neurotic about it. Generally, problems arise when the front door – or window– is obscured from the street by dense planting, often put there in the first place with the intention of creating some privacy. If any space in the front garden is too well screened, then a burglar can happily work away hidden from view, so you need to find a balance between suitable screening and an open invitation to intruders.

In many cases a few evergreen shrubs like *Pittosporum tobira*, *Escallonia* 'Apple Blossom' and *Prunus* 'Otto Luyken', intermingled with less dense deciduous trees and shrubs like *Cercis canadensis* 'Forest Pansy', *Amelanchier lamarckii* and *Kolkwitzia amabilis* 'Pink Cloud', prove the best option. Planting

ABOVE **If you pack your garden full of plants, do be careful that you don't totally obscure the front door and windows.**

a mixture like this doesn't create too much density, so the front door and windows aren't completely blocked from view.

Front gardeners can still get that much-needed privacy throughout the summer, without totally cutting themselves off from the outside world, by growing tall 'transparent' perennials. Try a drift of *Thalictrum delavayi* 'Hewitt's Double', an enormous crambe, or a swathe of long-lasting purple *Verbena bonariensis*. All these are big without being too heavyweight and when planted en masse they act like a veil and, since they don't obscure completely, they can be ideal for a small front garden where you want to see some of the house behind. Taller grasses like *Miscanthus sinensis* 'Flamingo', *Molinia caerulea* subsp. *arundinacea* 'Karl Foerster' and *Saccarum ravennae* act in a similar way in slightly larger spaces.

THROUGH THE BARRICADE

Railings with spiked tops don't actually stop anyone legging it over the top, but they do give off a somewhat threatening air, which just might be all that's needed to make the average casual burglar have second thoughts.

Resist the temptation to have enormous hedges: you only want them to be large enough to demarcate your space and to deter opportunistic thieves, so you don't need a 10-foot-high monster. Before deciding if you really do need tall fences or hedges, think about those around you and how your boundaries will affect them. Will your neighbours thank you for hiding them behind a dense barrier which leaves them sitting in deepest shade? Leylandii hedging is probably the biggest single gardening cause of neighbour disputes – so much so that in June 2005 new legislation was brought in which dictates that all hedging must be kept below 2m (6½ft) high or your neighbour does have a right to request you trim it. Aim for a height of about 1.5–1.8m (5–6ft), which is eye-height – for most of us, at any rate. This way a hedge will provide some privacy without being out of proportion with the garden as a whole and you'll be able to trim the top without too much difficulty. Go for spiky plants like holly or *Osmanthus* if you're at all worried. But never, never, NEVER even consider using x *Cupressocyparis leylandii* – the Leyland cypress – it's too dense and needs trimming a hundred times a year. Choose *Thuja plicata* (western red cedar) instead; it smells of pineapples, isn't aggressive and can be easily clipped into formal geometric shapes.

ABOVE Deciduous plants are often a better choice for use as 'veiled', translucent screening.

People often worry about having tubs and planters stolen. If you use very heavy ones, they're extremely difficult to walk off with, and if you still feel nervous about it you can always chain them to the house. Wooden barrels and terracotta pots can be secured by carefully drilling into the paving below one of the drainage holes, then fixing them to the ground with rawlbolts.

NIGHT LIGHTS

Lighting makes a statement about how passionate you are about your front garden. However, uplighting the house *à la* Elton John may not be exactly the statement you're after, so it's best to err on the side of subtlety.

Practical lighting is often needed for paths; simple bollards lining the edges will help visitors to navigate their way to the house without tripping over, and they are especially useful where there are steps or changes in level. Simple recessed uplights built into paving are trickier and generally more expensive to install, but they are a more charismatic alternative. Some models come with grilles to protect them from damage in driveways, or to protect you from the hot lens when you walk over them. Uplighting is ideal where there is obvious symmetry and helps to define the layout of a design after the sun goes down. Position low-voltage spots at the base of standard topiary balls or clumps of erect perennials and they will produce startling 3D effects.

As a general rule, any lighting used in a front garden needs to be restrained and not look like 365 Christmas decorations. Often one or two lights are more than enough to subtly light the entire garden – and they won't look too ostentatious either.

Spread lighting, in contrast, generally 'flattens' everything, but if the light source is strategically placed it can be used to throw imposing shadows against a wall or other backdrop. However, it is good at lighting up the whole scene, and so is often used in high-security situations. If you prefer to light from above, you could place spotlights in overhanging trees to delicately graze the branches and cast light on those paths that are particularly well screened from other ambient light sources, like street lighting.

Illuminating the front door might not sound necessary, but it sure helps you find your keys (not to mention the keyhole!) in the dead of night and it does make that front door into a feature – so do make sure it's had a lick of paint.

If you're worried about security, then opt for those big infrared-triggered spotlights which come on when movement is detected. These spots obviate the potentially expensive and un-neighbourly use of spread lighting; lights which are left on all night are anti-social, shouldn't really be necessary, and give out so much constant glare that you never see the stars.

PLANTING

ABOVE A simple water feature is an easy way to provide the main focal point for a small front garden design.

Simplicity is the key to any planting scheme for a front garden and this approach suits all except perhaps the most cottagey of designs. But simplicity needn't mean boring, of course; the front garden is still the chance to show off and create something spectacular.

In tiny terraced gardens, don't just gravel the whole thing; plant ribbons of perennials to create a simple patchwork effect. Evergreen *Ajuga reptans* 'Burgundy Glow', *Heuchera cylindrica* 'Chartreuse', barren strawberry, *Liriope spicata*, *Pachysandra terminalis* and *Luzula nivea* work well whatever style of house you have and all of them will thrive in a shady position. In a dry sunny spot, simple clumps of *Panicum virgatum* 'Rehbraun', *Pennisetum setaceum* 'Rubrum' or *Bouteloua gracilis* rising through lambs' ears, *Teucrium chamaedrys* 'Prostratum', *Cerastium tomentosum* and lawn camomile gives a gentle, restrained, informal look. All are easy to look after, help keep the weeds down and look far more interesting than a boring shingle beach.

Low maintenance is usually a desirable feature of front gardens, as we inevitably give more time and energy to the space at the back, but if you've got the room, why not fill the front with an exciting mix of tall herbaceous plants and ornamental grasses, bringing a generous slice of the 'wow!' right into the centre of the city? Traditionally, old-fashioned cottage gardeners planted giant perennials at the back of large herbaceous borders to tower over other plants and provide a dramatic backdrop. As well as helping create classic tiered or layered plantings, perennials such as *Solidago* 'Golden Wings', orangey-red *Helenium* 'Septemberfuchs', and tall perennial yellow sunflowers look really striking when planted together in large drifts.

However, if you grow nothing but herbaceous perennials you'll have little but bare earth to stare at during the winter; and as year-round appeal in the front garden is important, this means almost any planting scheme needs a good backbone of evergreens to hold it together. Be careful not to over-use dark evergreens, though, as they can easily overpower a small space. Of course, evergreen doesn't necessarily mean boring. Green comes in a huge variety of colours, from the light apple green of griselinia to the olive green of *Cistus* x *aguilarii* and the juniper colour of *Cytisus* x *praecox*. Evergreens help anchor a design, act as focal points in winter and during the summer they're the perfect foil for showy herbaceous perennials.

For some loud 'look-at-me' colour, try the flat plates of *Achillea filipendulina* 'Cloth of Gold' – these last for ages – and the devilishly hot *Crocosmia* 'Lucifer'. Having a fondness for red flowers, I find the red-hot poker *Kniphofia* 'Lye End' and *Dahlia* 'Bishop of Llandaff' hard to resist, too. Hot summer sun makes these colours ultra-vibrant and as a general rule all tolerate dry conditions well.

Spiky giants are like the lemon in your tea; planted in amongst a mixed front-garden border they perk it up, giving contrast to softer-leaved forms. *Acanthus mollis* has both architectural leaves and flower spikes which last for ages. *Eryngium agavifolium* is almost asking for a punch-up and *Echinops sphaerocephalus* (what a mouthful!) has silvery-grey, globe-shaped flowers that contrast beautifully with taller grasses such as *Miscanthus sinensis* 'Variegatus', rigid *Verbascum olympicum* and the vivid magenta of *Lychnis coronaria*. Tolerant of dry, free-draining soils these all need lots of sun to reach their desired height.

BELOW Be bold with your front garden planting but, as here, go for a balanced mixed scheme with plenty of evergreens for year-round interest.

ABOVE The archetypal English rose isn't, admittedly, particularly low maintenance, but many front gardeners can't live without them. Looking at this doorway, I can see why!

When growing giant perennials, allocate them loads of room; they need space around them to develop or else they'll crowd out the smaller competitors. Those with slender stems will need staking or they'll flop over, but this can be achieved invisibly by using willow or netting supports placed in position in spring. By summer you'll have straight stems and the supports will be hidden by foliage.

ROSES

The national favourite of the English, roses provide not only colour and perfume, but their thorns act as excellent deterrents – most thugs won't attempt to barge through a large rose-bush. Roses don't like salty air too much, but they do fine in cities, loving full sun but tolerating some shade. But they are *the* shrub for that heady combination of wonderful flowers plus exquisite perfume. Planted en masse they will give a period feel to your garden, but they lend themselves just as easily to being interplanted with most other shrubs and flowers. At the Chelsea Flower Show in 2004, Best in Show winner Christopher Bradley-Hole combined roses with miscanthus grasses in his very contemporary minimalist garden: a new and adventurous combination. There are hundreds of roses available so it's a good idea to get a specialist book on them. If you're fussy about scent, visit a rose specialist

in June to get a nose-full – you'll be amazed how different they all are. You'll be able to weed out those that have no scent whatsoever! I like species roses because they are tough and floriferous and those like *Rosa rugosa* 'Alba' and the vigorous *R.* 'Roseraie de l'Haÿ' have a wonderful spicy scent especially in damp weather. *R. spinosissima*, the Scottish rose, is a favourite too, which has some highly scented varieties, including double white and double pink. The Gallica roses are the oldest around and the most fragrant. The Portland roses like *R.* 'Jacques Cartier' and *R.* 'De Rescht' fit nicely into smaller gardens and also have a long flowering period. With these, you don't have to subject them to hard pruning as needed by hybrid tea roses, so for low-maintenance gardeners, they're ideal.

SHAPE UP

Front gardens are the perfect space for trying your hand at topiary; and if you feel a bit unsure about your artistic skills, then box, in its familiar clipped balls, cones, spirals, cubes or whatever, is commonly available at most garden centres. I prefer classical geometric shapes as they go well with everything and look equally at home in contemporary or cottage gardens,

BELOW I don't think there's a garden where topiary looks out of place – front or back.

ABOVE Bold minimalism, topiary-style.

but if you fancy a monster or two – a writhing snake, or a railway locomotive – go for it! Topiary always makes a theatrical statement, whether it's low-growing manicured mounds of evergreen azaleas, looking for all the world like stepping stones over a Japanese 'lawn' of moss, or two tall, tightly clipped cones either side of the front door, topiary broadcasts to the world that you have taste.

If you want your artistic or bohemian side to be given full rein, there is nothing to stop you filling your garden with whimsy. Box (*Buxus sempervirens* and varieties), is the all-time classic plant for topiary: it's so amenable, tolerates shade and will thrive in soils where anything else would just give up the ghost. What's more, it doesn't grow too fast and is great fun to clip. Importantly, though, trimmed box has presence; it can be used to anchor a design or, literally, be the sole design feature. I've yet to see a garden where it looks out of place. Lots of small box planted close together and trimmed into tiny hedges make the classic knot garden – I love these. A very simple design, based on traditional patterns, works best, and the 'knots' can be filled with whatever you fancy, such as dwarf lavenders or herbs, or perhaps gravel and a hefty container filled with agapanthus in the centre.

Of course, box isn't the only plant that can be trimmed tightly into different shapes. Yew, small-leaved privet, holly, *Prunus lusitanica* and many conifers

are also amenable to topiary shears. For the ultimate all-year-round architectural statement you could go for nothing but topiary in the garden: Packwood House, just south of Birmingham, is a perfect example. A circle of five or seven pyramids, a ring of large balls, or a forest of giant mushrooms underpinned with gravel makes for a wonderfully magical space, and requires little maintenance except for gentle pruning. Such gardens are perfect examples of less equals more.

BIG AND BEEFY?!

To avoid the classic front-garden disaster of a huge, dominant plant swamping everything and cutting out valuable light, you must take note of the eventual height and spread of the specimen you've just fallen in love with at the garden centre. A weeping willow is *not* a tree for a small front garden – and don't get me started on pampas grass! You can grow some whoppers if they are *very* slow growing, and/or you really don't mind regular maintenance work; for instance, *Buddleja davidii* can be a little on the large side but it's typical of shrubs that can be easily kept in check by hefty pruning. In fact, *Buddleja davidii* varieties positively love being hacked back each spring as this encourages loads of shoots which then flower. It's a plant which flowers on growth produced in the same year, just like *Clematis tangutica*, a rampant climber that also needs to be hard pruned in spring to promote flowering shoots.

POLLUTION

Tolerance to pollution is another consideration when choosing plants for a city front garden. Many main London thoroughfares and squares still owe their character to the pollution-tolerant plane trees which were planted during the late-nineteenth and early-twentieth centuries. Nowadays popular municipal trees include *Prunus* 'Spire', *Corylus colurna*, *Pyrus calleryan*a 'Chanticleer' and *Prunus* 'Kanzan' – a huge and rather loud, but fun, flowering cherry, equally impervious to city grime. But you'll be surprised what you can get away with: some southern city gardens even have cosseted banana trees growing in them. Many common perennials also brave the dusty air, plants such as *Acanthus*, lupins, *Achellia*, geraniums, *Veronica*, *Solidago*, *Liatris*, *Sidalcea*, *Aster*, *Euphorbia*, *Penstemon*, *Crocosmia*, *Anemone* and *Lychnis*.

You can't change the air in cities but you can make it smell better! Along the garden path is the perfect place for growing scented plants. Most such plants tend to be either up-close-and-personal such as cottage pinks and *Cyclamen purpurascens*, or touchy-feely such as rosemary and *Artemisia*. Positioning them right next to a path means you'll get maximum stroke-satisfaction each time you brush against them. If you're a night-owl, then night-scented stocks are a must; the scent it pumps out on July evenings will knock your socks off. Deutzias are a good choice, too, especially *D. compacta* and also *Elaeagnus*, which will have you chasing around trying to find the source of scent in the garden – until you realize it's from the inconspicuous white flowers. If you have some space next to a south-facing front door, why not grow *Chimonathus praecox* 'Luteus' against it? This winter-flowering shrub has yellow bellflowers and a fantastic scent and is the perfect plant to lift your spirits during the darkest time of the year.

ABOVE ***Prunus*** **'Kanzan' is what I call a 'seducer' – wonderful for two weeks of the year in spring but then an obstinate monster.**

The front garden is the first thing you see when you come back from work. Your mood can't help but be subtly affected for the better if it looks cared for and interesting, so reclaim that space and smarten up your bit of the street!

From up front to down under . . . fancy a chill-out zone below stairs, away from the bustle of city life above? The front garden may be a transition zone from the workaday world to your home, but more private spaces beckon once you've closed the front door. The ultimate in my secret-garden fantasy has to be the basement garden. Sometimes it's nice just to get away from it all . . .

DOWN BELOW

'Basement' isn't a particularly pleasantly evocative word, is it? It brings to mind a small, dark, cobwebby, forgotten space that's damp, smelly and creepy and acts as a kind of sump for all the street litter. As an added irritation there's also little privacy, with people looking down on you as they pass by. All in all, it's not the kind of place that you'd imagine could ever be packed full of plants or even just used and enjoyed as a garden.

Although the raw material might seem unpromising, basements do have exciting potential and present one of the strongest cases for transformation that I know. In the gardening world, basements are introverts while the ground-level gardens, with their apparent airy freedom, are the extroverts – the open courtyard invites chatter, the basement garden, contemplation.

BELOW Walls aren't all evil – in basement gardens they afford wonderful protection from the adverse weather.

But you wouldn't believe what can happen below stairs. Basements have a ready-made atmosphere that you can't simply take or leave and they provoke a reaction whether you like them or not. Think of a basement as a small stage: it's a self-contained space with no view and no ability to 'borrow' features from the landscape around it, so the focus is essentially completely inward. In addition, the enclosed character of basements gives them scope for intimacy and intensity – the perfect ingredients for a dramatic encounter.

Basements also have a real mood of their own. I always get a slight prickle on the back of my neck when I'm in a basement and whenever I think of them I find myself daydreaming about film noir, mysterious meetings, things secret and hidden, and I get drawn into their air of tension and suspense. Look beyond their flaws and you'll see that basements offer so much – their spooky personality and almost otherworldly presence should be exploited to the full.

MICROCLIMATE

Apart from their size, the main negative factor affecting basements is an obvious one: lack of light. What light there is falls mainly from above, and the deeper the basement, the less it will get. Some basements are lucky, in that they catch the sun when it's at its highest (around midday), but most of them will be in perpetual shade and may well be pretty dark, especially in winter. So therefore it stands to reason that you can't grow true sun-loving plants such as agave and pineapple broom (*Cytisus battandieri*), in such conditions, and you shouldn't try; the results will be very disappointing.

Take time out to learn about the particular microclimate of your space; in this respect basement gardens are unique. We tend to think of them as being cold places, but of course basement gardens are usually all walls, walls, walls and nowhere is the storage-radiator effect more evident. These walls also provide one advantage over ground-level gardens: because basements are protected from wind, you can grow plants there that wouldn't be happy in more exposed gardens. The downside of the basement microclimate is that many of them are in perpetual shade and most of them are pretty damp too – this is something that will need to be taken into consideration when you are choosing plants and hard-landscaping materials.

SOIL

The soil in many sunken gardens is often a token gesture; a squelchy mess devoid of organic matter, nutrients and beneficial micro-organisms, or a sterile, structure-less powder that runs through the fingers like flour. And that's if you're lucky – sometimes there isn't any soil at all, just a load of flaky concrete.

If this description applies to your basement, then you're going to need to do a little work on the soil before you can think about putting in any plants.

Unfortunately this means removing a good proportion of the bad soil and replacing it with good-quality topsoil, as well as adding lots of organic matter and grit to improve drainage and aeration. One word of warning, however – whenever you are digging down in a basement, be careful of the footings of the surrounding walls, so as not to disturb the foundations of your house. If you have any doubts or concerns, play it safe and do as many basement gardeners do and grow everything in pots. Constructing raised beds will create more planting space than lots of pots but, again, be careful where you put them – siting them directly against house walls may compromise your damp-proof course.

OPPOSITE An oasis of calm below the hustle and bustle of city life.

Design-wise, a basement garden demands that you go for broke in a big way, as these spaces have larger-than-life built into them. Half-heartedness just won't do. But don't worry, this all or nothing approach needn't cost the earth. For example, you can economize by using masses of different plastic pots (covering the edges with trailing ivy), which will help keep the budget down. Think big – nowhere else do a couple of flaccid bedding plants seem so out of place.

STYLES

So which design styles will work in basements? Not many, I hear you say, because the space is so small and dark. Well, surprisingly, the jungle-look is actually the easiest to pull off: filling a small space with large-leaved jungly plants actually makes it seem bigger, because those very obvious boundaries are hidden and the jungle seems to go on into infinity. If you can't see the walls, then how do you know how big the space actually is? Jungly gardens also have a supernatural charm that is enhanced by a spooky basement. More importantly, it's a look that works well with the dark, damp microclimate and which allows loads of different plants to thrive: hostas, *Rheum*, ferns, *Ligularia*, box, *Anemone*, vincas, *Aruncus* and mind-your-own-business are all really happy in such conditions.

The minimalist style is another look that works well and it's ideal if you want to keep maintenance down. Minimalism and basements can be a happy union, but more care and a sympathetic eye are needed with this look as it's easy to come a cropper and create a soulless, uninspiring composition. If you are laying down hard landscaping as part of your contemporary, minimalist design, use western red cedar or Karri decking, or slate, polyophry or quartzite slabs over the whole area. Position a loquat

ABOVE **Packing a small basement with plants is the last thing you should do, surely? But if you struggle to see the boundaries of this jungly basement, how do you know how big the space is?**

(*Eriobotrya japonica*) or weeping pea tree (*Caragana arborescens*) in a huge pot, or even a modern fountain in the centre and you will instantly create a really effective focal point. Tall coloured pots positioned along the back wall and filled with lush hostas, box cones or arum lilies and topped with hydroleca helps to define the space and makes a bold architectural statement against a neutral-coloured wall.

Although many basements have no neighbouring windows they *are* looked down upon, so the design has to be visually appealing from above, too. This isn't as difficult as it sounds, it's actually easier to imagine a design from a bird's-eye view – especially when drawing it on paper. Bold, simple geometric layouts usually work best: circles of paving leading to a larger one in the centre of the space; a spiral of box balls, starting with small ones and gradually increasing in size; or perhaps interlocking rectangles of brick pavers, each one edged in sunken sleepers.

Whatever style you go for, remember that not only must it link with the house itself, but also with your interior. Like a conservatory, the basement is more 'house' than 'garden', so steps must be taken to make the transition seamless. Rough slate paving running through the kitchen and into the garden is one way of achieving this, or perhaps you could continue the colours of the internal walls externally which will help blur the boundaries and knit inside and outside together.

FORM FOLLOWS FUNCTION

ABOVE Keep the heart of your city basement clutter-free – flexibility is key.

Flexibility is the key to getting the most out of basement gardens, as it is for all small spaces. The core of most basement-garden designs is an open, clutter-free centre which allows for bikes to be stripped down for maintenance, doors to be sanded, kitchen units to be easily assembled, as well as being a place where you could party well into the small hours with an entire hockey team!

In order to maximize your space, try building in furniture using brickwork or concrete-rendered breeze blocks – the surrounding walls will double as chair backs. I often make lids to seating benches using decking or reclaimed floorboards treated with a preservative, so cushions, gardening tools or children's toys can be stored inside. These storage seats can even be waterproof if you line them with plastic sheeting or make each seat according to the size of cheap plastic storage boxes – the ones you get from DIY superstores. Matching the materials used on the bench and the floor will blend them in and give a seamless, stylish look.

For the ultimate in flexibility, get some moveable furniture. Collapsible tables and chairs can be stored upright behind large planters when not in use, or when you need somewhere to pop a children's paddling pool. Clear plastic or glass tables are a good choice in larger basements, as you can see plants through them and they reflect valuable light, too. I've always wanted to create a table for a basement out of a giant terracotta pot with a large circular toughened glass top. I thought the container would look good planted with small ferns like the hard fern (*Blechnum spicant*) and the Himalayan maidenhair fern (*Adiantum venustum*) – rather like those tall bottle lamps your granny had twenty years ago. Perfect for a jungly design!

SURFACES

Because basements are protected from drying winds, damp and algae can occur, so any flooring must have a slip-resistant finish for safety. Slabs with a textured finish are ideal, but decking – a popular choice for basements – can be slippery, so choose planks with a grooved side for grip. Gravel has good slip resistance but it doesn't really work in a basement where you're treating the space as another room of the house. It's uncomfortable underfoot and as everyone wants to walk out first thing in the morning wearing a dressing gown, cup of tea in hand, it's not my first choice. Plus it gets carried into the house too easily.

Drainage is, of course, very important in basements – you don't want your sunken garden turning into a swimming pool after a torrential downpour! It's worth seeking professional advice if you're thinking of laying paving over the

ABOVE **Overhead beams draped with plants makes the perfect umbrella to shield you from prying eyes above.**

whole area as soakaways and drains must be taken into consideration. When choosing slabs, go for smaller paving units angled at 45 or 30 degrees, as they'll make small spaces appear bigger. If you are using a dark colour on the walls, use a lighter coloured flooring to keep a feeling of airiness. Of course, the opposite works too – darker slabs contrast well with lighter coloured walls.

PRIVACY

The major grouch of basement gardeners and, for that matter, those in ground-floor flats, is their lack of overhead privacy. It's bad enough being overlooked from the side, but to feel that people can look *down* on you can make you feel nervous and vulnerable: we like to see who's looking at us! This factor, more than any other, has to be resolved and it is a challenge. Creating total privacy means putting 'a roof on the box' and if you do that, you cut out the light, creating a pretty gloomy underworld. Perhaps privacy needs are more psychological than real – that's my mum's view and I tend to agree with her. Having a solid brick wall doesn't necessarily make you feel more secure – sometimes it's nice to be able to peep out and see who's on the other

side of it. So it is with basements. The object here is to make yourself feel that you're not being spied on in an intrusive manner. Frustrating those eyes from above, rather than trying to ban them altogether, is the best way to go about it. Think about old-fashioned net curtains: nobody bothers to come up close and look through the individual holes to see what's going on inside the house, but you can see out and light can get in.

Basements can be screened from above by several methods; some permanent, some temporary; and some ideas are a mixture of the two. Permanent structures would involve putting beams at intervals across the basement roof, rather like a pergola in an above-ground garden, and covering them with *Akebia quinata, Clematis armandii* or *Trachelospermum jasminoides* – that way you get a rather more fragrant version of the net-curtain effect. Think about safety, though, and make sure you support beams securely against the walls using joist hangers.

You don't have to be restricted just to wooden rafters; contemporary schemes look good with steel or ironwork, or even stout steel wires. Rusty reinforcing rods welded together suit the modern rustic style and old scaffold poles painted bright colours work well in more eclectic designs. But suppose you're doing a spot of summer socializing, or you fancy a quiet coffee in your pyjamas? Fixing a temporary pull-over canvas awning will give you the sense of uninterrupted seclusion you need, and in many cases this is better than a permanent structure as you can easily remove it to allow more light in and to let the whole space air properly and dry out. Shade sails have been popular in recent years and you can purchase bespoke as well as off-the-shelf canopies on the internet quite easily, but search around as prices vary. Cotton sheets are an inexpensive alternative – simply tie the corners to large eyehooks and yank the sheet up when required. Temporary canvas umbrellas are also perfect for ad hoc overhead privacy – they're cheap, weatherproof, light, easy to handle and come in many colours – but be sure to measure the width of your basement before you buy to be sure you've the space to let it open fully!

Making a basement private has to be an exercise in balance – you don't want to feel like you're hemmed in, but the skill lies in not cutting out too much available light, either. More often than not covering one half – or even just a corner – is sufficient to give you much-needed privacy.

MORE LIGHT

Mirrors are worthy additions in the basement garden. They help to inject light into dark corners and increase the sense of mystery, especially when plants conceal their edges. But the effectiveness of mirrors depends on what they are reflecting; they need to be angled so that the reflection doesn't catch *you* the minute you walk into the garden, but picks up on some quality planting instead. Cladding an entire wall with a mirror will undoubtedly double the space visually and force you to question where the garden ends, but it's often difficult to avoid including the reflections of the bins, storage cupboards and

ABOVE As most basements are dark and perhaps a little gloomy, if you've got a sunny spot it's a real blessing and somewhere to grow a prized acacia.

your collection of mountain bikes – all of which ruin the illusion you're trying to create. Remember less is more, and sometimes a small mirror enveloped in planting is all that's needed.

Acrylic mirrors are a light, easy to handle and inexpensive alternative to glass, and can be cut more easily into different shapes. If you have pets or children acrylic mirrors are a must, as being shatterproof they are much safer than glass should they get damaged. They are also simple to attach; just stick masking tape over where you want fixing holes and drill through the mirror using a metal bit. Finish it off with mirror screws to help maintain the illusion.

Polished aluminium or steel panels and containers have similar reflective qualities, and sometimes work better than a mirror as the reflected image is always blurred. They're perfect for almost all designs where such a contemporary material won't look out of place.

A fresh coat of paint goes a long way to lighten up a basement garden. Try to stick to different hues of the same colour, rather than mix colours. Neutrals work best – they don't 'impose' and always contrast well with your planting, whereas darker colours will often enhance the hemmed-in feel. However, in a small space you can afford to experiment, and if it looks ghastly it doesn't cost a lot to simply paint over your mistakes.

GARDEN WHIMSY!

In keeping with the theatre-in-a-box feel, the basement garden begs you to bring in touches of whimsy. With no view to borrow from the world around, it's vital to create sufficient interest within the garden. If ever there was a garden space suited to eccentric touches, the basement is it. Whatever you put there will appear to be twice as significant as it would in an 'up there' garden. A collection of shells or driftwood suddenly becomes magical, and you'll notice leaf shapes and individual flowers more keenly.

The basement can be a wonderful opportunity to bring out the hidden you, the creativity the normal everyday world doesn't see. You can treat the area like a three-dimensional picture, changing the objects and their arrangements whenever it suits, so when you look out of adjoining doors and windows you've something different to focus on each month. It's nice to have eye-catching objects like waterspouts and statues to distract from the small space, but every other element will need to work hard too. Focal points in basements aren't concerned so much with perspective as they are in a large country garden; rather, they provide the eye with a series of interesting little diversions and surprises.

Check out reclamation yards for unique knick-knacks; some huge barrel rings, a lead Statue of Liberty and a herd of rusty cast-iron cows are some of my most recent finds! Reclamation yards offer the chance for eccentricity to burst out. How about stone statues of nymphs, or lion's-head gate-guardians, huge stone balls, and all things gothic from gargoyles to griffons? But don't go *too* mad otherwise your design could end up looking like a dog's dinner.

At reclamation yards old doesn't necessarily mean cheap. I've learnt not to expect to find knockdown prices or bargain-basement pieces, you will find bargains – like beautifully kept butler sinks and buckets – but today's yards have a discerning clientele and prices can be high. This is certainly true of city yards, and especially those in London where prices are sometimes astronomical. I'm fast becoming an advocate of out-of-town yards – it's the perfect opportunity to throw together a picnic and spend a day out treasure-hunting. There are a couple of gems near where my mum lives in Somerset and sometimes they're the main excuse for the journey.

ABOVE Why have a basement focal point you can only see during the day?

ILLUMINATE

With such a unique atmosphere, you can only add to the drama in basements with garden lighting. A lot of the time basement gardeners don't bother with it, but it can be used cleverly to create different moods, much like the way that banks of lighting in a theatre can manipulate the emotions of the audience. There's a huge range of garden lighting available now and numerous suppliers are selling lights to suit all budgets and tastes, from cheap plastic sets to swanky ones made in copper, steel, aluminium and stone where the fitting is an attractive feature in it's own right.

To get the most out of the lighting in a garden, any garden, careful placement is key. Basement walls are fantastic projector screens: angle a spotlight in front of clumps of *Miscanthus sinensis* 'Flamingo' or other giant perennials like *Macleaya cordata*, foxgloves, *Angelica*, *Eupatorium* and *Filipendula rubra* and you can create a wonderfully atmospheric effect by casting their silhouettes and shadows on the wall behind.

I love uplighting tree ferns and tall cordylines with spotlights placed at the base as they throw the rough texture of the trunks into relief, but try and hide the origin of the light to enhance the mystical feeling. In contemporary

minimalist designs downlighters can help to highlight the shapes of topiary and boldly planted containers where plants would be in shadow if they were lit from below.

Spacing narrow spotlights equidistantly and positioning them tight to the wall will provide a dramatic night-time focal point, or you can add an ethereal feeling to any planting scheme, be it in a basement or courtyard, using tiny plastic lights positioned every so often – but make sure the fittings are hidden. You can add some glamour to decking by setting LED lights into the wood, which will twinkle like stars and can be positioned sporadically or in a defined pattern to suggest a direction to walk or simply the edge of the decked area for safety.

Fire also enhances the moody atmosphere of a basement garden, as well as keeping you warm and thereby extending the time you spend outside. For complete flexibility, get some temporary braziers which can be easily cleaned and hidden when not in use. If there's room and you don't mind a permanent feature, a sunken fire-pit made from firebricks will become the hub of any seating area. A metal basket ensures you can pull all the spent ashes out without too much bother and when not in use you could cover it with a timber lid or a deep, recessed drain cover which you can disguise with pieces of the surrounding paving to help it blend in.

You could, of course, get really creative and make some lights. Tea lights in olive-oil cans punctured with a screwdriver so the whole container glows, or tapers pushed into lengths of copper pipe cost virtually nothing. Bottles, vases, coconut husks, antique saucepans and buckets of sand can all be filled with candles for a cheap and quirky effect, or why not drape exterior fairy lights over your favourite architectural specimens?

WATER

Nothing beats a secret pool in a basement garden, especially when surrounded by luxuriant planting. Masks, lions' heads and small cascading wall fountains not only provide a valuable focal point but enable you to grow beautiful marginals at their feet. Water irises, *Kirengeshoma palmata*, *Trillium*, *Ligularia* and *Filipendula ulmaria* 'Aurea' are perfect for basement water features as they all thrive in a boggy, semi-shaded position.

Alternatively, a raised pool built of stone, rendered concrete blocks or untreated sleepers is the perfect tranquil spot to sit quietly with a glass of wine, trailing a hand through the water. Lighting water features in basements

ABOVE **The soothing sound of running water always provides a welcome distraction from unwanted city sounds.**

will deepen the sense of mystery and waterproof spotlights under spouts and wall fountains will produce a mesmerizing flickering effect on the wall behind. If midges are a problem around your water feature, lighting a few citronella candles will help stop you being eaten alive or – if the pond gets some sun – try a few small ornamental fish that will eat any larvae.

PLANTS

Contemporary minimalist or modernist planting schemes rely heavily on a few key plants which almost always have architectural merit and generosity of form – plants like *Cirsium*, *Astelia*, box, *Persicaria*, *Melianthus*, *Phormium*, *Euphorbia characias* subsp. *wulfenii* and bamboo. Whilst minimalist planting schemes may appear over-simplified to some people, the whole concept is about tranquillity, serenity and the relationship between mass and void; less is definitely more. A restricted plant palette can make a minimalist design in a tiny basement look sterile and bleak, so choose plants that work hard for their space: those that look good right through the year and, ideally, that change with the seasons. Take *Prunus serrula*; it has gorgeous ruby red bark over the winter, tiny confetti-like white flowers in spring with graceful, almost

translucent leaves, and good colour and cherry-like fruit in autumn. All of this and it has a simple, mounded shape. It's a tree that begs your attention all year round so it suits pared-down minimalist design perfectly. (I will admit to some bias against minimalist planting schemes only because the jungle look lets you go mad with plants!)

Many evergreens may appear dour and uninspiring for much of the year, but they are perhaps our most important plants. Think of them as anchors which provide the foil for and 'hold down' other plants all year round. These evergreens are especially important in the 'picture' garden.

EVERGREENS

As light is limited the backbone of basement gardens is going to be made up of evergreens – bamboos, dramatic shrubs, quirky topiary and a small tree or two if you've got the space. *Fatsia japonica* is a superb shade-loving, glossy plant with leaves like huge hands straight out of the Addams family; its new foliage even unfurls like claws. *Mahonia aquifolium* 'Smaragd', *Skimmia japonica* 'Redruth', *Prunus laurocerasus* 'Camelliifolia', *Aucuba japonica* 'Rozannie', *Itea virginica* and *Daphne odora* 'Aureomarginata' are also easy to grow in shade and their new shiny green leaves are useful light reflectors, too. Camellias are some of our most valuable early-flowering, shade-tolerant evergreens that just need a rich, acid soil to thrive. *Camellia japonica* 'Adolphe Audusson', which sports clear red flowers right through the spring, is an entry in my top fifty ultimate favourites. However, *C. japonica* and its cultivars are a poor choice for a really tiny basement garden as many will grow to more than 8m (25ft) in height and spread; better to choose *C.* x *vernalis* or *C.* x *williamsii* varieties instead, as both only grow to a height of 2–5m (6–15ft). *C.* 'Francis Hanger' has clear white flowers, *C.* 'Elsie Jury' is tall and upright with huge pink flowers, and *C.* 'Yuletide' has a dense habit smothered in dots of red. Watch out for the pink-flowered cultivar *C.* x *williamsii* 'Donation', it's available everywhere but it is one of the biggest.

Variegated evergreens are a good choice if you want to hide any oppressive walls and will act as a foil for surrounding perennials but, perhaps more importantly, they introduce year-round variation in a scheme of green. It's true that most variegated plants dislike deep shade, but unless it's a plant that demands full sun the chances are it'll thrive in a semi-shaded basement. *Euonymus* 'Emerald 'n' Gold' and *Pachysandra terminalis* 'Variegata' are tough ground cover plants, whereas *Aucuba japonica* 'Crotonifolia', *Elaeagnus* 'Gilt Edge', and *Griselinia littoralis* 'Variegata' are perfect for some reliable structural planting. All these plants are a little big for space-hungry plots, but they will tolerate toughish pruning to keep them in check.

JUNGLE FEVER

For the ultimate in Jurassophile plantings, however, nothing beats a tree fern or two, and for some all-important height a rigid *Typha maxima* or a tall *Cyperus papyrus* (the Egyptian paper rush) is a must. These three plants will all grow well in a damp basement garden; just give them as much sun as you can.

Ferns should top the list for essential plants in a basement garden – the only bad thing about them is their horrible, unpronounceable names! Deciduous ferns like the mountain fern (*Oreopteris limbosperma*), and the buckler fern (*Dryopteris erythrosora*) are favourites but in basements where space is a premium, be sure to include evergreens like spleenwort (*Asplenium scolopendrium*), soft shield fern (*Polystichum setiferum*), and the common polyopdy (*Polypodium vulgare*) for year-round interest.

To fill in the gaps within a jungly scheme, encourage small mosses and plant European wild ginger (*Asarum europaeum*) and mind-your-own-business – both can be a little rampant, but are welcome additions to a basement garden where they'll quickly carpet themselves between all the cracks.

ABOVE The jungle look has a spooky ambience which is perfect for city basements.

BREAK UP THE GREEN

If you're finding all this heavyweight green planting a bit much, you could lighten it considerably by adding loads of shade-tolerant perennials, selected for both their striking leaves and flowers. Meaty *Rodgersia podophylla*, hostas and *Heuchera* 'Palace Purple' look sensational when combined with dainty toad lilies, *Geranium phaeum* 'Variegata', *Epimedium pinnatum* subsp. *colchicum*, *Symphytum alba, Dicentra spectabilis* 'Alba', pineapple mint (*Mentha suaveolens* 'Variegatum'), *Luzula nivea*, *Euphorbia palustris*, *Polygonatum* x *hybridum* and *Astrantia* 'Hadspen Blood'.

Every wall in a basement garden can be primed for climbers: add strong 'invisible' or translucent wires for supporting them. Tempting as it may be to cover every available inch with plants, do try to leave gaps, otherwise green will dominate and make you feel you're being taken over. You need a balance between exposed wall and planting. Ivies like 'Eva', 'Pedata' 'Ivalace', 'Atropurpurea' and 'Green Ripple' are perfect; none of them are

particularly invasive, they will stick to walls tenaciously and they need no maintenance or support.

If you crave seasonal colour, then pots of red or white busy lizzies mounding though *Chlorophytum* or *Tradescantia pallida* 'Purpurea' could be thrown in wherever there's room. Although both are tender and are often grown as houseplants, in cities where the temperature is higher they'll usually survive right through the winter.

SCENT TRAP

Scented plants are a must in the basement garden. Whereas roof terraces are open to the elements, the advantage of having any strongly scented plants in an enclosed area like a basement, courtyard or side passageway is that the fragrance hangs around for longer, rather than being blown away. Because the space is small, the plants make a much bigger impact and as a basement is so close to the house, powerful free-scented plants will perfume every room.

If your's is a semi-shady spot, why not grow sweet-scented lilies and mix them up for continuity? *Lilium regale*, the Madonna lily, will add scent and colour in early summer, then plant *L. candidum* for midsummer, and *L. speciosum* var. *album* or *L. auratum* for late summer and early autumn.

The sweet-smelling *Nicotiana sylvestris* is a sumptuous plant that is festooned in ginormous trumpet-like white flowers throughout the summer, but it does need to be given as much sun as possible. For early-evening scent, grow evening primrose (*Oenothera biennis*) for its intoxicating lemony smell or lily-of-the-valley – a much-underrated, fragrant perennial with a pernicious zeal which won't mind a shady position either. If you're lucky enough to have a sunny spot, get some perfumed night phlox (*Zaluzianskya capensis*) for a knockout fragrance.

Next up is the classic backyard – the one city garden which is most neglected. It's a place to party, relax or exercise some creativity – and above all else it provides the opportunity to extend your living space. No matter how small, out the back can and does fulfil the need to expand one's territory.Just don't forget the plants, please!

'Although the raw material might seem unpromising, basements do have exciting potential and present one of the strongest cases for transformation that I know.'

ON THE LEVEL (COURTYARDS, BACKYARDS)

This is *the* city garden space with potential. Picture those idyllic courtyards of old: painted wooden arbours dripping with climbers; espaliered fruit on every wall; and a crystal-clear fountain in the centre, cooling the air. Sounds good doesn't it? Well, let me bring you back down to earth with a bump. In reality most backyards are dull and dismal – the most neglected of all city gardens. Many aren't much more than a dumping ground for bins, used paint pots and dead furniture and they're usually covered in grey concrete or tarmac. Sin City indeed. Your backyard may look like this (now); but things are going to change. Think of your backyard as both an asset and a luxury – it's often the closest us city folk have to a proper garden, so neglect here is tantamount to heresy. Those of us with no ground-floor space, nowhere to play petanque, play-fight with the dog, store our tools or wash down our bikes, have got good reason to be jealous.

BELOW Pick a style and go for it with gusto. (I don't like the broom, though!)

STYLE WISE

All city backyards have one thing in common – boundaries. So, what's new? Well, boundaries provide the all-important distance between you and your neighbours' gardens. As a result your garden exists in isolation, which means you can literally go for any style you like because adjacent gardens won't dilute your design.

ABOVE Restrained and effortlessly simple, this wonderful retreat demands that you relax.

ANYTHING GOES!

Unlike front gardens, where more self-restraint is sometimes necessary, and roof terraces, which are often governed by the building itself and its backdrop, the backyard is the place for self-expression. I love Moorish-inspired designs: cool, dark outdoor rooms with terracotta-coloured tiled floors that are partly roofed over to give shelter from the sun and feature a simple fountain, pool or rill running down the middle. Or how about an urban jungle? Luxuriant tree ferns, hardy bananas, cordylines, *Astelia*, hostas, *Ligularia* and Egyptian paper rush enveloping a simple circular seating area. Or imagine romantic liaisons in a garden filled with scented roses, forget-me-nots, foxgloves and other cottage perennials, a look that works in all but the very tiny space. Or what about going in completely the opposite direction and creating a rustic, minimalist design using materials like soft willow, granite and verdegris copper? If space permits, the oriental garden is a favourite low-maintenance option, and so is the modernist courtyard – a liberating garden style that uses the ideology of Mediterranean gardens but cranks up the drama. And if you want to be knee-deep in foliage, go for a gravel garden where plants pop up everywhere, blurring the boundaries between borders and paths.

Defining the style you want right from the off is imperative to the whole design process, but don't be a slave to it. Use the chief principles that are appropriate to that style, but only as a starting point. These, moulded with your own ideas, will allow you to create a garden that's unique, *and* one that fits comfortably within your plot. Be warned that carbon copy recreations of designs that you see in books and magazines will often fail to work as, obviously, every garden is different. Sometimes all that's needed is the subtlest touch: a statue or even just a couple of distinctive plants in pots will help suggest a particular style.

BUT DON'T FORGET A FEW RULES . . .

Whatever style you go for, again the appearance and architecture of your house will have a huge bearing upon the success of any design. Even if your chosen garden style is dramatically different (and it often is) to that of your house, you must be sympathetic to the make up, age and appearance of the exterior. Small city gardens are 'outdoor rooms' and, as I've said before in this book, marrying house and garden together will make both spaces feel bigger. It's such a simple thing to achieve and can be easily done just by using flooring of a similar ilk, or by painting the walls outside the same colour as those in the living room.

Treat garden fashions with caution, too. Every garden style has its day; just look at the Chelsea Flower Show, what's hot one year will be passé the next. Fashion is a terrible thing in garden design as it seduces everyone into plumping for the same materials, plants and accessories, thereby forcing individuality out the window. Gardens that are designed purely with the 'next big thing' in mind date terribly; look at cobalt-blue painted fencing – once it was the height of style and now it's a pariah.

As in every garden space, you will also need to consider the practicalities of gardening in Britain. The personality of your space will be determined by many factors: orientation, soil type, open or enclosed space, windswept or sheltered. Some of these characteristics you can't change, and many you wouldn't want to. Working up your design ideas in conjunction with what you have is key. For example, you want to build a tropical-style courtyard out back, but you live in Edinburgh where the shorter summer and cooler northern climate mean you have to adapt your planting scheme to suit the locality. Invariably, half-hardy exotics such as *Alocasia*, *Neoregelia*, *Aeonium* and *Hedychium coronarium* (ginger lily) will have to be substituted for hardy exotic plants such as cordylines, *Euonymus alatus*, *Sedum* 'Matrona' and *Catalpa* x *erubescens* 'Purpurea'. You may well have to concentrate more on the suntraps instead of shady corners where you can hide away from the sun.

WHAT TO KEEP?

When you move into a house you inherit all the additions of the previous owners. The garden is an inheritance, too. Before starting work outdoors, decide what to keep and what to ditch. With a winter move, bulbs and perennials will be dormant, and you won't know exactly how deciduous trees and shrubs will look until the spring. Fortunately, the garden is generally the 'last room' in the house that gets attention, so at least there'll be a fair amount of time for you to watch how your new garden develops. There might be hidden treasures in the garden, some you'd like to keep – if you knew they were there!

WHAT DO YOU WANT FROM ME?

In a backyard where there is so much potential you will need to be realistic. Where space is at a premium, lots of practical necessities will jockey for position, and this usually means making many compromises.

Write two lists: the first should be a fantasy wish list, and the second should itemize all the everyday needs that your outdoor space must fulfil. Then weigh them both up, side by side. Dining and entertaining versus the rotary washing line; expansive prairie-like borders versus a kids' football pitch; hot tub and chill-out zone versus bike rack and tool shed – I know which one will usually win here!

Bear in mind that practical needs do change as time goes by, too. Initially there might be a sandpit for young children, but a few years later a mini-football pitch might take precedence and after that, an entertaining area. Wherever possible, allow for the garden to grow with your needs. Plan ahead so that any hard landscaping that is done now won't block future plans. Soft landscaping is much easier and cheaper to adapt later than hard landscaping – a full-on brick and timber pergola is costly to build and costly to ditch. Even large shrubs can be moved if necessary, and moveable gardens (such as large tubs and planters), are very easy to rearrange as your needs evolve.

BELOW Keep things flexible – it's no good having a garden which can't be used properly. Form should follow function!

ABOVE **Always, always, always make seating a priority in your garden – it's probably where you'll spend most of your time.**

Families with young children have to be especially forward-thinking. However, I'm not a fan of creating gardens that are purely kids-orientated. Even though most of us move home regularly, before too long your kids will be playing football in the park down the road. I much prefer making 'family-friendly' gardens – spaces that don't prohibit children but just aren't dominated by permanent climbing frames and paddling pools.

PLAN FOR SPACE

In the majority of cases, an open centre is the starting point for backyard designs because it permits the space to be as multifunctional as possible. A formal layout based on a traditional courtyard is the most common one. Typically, the focus of the design will either be a fountain or small tree in the centre, or if the space is longer than it is wide, it might have a bench beneath an arbour positioned centrally in front of the rear boundary. Admittedly this is being overly simplistic, for there are hundreds of designs which blow this principle to the wind. But, nevertheless, it's a useful starting point if your head is spinning with ideas.

In many cases, backyards tend to be focused around a table, as eating outside is perhaps the most important consideration for city dwellers. Where space is limited the table and chairs are always the most dominant feature – if only because they need room around them on all sides for diners to pull back their chairs and relax in comfort.

A simple square or circle of paving (or a combination of them both) positioned in the centre of the yard always works well, because not only does it help keep things bold yet simple, but it also enables you to envelop the garden in plants and in turn blur the boundaries. Both these shapes are static, too, and don't inspire movement. This is useful in a small city space surrounded by neighbouring eyesores, as it helps to keep the eye focused inwards. The downside of a design like this is that for many (myself included), it's all just a bit too rigid. Instead, you could go for a more relaxed, asymmetrical layout. This still gives a sense of order, but it isn't quite so strict. Imagine a low wall fixed to one side of the garden and built out partway across it, or a raised rendered pool just off to one side of the central line of symmetry that runs down the garden. Look at the paintings by Piet Mondrian and you'll get the idea.

Asymmetrical designs also allow you to easily break up the space to create a little bit of mystery. What's round the corner? Picture tall planting with 'opaque' perennials' like *Actaea simplex* 'Scimitar', purple cow parsley, *Thalictrum delavayi* 'Hewitt's Double' or a simple heather screen; it inspires you to investigate the other side.

If a table and chairs or a bench positioned at the end of your garden is the focus of your design make sure you go for something that's in keeping. Splash out for the good stuff or shop around for something sympathetic. Under no circumstances go for white plastic furniture – it goes with nothing.

OUTSIDE ENTERTAINING

Talk to any city gardener about their space and the number-one flaw is 'we can't eat outside!'. The tricky thing is that dining areas need space, and lots of it – not easy if the garden is no bigger than a postage stamp. When planning your dining area remember that seating areas need more room than you'd think. To check you've allowed the right amount of space, measure the dimensions of the set that you've got your eye on and make a cardboard template of the table and each one of the chairs. Then lay these cut-outs flat on the ground to check you've planned for enough legroom – it'll also help you work out how much paving you'll need to buy. Alternatively, measure the space taken up by the table and chairs in the dining room and transfer your findings to the ground. Better still, drag them outside! For four people to sit comfortably, I try and allocate at least 3–3.5 square metres (32–37 square feet).

ABOVE What a place to sit and entertain!

If you intend to entertain four people, try and plan for six. You never know when you'll get gatecrashers.

Remember to keep things flexible. The area you're considering for some al fresco dining may have to facilitate some sunbathing, too. Collapsible furniture sets are best here. Plus they enable you to chase the sun around the garden.

Form follows function. Make sure chairs are comfortable before you're seduced by their appearance.

Some protection from the sun might be necessary. Temporary parasols or sails are best, as they can be removed when not in use. Choose one in a neutral colour so it doesn't dominate. Roller blinds are definitely a more expensive option, but they do negate storage problems and, again, because they're not fixed in position they don't block out valuable light either. Permanent structures, like wooden beams running from the house, covered with wisteria, or a sail tensioned on wires, might be necessary for all-year-round overhead privacy.

THE GARDEN'S COOKING!

The barbecue – that essential summer gadget! Let's face it, we've all got them and they do come up as a design consideration. You need to carefully consider where you're going to put a barbecue because it needs to be sited away from doors and windows, yet within easy reach of the kitchen.

Where space is limited, go for moveable barbecues rather than built-in ones. If you only use the barbie during the summer, why create a fixed area for cooking? Built-in barbecues often look ugly, especially in winter. Barbecues on wheels also allow you to move to a sheltered spot if the wind gets up.

If you go the whole hog and create an outdoor kitchen, worktops in the garden should be able to accommodate a few pots of seasonal colour when the barbecue is not in use. Always try and build cupboards underneath so you can hide the gas bottle, trays and cooking utensils, too.

A heater will prolong the time spent outside, even in summer. A gas-fired 'mushroom' (like the ones you see on the continent) is very effective but can be an unwelcome focal point. Plus it can cost a fortune in gas to use it every evening. Small electric heaters are a better solution, as they can be fixed to a wall and are therefore less obtrusive. Braziers, fire-pits or Mediterranean clay chimineas are the cheapest option and are perfect for those who love the sight and sound of a roaring open fire.

Choose surface materials that can be cleaned. Natural sandstone isn't ideal as it picks up stains easily. I've used smooth dark slate before, and with minor scrubbing all but the worst stains come off. Gravel works well as you can 'ruffle it up' to get rid of spills. You don't need a sea of the stuff, just enough to surface where you might cook.

THE CONCRETE NIGHTMARE

Concrete slabs are much maligned and, in my opinion, rightly so. Exit stage left! They look cheap, they're not cheerful, and although plain grey concrete slabs are bad enough, yellow- and pink-coloured ones look even worse. Fortunately, they are easy to remove, so dumping them in a skip is not bad news. If you do want to keep them (maybe you can't afford to replace them with anything better), then all isn't lost, just chuck the ones that are broken. It's actually worth taking all the broken ones up, anyway, and re-laying them.

Don't bother to clean ugly concrete slabs regularly with a pressure sprayer, unless they're slippery. Weathered, they're at least tolerable.

ABOVE Brick pavers turn the floor of this concrete yard into a more interesting chequerboard design.

To be honest, in many cases you'll simply wish that you'd replaced them, so perhaps save up or choose smaller plants so that you can budget for some attractive paving. To do the same-sized area, some imitations will cost half the price of natural stone, and many are cast from moulds of the real thing, so the finish is pretty authentic-looking. Gravel, or even bark, is cheaper still – although perhaps not as practical as you can't just wander out barefoot first thing in the morning or late at night.

A thick concrete pad, on the other hand, is a different story, and you'll find it the very devil to dig up. This is definitely an instance where hiring a builder to break it up pays for itself ten times over! When the concrete has gone the soil underneath is going to be old, compacted and sour. I call it 'dead' soil. So whenever you rip up any concrete and plan for planting in its place, chuck out the soil to a depth of at least 30cm (1ft) and replace it with good quality topsoil. It'll cost less than you think; a 1-tonne bag will set you back about £60–80 and will do approximately 2 sq m (21 sq ft) at this depth.

I appreciate that sometimes this is too much like hard work, so why not treat your concrete like the perfect blank canvas? Out back you can opt for a pot garden, leaving the concrete as excellent hard-standing for laying gravel underfoot and arranging seating and planters on top in a design which provides a lush green backdrop to dining alfresco. As long as it's not badly cracked, in many cases a concrete backyard is the perfect foundation for paving slabs. (However, when you lay them, remember that they mustn't bring up the level of the ground to the extent that you then compromise the damp-proof course of the house.) Decking is also ideal for covering concrete, as it provides the perfect firm footing for the timber frame (if it's level, of course). With a concrete desert it's a case of weighing up the options. Do you leave the concrete and cover it? Or do you break your back (or the bank!) trying to remove it? If access to and from the garden is particularly difficult, then I know which option I'd settle for!

To break up a sea of grey concrete slabs; intersperse rows of slabs with treated wooden stretchers, or leave some of the slabs out and in-fill with gravel, old tiles laid on edge, cobbles set in cement, or even pieces of driftwood you lugged back from the shore. Or why not lift the occasional slab, dig out the sand cement foundation and replace it with fresh topsoil. You've then created some little planting pockets for tough ground cover like *Vinca minor* 'Atropurpurea', *Ajuga reptans* 'Burgundy Glow', *Pachysandra terminalis* or even common ivy. You could go the whole hog and create an abstract checkerboard effect! (Although don't forget to keep an area free for a table and chairs.)

GARDEN SHEDS, LEAN-TOS, AND GREENHOUSES

Give these a good check over. If you've inherited a greenhouse, then there's a good chance it's falling down, because keen gardeners usually take sound, expensive greenhouses with them! If the greenhouse's framework is in poor repair then, sadly, it's often easier and cheaper to buy a new one. If the framework is in reasonable condition, though, and all you've got is dirt and some broken glass, it's pretty straightforward to repair: panes of horticultural glass are cheap, and can be re-installed quickly.

Outhouses, like toilets adjoining old Victorian townhouses, needn't always be knocked down. Storage space in city gardens is like gold dust, so if the structure is at all sound, try and renovate it into something useful. An old outside loo can easily be converted into a potting shed or dry store for garden tools. Give the outside a general tidy-up and a good lick of paint, then cover it with trellis or a wire framework for a climber to scramble over. Voilà! Transformation complete.

I must confess that the old adage 'a shed is a man's best friend' doesn't ring true with me. Yes, they might be prime storage space and practical essentials (especially for families), but more often than not they're a garden eyesore. Paint them, cover them with climbers or screen them with bamboos – anything to prevent them being an unsightly focal point!

EXISTING PLANTING

When it comes to existing planting, care needs to be taken when assessing what to keep and what to chuck. It takes just minutes to chainsaw down a tree, but it might take a lifetime (or cost a fortune) to replace a fully grown specimen. Mature hedges and evergreen shrubs are almost as difficult to replace. So, think twice before whipping them out and do check what they might usefully be hiding – you don't want to fell an old yew only to be faced by an ugly concrete cooling tower that was previously concealed from sight.

Be warned that many specimen trees have Tree Preservation Orders (TPOs) on them; so if a tree has to go, check with your local council that you are allowed to cut it down. Once you've got the tree felled, you've then got the roots to worry about. Most tree surgeons will have a stump grinder to tear and smash the stump to pieces, but if access is poor and they can't get the machine in, you'll have to do it by hand, which can be seriously hard work! Once the area is clear, the soil that is in close proximity to the old tree trunk will need revitalizing before you can plant up with anything new. Lashings of well-rotted organic matter does the trick here!

If a tree casts too much shade, or is just too big for its allotted space, don't just chop it down. All the tree might need is its crown lifting or some judicial thinning. This is particularly true when the tree acts as an anchor in the garden, or is an important focal point. So, before you make that irrevocable decision to remove the tree, see if it can be incorporated into your design.

ABOVE To keep or replace? Now that's the question . . . Here the lawn works wonderfully, but mowing it once or twice a week in summer might not be to everyone's liking.

In many cases it's often a great starting point. Why not tile round it in slate or clay pavers and create the perfect spot for a simple wooden bench?

If you are going to do any remedial work, do get a certified tree surgeon in and don't scrimp and get lumbered with a cowboy. I've seen lots of squared-off, flat-topped and otherwise nastily maimed trees on my travels and they're not a pretty sight! Pruning a mature tree is a highly skilled and dangerous job, so leave it to the experts.

Apart from trees and shrubs, most other plants are easy to move, adapt or replace. Bulbs are different, though. I don't know about you, but I only ever find these when they come up speared on the end of my garden fork. The choicer perennials you wish to keep are worth dividing and replanting and you'll end up with two or three times more that way.

THE LAWN QUESTION

The English love their lawns. Grass is a wonderful child-friendly surface, and the perfect natural foil for plants. If you inherit a garden with a lawn it will, at the very least, need renovating. But before you pull out the scarifier, lawn sand and moss killer, ask yourself if you actually need a lawn at all.

In a tiny garden a lawn needs to be pristine and requires constant upkeep and regular maintenance. It's often a waste of space – especially if you want to use the garden all year round. In winter, lawns are soggy, unsuitable for playing on and can't support dining chairs and tables either. It may well be worth ripping the lawn up completely and paving the whole garden instead. Remember, in a small space everything has to work hard for its inclusion, and where are you going to store the mower? In generously proportioned gardens, don't be too hasty to get out the turf lifter, though – a lawn is a cheap and viable addition to the larger garden – especially from a design point of view as they can be easily cut into any shape you want.

If you're desperate for a green sward but don't like the idea of all that maintenance, then camomile lawns are a realistic alternative. The non-flowering variety, *Chamaemelum nobile* 'Treneague', is the one to go for as it stays low and bushy and needs minimal maintenance, just a soaking with water in very dry spells. Do give them lots of sun, too. Walking over a chamomile lawn is an experience to treasure; the fragrance when you crush the foliage underfoot is heaven-sent. But, like thyme and Corsican mint (which you could use instead), camomile won't tolerate heavy wear and tear, so it's best used in low-traffic areas. Like grass, camomile will soon rot and go brown if it's not in an open, sunny position and remember to cultivate deeply, too, or otherwise it will become waterlogged.

MANIPULATING THE SPACE

Whilst most backyards are square (meaning the traditional open courtyard layout works well), of course many come in other dimensions. The challenge for most city gardeners is how to get the best from your space and how to create an attractive garden without feeling hemmed in, something that can often be achieved simply by tricking the eye into believing the garden is bigger than it seems!

PLAYING WITH PERSPECTIVE

Wherever you find the more up-market Edwardian and Victorian city housing you are likely to encounter decent-sized backyards. They are often long and narrow rather than wide – what I call the runway look! Deep, thin gardens give you the scope to create a series of rooms down the length which disguises the elongated nature of the space. A simple solution is to position tall hedges, walls or screens at right angles across the garden to obstruct the view.

However, even though this will divide up the space, it's usually too clumsy for most city gardens – it tends to make them feel smaller because you can't see what's beyond. What you need is a little subtlety. Where possible, work with diagonal lines, using rectangles, squares or interlocking circles, for example, so that your eye is led across the garden, rather than straight to the end. The space around the edges then affords the opportunity to screen a little of the garden beyond, without blocking it off completely. Even something so simple as cutting the lawn up into diamond squares with an off-set path linking them and planting either side of the path with arching bamboo, will effect a simple transformation. Carefully positioned focal points such as statues, pillars, sundials, or merely distinctive architectural plants, come into their own. They provide welcome punctuation to the larger page and together they will act to lure visitors along the route you've planned down the garden.

With enough space for separate garden rooms you can have a huge diversity of themes. But keep each separate theme and space simple: you could have a bountiful perennial garden in one, a knot garden in another, a fountain, pool and shaded seating area in a third, and each one could be separated and united by trellis, fencing or hedging. It's quite possible to juxtapose a gravelled garden of low mat-forming plants, such as thymes and other rock-garden flowers, in the sunny side of a covered dining area, with a jungly herbaceous border screening the neighbours on the other.

For me, short, fat, wide gardens are the most difficult to design as the back boundary always dominates the space. It's very hard to appreciate the actual size of the garden because you inevitably feel hemmed in. Strategic planting just outside the house, which helps obscure both the boundary and much of the garden, will help no end. Again, using the diagonal line is useful, too, because it pulls the eye to the side of the garden, rather than allowing it to focus directly on the back. Imagine a simple swooping serpentine curve, an elliptical or kidney-shaped lawn or, again, interlocking diamonds running at 30 or 45 degrees across the space.

A focal point should always be dramatically different to its surroundings if it is to stand out and be noticed. It's no good positioning pots filled with foliage plants or green box topiary in front of a yew hedge, for example – where's the contrast there?

FOCAL POINTS

Focal points are vital to all gardens, especially small ones where the focus is inwards. Almost anything can be used to attract attention as long as it's different to its surroundings. Obelisks, statues, pools, rills, summerhouses, arbours, garden canopies or even striking container displays work well, as long as the object has dramatic form and/or it's a different colour to the norm. The effective and successful use of focal points can help make a small garden feel bigger, because it provides relief for the eye as it wanders over the space. Plus, they provide suitable distractions from dominant boundaries.

How far a window opens, or whether doors open inwards or outwards, always has an impact on the positioning of features, but their location also

ABOVE Taking a lead from surrounding planting, the bamboos help blur the boundaries between this garden and its neighbours, in turn making this space feel so much bigger.

determines the siting of focal points. Usually, the best spot for a focal point in a tiny garden is in line with the main window that overlooks the space or the patio doors, as it helps to draw interest and makes you venture out into the garden. In a small garden this may simply be a box cone in an attractive pot, or a small nymph spouting water from its mouth. A larger, primary focal point, such as a tree in the corner, could then take over. But, don't think that loads of different focal points are a good thing – less is most definitely more! If more than one focal point is visible at any one time, confusion inevitably occurs.

BORROWING SCENERY

Focal points do not necessarily just have to be inside your space, as visually you own everything you can see from your garden. Admittedly, this might be an electricity sub station or a gas tower (or another such unwelcome focal point that needs screening), but equally it could be something attractive such as church spires, large trees, a coastline or the city skyline. These are welcome additions to your horizon and 'borrowing them' will extend your boundaries, which will in turn make the garden feel larger. Framing a view with planting, or positioning a tree so the eye is bounced still further into the distance, is the simplest way to direct attention away from the fact that your backyard is tiny.

You can achieve the same effect on a smaller scale simply by merging plants in your garden with those found in adjacent gardens. Don't just go mad and cut back the trees, conifers and tall shrubs which overhang your boundary; make the most of them. When you can't see the back fence, how do you know where your garden ends and your neighbour's begins until you're right on top of it? Using the same plants or those of a similar colour will help, too. If it's a bamboo that spills over, then consider using the same bamboo elsewhere to provide a little continuity between your garden and your neighbour's. Don't look at it as stealing, just borrowing!

LIGHTING

In tightly enclosed spaces, night-time lighting turns the courtyard into a fantastic drama-scape, extending the use of this outdoor room from late evening into night. You might not have the skyscraper skylines of Manhattan, Hong Kong, Singapore and Shanghai to play with, but lighting can transform your night-time space just as much as it does these cities. If you have trees, you could position spotlights to cast ambient light down on to a patio, or put an uplighter at the base to illuminate the bark and cast graceful shadows in the canopy. Fairy lights and light strands can be very effective and subtle when trained over arches or up through a temporary awning; many are programmed so that at the flick of a switch the colours change. In a small space, LED lights could be arranged to form different shapes which at night create an all-new dimension to the tiny backyard.

PLANTING

In small backyards the mixed garden works best. Spectacular seasonal displays of perennials or massed bulbs are often inappropriate because they're so short-lived and therefore don't maintain interest throughout the year. So use everything the plant world has to offer: small trees, shrubs, grasses, bulbs, perennials, ferns, climbers, roses, wall shrubs, ground cover; and for those who are happy replacing them – biennials and annuals too. All these plants will create a scheme that's appealing both at the height of summer or in the depths of winter.

TREES, TREES, TREES

I haven't mentioned trees enough in this book so far. Trees . . .? Matt – that's all you ramble on about! But I've reserved my passion for the one place that you can go mad – the backyard. I'd like to think that every gardener would contemplate having a tree in whatever sized garden they have. For small gardens trees like *Caragana arborescens* 'Pendula', *Mespilus germanica* 'Nottingham', *Acer palmatum*, *Morus alba* 'Pendula' and the fastigiate *Prunus* 'Amanogawa' can be grown in containers; they don't just come house-sized, you know!

Trees give you so much. They screen out ugly eyesores, they provide privacy and they also act as superb focal points. Even a tiny tree in its fourth year will somehow give a garden a sense of solidity and the feeling that it's grown well beyond its years. For such small spaces as city backyards, it's important to make your tree work hard for the privilege of being in your garden. This means that you should have high expectations of them providing interest all year round and should think about flowers, possibly scent, fruit and coloured bark as well as a shapely form that will look great as a winter skeleton. I'm not saying you'll get the lot with just one choice, but be greedy and go for those specimens that offer as much as possible.

Crab apples and ornamental cherries are without a doubt the two hardest working groups of trees. Most have attractive spring foliage, are smothered in dainty flowers, then produce fruit and, lastly, marvellous autumn colour. Contrary to popular belief, many don't suffer greatly with pest and disease problems either. Birches are good too. For tiny gardens choose *Betula pendula* 'Youngii' – a weeping tree that won't grow taller than 3m (10ft). Or what about the pure white bark of *Betula pubescens*? I'm particularly partial to the Chinese red birch, *Betula albosinensis* var. *septentrionalis* – the bark has to be seen to be believed! Acers are always worth including, again, because they try to impress all year round. Excellent choices are maples such as *Acer capillipes*, *A. rufinerve*, or *A. davidii* 'Serpentine' for its stunning bark – it's commonly know as the snake bark maple. Buy one and you'll see why.

When choosing a tree you obviously need to take into account its eventual size. Do you actually have room for the mature version? Coupled with this is vigour, or how fast it will grow. Some trees, such as *Prunus* 'Kanzan' are what I call 'seducers'. This one has the most jaw-dropping, lurid pink flowers in late spring. That, coupled with the fact that it's the most common ornamental flowering cherry available, means that it's often a dead cert at the garden centre. However, it is a wolf in sheep's clothing and will reach a height and spread of 10m (33ft) in fairly quick time, so it's not the best choice for the small city garden.

Any household with small children should be careful planting a tree which has thorns or poisonous seeds, such as a laburnum. Watch out, too, for those that dump loads of fruit or leaves, leaving you with a mammoth clearing up job. Then there's shade. When a tree is small it hardly seems worth thinking about, but in ten years the canopy could completely cover a small garden. That's fine if that's what you wanted, but it's not much fun if you didn't. If in doubt, go for those trees with small, almost translucent leaves such as *Alnus glutinosa* 'Imperialis', or tight, conical-shaped trees like *Pyrus calleryana* 'Chanticleer' or *Malus tschonoskii* that don't cast too much shade. Ask lots of questions at the nursery, such as will the tree's roots undermine the foundations of your house? Some trees, such as eucalyptus, are notorious for doing just that, and for sending roots into cracked drains, too. Or some, such as rhus (commonly known as the 'stag's horn sumach'), will send out foraging suckers, which might come up in the middle of your lawn when you least expect it!

Trees give you so much. They screen out ugly eyesores, they provide privacy and they also act as superb focal points. For such small spaces as city backyards, it's important to make your tree work hard for the privilege of being in your garden – be greedy and go for those specimens that offer as much as possible.'

TIERED PLANTING

'Tiered' or 'layered' planting is usually the most appropriate planting scheme for a design with an open centre. Tiered borders make good use of space and work hard to hide the boundaries. Layering simply means arranging your border with taller plants at the back, gradating down to smaller ones at the front (nicely concealing the stems of their taller cousins). If you have plants of all one height, you just look straight at them and that's it, you've seen the lot in the blink of an eye because the planting is so static and boring! With tiered planting there's more to look at, more interest, more movement, as the eye wanders up and down the bed, from front to back. It's the best way to arrange a narrow border, in that each plant is positioned to enhance, and not obscure, another. It makes sense. Why have small ground cover plants such as *Stachys byzantina* 'Silver Carpet' and *Rosmarinus officinalis* Prostratus Group at the back of a border and taller, denser evergreens in front hiding them?

To help put together a successful tiered border, try arranging selections of plants in pleasing combinations when you're at your local nursery. Set them out with shape, colour, texture, habit and, of course, size in mind. 'Try before you buy!'

The back tier is usually made up of climbers and larger evergreens such as *Choisya ternata* 'Sundance' and *Olearia* x *haastii*, which provide the all-year-round structure to the scheme. Remember, the more dramatic and dense the plant, the smaller it will make the garden feel – sometimes this is welcome, but most often it goes against the grain. Don't pack plants in; you only need a couple to hold a scheme together. Too many and not only will they dominate but they'll take over, swamping the plants in the foreground. Many common 'backbone' evergreens, such as *Photinia* x *fraseri* 'Red Robin', *Viburnum tinus*, and *Carpenteria californica* need to be kept in check if space is at a premium.

Taller grasses such as *Miscanthus sacchariflorus* help break up evergreens and provide all-important juxtaposition of shape and form. In borders that are no more than a metre wide, perhaps use them in conjunction with wall shrubs such as *Garrya elliptica* 'James Roof' and evergreen climbers like *Clematis armandii* forming the back layer. They'll stick tight to the boundary and act as a foil for showier planting in front, but they won't take over. Structural plants needn't always be thrown against the fence, though; box cones or small yuccas in the middle tier make perfect focal points and help make things more 3-D.

The middle tier should be made up of smaller evergreens such as *Cistus* x *aguilarii* 'Maculatus' and deciduous shrubs such as *Ceratostigma willmottianum* and *Philadelphus* 'Manteau d'Hermine', with taller perennials like golden rod, lupins, red-hot pokers and *Agapanthus* 'Albus' placed in clumps or weaved in 'ribbons' throughout. The front tier is usually made up of mounding and prostrate shrubs, small perennials, low-growing ground cover such as *Stachys byzantina* 'Silver Carpet' and a variety of small bulbs.

How do you get to your back garden? You probably have to walk down a boring concrete passage that you edit out of your sight as you pass through it. Is it really worth transforming? You know what my answer's going to be! Remember: 'it's better to travel than to arrive!' Be greedy and have both!

PICKING PLANTS FOR BORDERS

It's often overwhelming to visit a garden centre and see the huge range of plants that are available, and it's often difficult to appreciate how they will look when they reach maturity. But don't despair, here are a few golden rules that will help guide you towards choosing the best plants for your space:

- Avoid impulse buys. Research, research, research and plan, plan, plan! Make a scale sketch of your border, and you can then add on each individual plant using a circle to represent how big they may get and their preferred position.
- Pick plants that are appropriate to your microclimate. Shade-lovers for shady spots, sun-lovers for sunny spots and acid-loving rhododendrons for acid soils. Remember: right plant, right place.
- Note carefully the mature height, spread and vigour of your plants and position them with this in mind.
- Watch plant spacing, especially when it comes to trees and shrubs. Always give them enough room to develop; you don't want to absolutely cram them in only to find that maintenance is a problem, nor do you want loads of gaps which take ages to fill out.
- How much maintenance will your plants require? Can you devote the appropriate amount of time to them?
- Are the plants suitable for the job you have in mind? Will that tree screen your neighbours or, come winter, will it shed its leaves, leaving you feeling over-exposed?
- Consider the shape, colour and texture of the foliage and the stems. Flowers are not the only source of interest and trying to achieve continuity of flowering can be tricky, so use everything that plants have to offer.
- Consider the style of garden that you're after and choose plants accordingly – cottage perennials for cottage gardens, single architectural specimens for more contemporary designs.
- Try and get an all-important rhythm to your planting scheme. Repeat certain colours, shapes, individual plants or associations to link your scheme together.
- The best piece of advice I ever read was: 'Less is more! Write out the plant list, halve the species and double the remainder!' It's easy to get seduced into buying everything, but that only contributes to a chaotic look.

FROM A TO B (PASSAGEWAYS/ SIDE ALLEYS)

ABOVE Don't think that your narrow passageway is just for the rubbish bins!

It's easy to forget the side alley and to think of it just as something that lets you get from one place to another: a kind of transit zone from front to back garden. As such, neglect is usually the order of the day; the passage becomes a store for the bin, somewhere to hang ladders, park bikes, or cram in the dog kennel, and pretty soon it's an obstacle course stuffed with spare pots, watering cans, hosepipes and bags of compost.

So the side alley is often the biggest challenge for a gardener – too shady for plants, too cluttered and seemingly devoid of potential, it can be a nightmare. But for many city gardeners this narrow, walled-in space is, unfortunately, all they've got to play with.

The most effective way to handle the area is to treat it like any other tiny space: look at what you need it for and be flexible. Ask yourself what you actually want from the space, what you need to use it for and be prepared to compromise. A transit alleyway needs to be kept clear; people, barrows, bins and bikes need to be able to get through, so you can't fill it up with clutter or even permanent features. Of course, many people are blessed with larger side passageways which are more in keeping with what we perceive a typical garden to be, so in that situation the wish list needn't be honed down so ruthlessly. However, if the space is so thin that you can't have a dining area or a sun terrace for a couple of deckchairs, it doesn't mean you can't brighten the walls and fences and create something that looks welcoming. At the very least, decorating a narrow side alley is the opportunity to create that optimistic feeling that the alley is leading somewhere special.

THE SIDE RETURN

Gardens that wrap themselves around the house are commonplace and this usually yields a side return that's ignored and thought of as alien to the garden-proper. It's often an awful waste of space, yet the alley part is like a surprise introduction – what's around the corner? It makes you want to find out.

Contrary to popular belief, the side return is a welcome addition to a garden for many designers, as the angles of the house offer inspiration for a garden's layout and present numerous opportunities to tie both house and garden together. You might think a square garden would be easier to design since it doesn't have that bothersome dog-leg. Actually, square gardens are

ABOVE Of all surface materials, gravel is the most cost-effective by far. There are loads of different colours and sizes available, so it shouldn't be seen as tacky alternative.

amongst the hardest to plan because they're static and very often there's no starting point – they're 'square'. In gardens that extend down the side of the house, however, you've got an 'L' shape that you can work with immediately and you've got all that potential for a grand entrance.

UNITY

The easiest way of uniting a tricky alleyway or side return with the rest of the garden is through repetition of materials. Granite setts or cobbles running across the area will make the space feel wider, and these can be repeated in the main part of the garden beyond to bring the design together. Equally, large squares of decking laid down the alley and leading to a decked backyard look great, as well as tying in both parts of the garden. If gravel is your thing, a large arc of weathered flint gravel edged in dark grey granite setts swinging right round the house and into the alley would have the same result.

Repetition of plants will also help create a sense of continuity. Look at the plants you're using in the main part of the garden and think about repeating particular shapes, colours, associations or, if aspect allows, the specific plants themselves. Again, it all helps to knit the two spaces together.

ON THE GROUND

Hard surfaces need to be functional, solid and wide enough to accommodate a herd of removal men or a stampede of kids. In all slip-prone areas – and many alleyways generally don't get much sun – paving with a coarse, riven finish is preferable to smooth tiles, for obvious reasons.

In very dark alleyways, again choose a light-coloured stone for that old trick of boosting light levels, but if re-laying a load of new paving sounds expensive and too much like hard work, you can always make the space seem brighter simply by pulling out the pressure washer. If you're lumbered with monotonous concrete paving and you want to add some life to it, lift up the occasional slab and replace it with pebbles, bricks, cobbles or whatever takes your fancy – it'll be cheaper than replacing the whole lot.

Very often alleyways are the favoured home of that English favourite: dull grey concrete, with manhole covers and drains as 'special' features. Here, gravel can come to the rescue with its many sizes and colours. Choose a variety that's easy to walk on, preferably in a light, natural colour. A 25kg (55lb) bag will cover nearly half a square metre to a depth of 5cm (2in). If you're using fine gravel, first cover drainage grills with permeable gauze then simply spread it around evenly. With gravel you needn't worry about compromising the damp-proof course either; water simply drains through it double-quick.

'Hard surfaces need to be functional, solid and wide enough to accommodate a herd of removal men or a stampede of kids.'

TAKE COVER
Applying dark period greens to structures can help hide garden eyesores like sheds, but don't use too many murky colours in an alley as it can create an oppressive effect in small, already-dark spaces. For walls, go for colours like distressed whites and creams; these blend in, boost light levels, and act as a suitable foil for plants. Whatever colour you use in a small space will dominate, so choose with care and stick to light neutrals if you're in any doubt.

Have a good look at your walls, though, and don't be too quick to slap on the paint – unless, of course, it's an ugly breeze-block wall that screams to be covered. If your boundaries are made of worn London bricks, or you have a classic flint wall, or even a weathered fence – all of which blend well with their surroundings – leave them well alone. Painting them a completely different colour makes them dramatically different from their surroundings, creating a focal point you don't want to be drawn to.

Down-pipes in side alleys are a necessary evil: you can't get rid of them, but neither do you want to draw attention to them. If these are cast-iron, paint them black. This always looks classic and timeless and, since it's the colour we have come to expect them to be, oddly we don't 'see' them and they just get edited out of our visual awareness. Personally, I even like to paint the plastic ones. I know they're usually black already, but the plastic is too smooth and shiny and I find that painting them adds a subtle texture to the surface, which somehow makes them less obvious.

Downpipes should never be painted the same colour as windows and doorframes (unless it's black, of course). Why draw attention to them? If you really hate your pipework you can erect trellis along the wall, boxing in the pipes as you go, but be careful that you don't replace one eyesore with another. If that sounds like too much work, evergreen ivy and *Hydrangea anomala* subsp. *petiolaris* will both climb readily without need for support and will provide cover on even the shadiest wall right through the year. To encourage evergreen ramblers and climbers like *Berderidopsis corallina*, *Lonicera henryi*, *Trachelospermum jasminoides*, or *Clematis cirrhosa* var. *balearica*, tie netting or garden wire around the downpipe to give the plants a toe-hold to scramble up.

ALLEY CATS

If your side passageway is wide enough to squeeze in borders for plants, use them to frame the space – climbers hugging the boundaries with appropriately sized shrubs and herbaceous perennials in front, and ground cover carpeting their feet. In alleys where access is key, tough ground-cover plants are perfect, and they won't mind a bit of bashing. *Ajuga reptans*, *Mitchella repens*, Scotch moss (*Sagina*) and barren strawberry (*Waldsteinia ternata*) are all tolerant of shade, tough enough to accidentally walk on, don't need a lot of watering, help keep weeds down and serve to soften the linear edges of paving as well.

FOCAL POINTS

Every design in this situation needs a focal point at the end, something to arrest the eye as it looks over the space. You might think that focal points only apply to bigger spaces – we've all seen an imposing statue at the end of an avenue at a public garden – but you don't need such grand perspectives to achieve some focus. In an alleyway a focal point is nothing more than a bit of garden punctuation, appropriately sited against a different backdrop. The positioning of the focal point means that it is intended to stand out and should have a kind of bold, 'look at me' quality. In an alleyway a focal point is essential – you need something for the eye to settle on.

A focal point is especially important if the alley is viewed either from a window or French doors. A statue, a collection of pots, a tree, or a simple waterspout positioned at the end, makes your senses perk up and helps to pull you into the main part of the garden. If the kitchen window looks out over the passageway, be sure to create a feature opposite it. This can be something really simple, even understated, like a band of light grazing the wall and shadowing a green topiary sculpture, or a mirror with its edges covered in ivy and angled so it reflects the rest of the passageway, not you doing the washing up! Or how about a collection of pots hung from the wall, each spilling with striped petunias, to catch that precious shaft of sunlight? (Or busy Lizzies for those with shadier spaces.)

HOW GREEN IS YOUR ALLEY?

I prefer the boundaries of a side passageway to be hidden, just like in a basement garden. If you can't see the wall because it's smothered in green, then who's to know that you're not looking into a vast expanse of jungle? Climbers rambling up trellises or encouraged to grow over unobtrusive wires are a must. I'm a big fan of using graceful bamboo in alley gardens, especially when it droops persistently across the space or is positioned so that you have to walk around each plant. It helps create an otherworldly atmosphere, especially if together the plant blocks the view to the end; even when bamboo is glistening with water there is nothing like parting it to see what's beyond. If you want to use bamboo, go for *Fargesia nitida* in shady spots; it's a well-behaved variety that won't mind being trimmed if it gets too tall. To get a bit of interest at ground level, too, underplant with soft plants like *Geranium*

ABOVE **Every alleyway needs a focal point to draw you into the garden-proper.**

phaeum 'Samobor', *Dicentra spectabilis* 'Alba', dead nettle (*Lamium*) and *Symphytum* to create a woodland feel. Add a few simple uplighters every few paces along the passage and you've got a real magical mystery tour!

In wider passageways you might be able to dig down and create borders along one or both sides. Shady alleyways are not a poor relation, instead they will allow you to grow arrangements of wonderful, lush, shade-tolerant perennials like *Allium* 'Globemaster', *Carex pendula*, *Astilboides tabularis*, *Polystichum setiferum*, *Heuchera cylindrica* 'Greenfinch', *Hosta ventricosa*, *Sanguisorba officinalis*, Solomon's seal, purple *Actaea* and *Pulmonaria*. If this sounds like too much hard work, then plant up some raised beds built in a soft sympathetic material like brick, French oak or treated timber planks. As in basement gardens, do remember your damp-proof course when considering constructing raised beds against house walls.

Of course, if it's a sunny alleyway then smother the walls with fragrant chocolate vine, jasmine and honeysuckle, and why not have a few arches going across the space, too, maybe with a grapevine growing over them, or a scented rambling rose?

Even in shady alleys scent is a must. If you've got the room, grow fragrant shrubs like *Daphne odora* 'Aureomarginata', *Osmanthus delavayi* and *Lonicera* x *purpusii* 'Winter Beauty'. There's something especially cheery about a shady spot having a sudden stunning blast of scent during the bleakest months of the year, and the Christmas box (*Sarcococca confusa*) will fill the air with its sweet, spicy fragrance, without taking up much precious space. Add a plain collapsible table and chairs and it becomes a welcome escape-spot, somewhere to retreat from the sun when it's too hot elsewhere.

If the alley is narrower than five foot there won't be as much opportunity to fill it with plants, otherwise you'll be hacking your way through a jungle every time you want to get to the garden-proper. In very tight areas you may be able to get away with a few narrow, flat-backed troughs or window boxes planted with ivy, *Cyclamen*, *Lirope*, *Athyrium niponicum* and drumstick primulas (*P. denticulata*) to break up the space, but you only need a couple for effect. Of course, check the height and how far into the alley these boxes are going to jut out, or they will come across as a feature to be wary of rather than enjoyed, and if a window box is placed too high, all you'll see is the underneath of it and it will be difficult to water. In very narrow alleys, temporary pots of seasonal colour work well too and if they are positioned on castors they can be moved out of the way at a moment's notice for easy access. *Lilium regale*, flowering in mid-June, is ideal for temporary containers, and its scent carries well. Surprisingly, lilies actually like semi-shade and their flowers will last longer than on those grown on a sunny patio.

ABOVE A veritable collector's lot! And why not? As long as the access/thoroughfare is clear.

Sometimes, though, you just get the bug and in no time your alley is crammed with pots and the walls and fences are bursting with window boxes, hanging baskets and just about any container that can be pressed into the service of growing a plant. I've seen alleys like this and they look beautiful, and I have to say that once in a while it's good to go OTT and enjoy it, and if you really do have to get a sofa from one end of the alley to the other, you can always move all the pots!

MESSING WITH PERSPECTIVE

You know how painters can create the illusion of distance in their paintings? Well, in a narrow space like a side passageway you can play the same visual tricks with patterns creating different perspectives. If you have a gravel path merely adding a circle of bricks, a gravel mosaic or a stretcher of cobbles will make a passageway feel wider, as does laying sleepers or large weathered slabs *across* the space. Granite setts laid in fan shapes work well and laying uniform modular paving at 30- or 45-degree-angles has a similar effect, drawing the eye across the space rather than straight down it.

Diamonds, rectangular cobbles laid in a herringbone pattern, or paving laid in a 'continuous' or 'stack' bond (where the paving is laid end on end) encourage you to speed down the alley to the garden beyond and will make the place feel more like a tunnel. However, sometimes you don't want to rush down a space but stroll down it gently, taking in your surroundings. Of all the paving bonds, bricks laid in a basket-weave pattern appear the most static and don't inspire rapid movement; ideal when you want to slow down and linger. Gravel acts in the same way, too.

To make an alley feel longer, position something to hide the end or have a simple gravel path which tapers as it recedes into the distance. (Use metal strips on either side to maintain a crisp edge and keep gravel from straying.) To make the passageway feel shorter, position larger plants in the distance and smaller ones in the foreground – get out there with your pots and move them around, you'll be surprised at the various different effects it's possible to create.

Dead-end alleyways can be host to the most effective garden knavery of all –the use of trompe l'oeil. Basically this is the deception of the eye by putting up a false-perspective trellis, a fake door or a mirror. A large mirror with its edges completely hidden by plants will reflect all that goes before it, and you can have great fun positioning plants so it looks like the garden goes on for ever.

STORAGE

Passageways and storage are not a happy combination, simply because the alley is supposedly to get from A to B, while storage has to stay put, and once you start storing things in an alley it soon gets junked up.

If you can, store the bin, or whatever, elsewhere. Unfortunately, a lot of us can't do that so disguise is the next best option. One idea is to build a cupboard from reclaimed timber, treated with an environmentally-friendly preservative. You can buy kits from DIY stores, but in my opinion they look too obvious, and lack character. On top of the cupboard there's plenty of room for terracotta pots spilling over with seasonal bedding like *Lobelia*, heliotrope and *Bidens*.

So, onwards and upwards, literally. Steps link one place to another and are seldom considered to be worth prettifying. Think differently: steps are a ready-made vertical display for all sorts of plants. Sitting on the step reading a book or doing a spot of contemplation was a bygone pastime, so let's resurrect the habit!

'If you can't have a dining area or a sun terrace for a couple of deckchairs, it doesn't mean you can't create something welcoming. Decorating a narrow alley is the opportunity to create that optimistic feeling that it is leading somewhere special.'

GETTING THERE (STEPS)

Like alleyways, steps are often seen simply as a means to an end: a route between two places. Many city gardeners have a fire escape or a couple of steps leading to their front door; some of us have a longer flight of steps leading from a first-floor maisonette down to a private back garden. Basement gardens by their nature have a lot of steps – some beautifully ornate – and, of course, steps are essential to link levels in terraced gardens. However, as places for gardening potential they're all but invisible to us. But we should cherish steps, especially in gardens where space is at a premium: steps offer a home for fantastically colourful seasonal displays, as well as providing the opportunity to seamlessly connect different parts of the garden together.

Part of the problem is that we think that steps should be kept absolutely clear for safety reasons, that it's never a good idea to clutter them up. This may well be the case if you have narrow steps barely big enough for your size nines, but some steps are very wide indeed which gives ample room to line the edges with plants in perfect safety.

POSITIVE DESIGN ELEMENTS

Any change in level is exciting. We get a sense that something is happening, that design has moved away from the static – and with steps we literally feel that the garden is going somewhere else, moving towards more interesting possibilities.

If you think of steps as simple changes in levels you can see how everything becomes a little more 3-D and lively. Steps introduce us to garden surprises – they sweep down in a curve so that you don't know quite what you're going to find at the bottom. Young children (and big kids alike!) seem to love them, and always want to climb up and down as if they are innately aware that each step is leading them on to something hidden.

Steps make you feel you want to explore and by using that underemployed, vertical dimension, they help to counter the effects of enclosed spaces. They're also a very strong architectural element within a garden that can be viewed from numerous angles. Because of this they're often used as major focal points and people automatically walk towards a flight of steps because they have a magical pulling power. I'm a big fan of putting steps into a garden to act as bridges between one area and the next, or to link up sections of a garden that differ in character from one another.

SAFETY

Of course, ultimately, steps have a prime functional quality: to get you comfortably from one space to another. Safety, therefore, is paramount. They should be level (or you'll lose your balance), and in good repair. Sometimes all that's needed is a re-paving job.

If you're thinking about including steps in your design, be warned that there's quite a lot of step lore (as well as some precise measurements), which is nearly all to do with safety and so should be carefully followed:

- Steps should be gradual, low and wide. Wide steps are inviting and with a cushion can double up as comfortable seats, but shallow ones almost feel 'spiky' and don't invite you to sit on them at all. Think of a stairwell in a building: it doesn't allow you the time to look around, you have to be conscious of where you're putting your feet, so you tend to go up or down these stairs quickly. There is considerable difference in the sizing of indoor and outdoor steps, and you can't base the garden variety on the dimensions of indoor stairs; they just won't work. Long stairwells based on typical domestic indoor dimensions are not appropriate for outdoor use as they feel cramped and could even be dangerous. The minimum tread should be no less than 350mm (14in) and the riser should be between 100–160mm (4–6in).
- Flights of steps shouldn't rise more than 40 degrees, as this would be too steep.
- Sometimes straight flights of steps can feel scary to climb up and they may not be feasible in very steep gardens, and they . A combination of sweeping paths interspersed with steps allows for an easier, more relaxed, climb. Breaking up long flights of stairs with generous platforms also creates a place to site a bench so you can sit and catch your breath. At stopping places like these, try to plant scented flowers, because this is where you'll notice them most. Changes of direction are beneficial as they make a design more interesting; they give the opportunity to plant evergreens like *Olearia*, *Choisya* and *Euphorbia mellifera* to screen the eye from what's around the next turn.
- Steps often need handrails, especially if you have young children or older visitors, but they should also be present if the vertical drop at the side exceeds 600mm (2 ft) , otherwise you'll feel insecure as you climb. Some people say that on stairs with no handrail they feel horribly drawn to the edge – with dangerous consequences!
- One obvious point about balustrades: make sure they are at a useable height: too low and you'll fall over them, too high and you'll have to grow.

Steps are more complicated to construct than you might think; however, it's not an impossible job for an amateur, but it is a slow one and involves accurate levels and precise measurements. If you were building a brand-new set of steps – if you were in the process of terracing the garden, for example – I'd advise getting a contractor in to do it for you. An ambitious flight of steps is a bit like a series of mini retaining walls and their construction is rather like an iceberg: what you see above ground doesn't show all the underpinning and construction underneath which is necessary to keep them there.

ABOVE **See-through steps make wonderful use of space as they allow you to plant underneath – a real luxury in a tiny garden where space is at a premium.**

Whatever material you decide to use, always build steps with the dimensions constant. The risers and the treads must be the same all the way up, otherwise there will be accidents. Admittedly, this is harder when using natural materials like logs, but the extra effort is necessary to avoid slip-ups.

UPLIGHT

Incorporating lighting effects helps dramatize the texture of the steps and the surrounding materials, but it also has a built-in safety factor as it prevents you from missing your footing in the dark. Lights in risers, or downlighters focused on each step really add a different dimension. If you can incorporate them into the construction, then go for it, just make sure the light cast by each fixture subtly overlaps, so as to avoid hazardous shady spots. Linear lighting (strips underneath the nose of each step), is also very stylish and almost invisibly lights each step; even though it can often be a little too bright, it makes a wonderful architectural statement and is perfect for ultra-modern designs.

Don't forget to watch out for consistency with other lighting elements in your design when deciding how to illuminate steps, and keep them safe by avoiding the contrast of deep shadowing with sudden glare.

MATERIALS

Obviously, steps must be solid and level and be able to put up with a lot of wear and tear, but if you have very old stone steps which are dipping in the middle, don't feel you have to repair them – the passage of time and many feet can make steps charming and evocative. The test of whether steps need repairing is not necessarily looks alone; safety is paramount and, regardless of how good the steps look, they must be slip-resistant.

If you have retaining walls, as in terraced gardens, it's easy to plump for using the same material to give unity and harmony with the rest of the hard landscaping. But although steps shouldn't be viewed simply in isolation and ought to appear as part of the cohesive whole, almost anything can be used; a different material can highlight their importance within the overall design. Bricks, granite, limestone, sandstone, slate, even rounded cobbles, can be used on wide steps. If steps are laid properly and are level they can give good grip, but if they stick up or wobble they can cause you to trip. If you wanted an informal woodland garden or a more natural look, you could use logs to retain stepped runs of bark; these are quite secure to walk on, and blend easily into the garden.

Gabions are a modern garden equivalent of seaside defences: great strong wire cages filled with knapped flint, Lomond boulders, Cornish paddlestones, white marble . . . whatever stone you like. You don't need a bricklayer for these, and they make great focal points in their own right. Some companies sell cages for flights of ready-made steps, small enough for the tiniest garden; all you have to do is fill them.

Steps made from wooden decking are easy to construct and well within the scope of the amateur carpenter and you can even get simple kits for basic steps. Decking is ideal if you're gardening on a slope and want to terrace it, but it's important to lay the wood for the treads with the grooved side uppermost for good grip underfoot. Decking steps will need regular treatment if they aren't to rot – unless, of course, you're using tanalized or pre-treated timber, which should last for years with minimal maintenance.

Metal-grille steps are now commonplace, and unique in that you're not restricted when it comes to planting underneath them. They help to make a space feel bigger because of their partial transparency and allow excess water to drain through. Galvanized steel looks the biz in modern gardens, or use rusty ironwork for more period designs (try your local reclamation yard).

Balustrades don't just have to be made of wood. Perspex or glass works well in contemporary gardens, although glass does look beautifully elegant with Edwardian and Victorian buildings. Their only disadvantage is that you can't grow climbing plants along them. Metal balustrades can be painted, or left 'naturally rusty'; you get plenty of the latter at reclamation yards, and a visit to one is the best bet if you have a period property and want to buy something sympathetic to its style. Some of the most breathtaking features I've ever seen in gardens have been bespoke balustrades made by local blacksmiths. These are expensive as they're custom-made, but they're worth it.

ABOVE Use the walls and always group plants to the side so that the central part of the stairwell is kept clear for safety.

PLANTS FOR STEPS

It sounds strange, but even a flight of steps has its own microclimate. The sunlight falling on them can change throughout the day and what was in sun first thing in the morning, can by the afternoon be in full shade. Open stairwells, too, can be cold and windy, whereas those steps which are enclosed can be warm and sheltered – especially if they're made from brick. Make a note of where the sun hits your steps as it swings round during the day, then you'll be able to pick the best plants for the site.

Simplicity is key for any planting scheme. Organizing your planting in a recurring theme or to mimic the steps themselves works well; try placing a set of matching pots or a run of scarlet pelargoniums on every other step. Bright colours, like pots of *Canna* 'Lucifer', and gardener's garters (*Phalaris arundinacea* var. *picta*), or gaily painted containers full of salvias, *Nemesia*, monkey flower and snapdragons look good in eclectic cottage-inspired

gardens. Pots of *Nicotiana* 'Havana Lime', *Heuchera* 'Palace Purple', cream petunias, *Osteospermum* and *Convolvulus sabatius* are perfect for period designs. Or why not put two standard bay balls at the foot of the steps; two sentries to check your credentials as you pass!

Obviously you have to think about the 'habit' of plants (the way they grow) when choosing them for step-planting. They need to be tight rather than open and sprawling – although a waterfall of tumbling plants down one side of a flight of steps does look lovely. Smaller herbs are ideal, particularly as you can clip them back if they get too big. It's a nice touch to have plants with scented leaves like southernwood (*Artemisia abrotanum*) so that when you caress them the scent is released. On the stairwell outside my flat I've got pots of scented-leaved geraniums: 'Attar of Roses', 'Lady Plymouth' and the delicious 'Chocolate Peppermint'. However, my favourite would have to be *Pelargonium* 'Rober's Lemon Rose' which I purposely make a bee-line for every time I go out just to catch the delicious whiff of lemons!

Due to restricted space, containers will undoubtedly have to be on the small side – meaning they're better with temporary displays which get changed two or three times a year, rather than permanent planting which requires bigger pots. However, sempervivums (houseleeks) or smaller *Sedum* species do well in terracotta for years, and they don't mind if you occasionally forget the watering. The same goes for Mediterranean herbs such as dwarf lavender, thyme and prostrate rosemary.

CLIMB UP

Climbers find railings and banisters the perfect support and using them keeps the actual step area free. If you can't plant at the bottom of the flight, then you'll need to position a fairly substantial pot there instead, one that's large enough to allow the climber to reach maturity – you try potting an established climber once it's wound itself round a support, it's impossible! Climbers such as *Clematis* 'Niobe', *C.* 'Ruby', *Rhodochiton atrosanguineus*, and *Lapageria rosea* 'Nash Court'are perfect for small space because they aren't too vigorous and won't need regular pruning. Admittedly, you can also grow vigorous beasts such as *Clematis* 'Elizabeth', *Passiflora caerulea*'Constance Elliott', *Vitis vinifera* and *Wisteria sinensis* 'Alba' which in many cases are the most breathtaking when in full flower – just be prepared to attack them with your secateurs regularly, to stop them taking over. Do avoid climbers and wall shrubs with prickly spines or rough leaves; remember, the prime purpose of a handrail is that you might need to grab hold of it to steady yourself from time to time.

For continuity's sake it's a good idea to grow more than one climber together so you get flowers and scent right through the year. For a shady stairwell – why not grow *Clematis macropetala* for the spring, *Lathyrus latifolius* (perennial sweet pea) for the summer and *Lonicera periclymenum* 'Graham Thomas' for the autumn. For sunny stairwells you could plant *Clematis* 'Apple Blossom' for the spring, *Jasminum officinale* for the summer, followed by *Lonicera periclymenum* 'Serotina' for the autumn. If you are growing more than one climber, be warned that some judicious pruning may well be required on occasion to stop any thuggish behaviour!

Annual climbers are perfect for training up balustrades as they're never around long enough to become a nuisance. My favourite for its remarkable intensity of scarlet colour is *Ipomoea lobata*, or you could use *Tropaeolum peregrinum*, the Canary creeper, for its lemon yellow flowers. *Cobaea scandens* will grow happily in protected sunny sites, 'Empress of India' is a nasturtium which throws up a blaze of dark red flowers (that you can also eat), or if you mainly spend time in the garden in the evening then try the moonflower, *Ipomoea alba* – it has flowers like white saucers and a stunning scent.

If you have no proper flat area that you can use as a garden, and only a series of steps to press into use, why not create a private plant-tunnel over them by constructing arches with trellised sides, then smothering the lot in fragrant sweet peas? Very private – and very romantic!

PLANTS AND SAFETY

When choosing your plants for steps, think safety. You're probably going to brush past them at times, no matter how wide the steps are, so avoid pots of spiky agave or anything nasty to the touch. Plants that shed lots of leaves have their own problems as you'll have to keep picking them up or they'll make the steps slippery, and blowsy trailing plants always seem to go where they shouldn't. Don't pick plants with leaves that act like sails either, or the whole lot will take off in a strong gust of wind. If you want to hide the sides of the steps altogether and just see the treads and risers, grow shrubs like *Cytisus* x *beanii*, *Viburnum davidii*, *Cotoneaster procumbens*, *Ceanothus thyrsiflorus* var. *repens* or annuals like *Amaranthus* or *Cerinthe major* 'Blue Kiwi' – tidy plants which have a mounding habit and will arch over the edges without becoming a nuisance. At the time of writing I'm addicted to red valerian (*Centranthus ruber*) – you see it everywhere in early summer spilling from cracks in old stone walls and never is there a plant more suited to growing by a set of old winding steps. But whatever you choose, just think about safety as well as enjoying the sense of mystery. All you'll feel like doing with steps like these is climb them like Jack and his Beanstalk, but you won'twant to take a tumble.

It's very tempting, but don't go mad with masses of pots; you can end up with so many that they're crammed together and encroach on where you would naturally tread. Eventually you end up having to mince your way through them. You need to feel comfortable walking up or down steps, so make sure pots are secure – don't have them teetering on the edge of the treads. If the steps are particularly narrow, avoid putting pots on them at all and use wall-mounted containers spilling with trailing fuchsias instead.

Next we look at balconies and roof terraces. Those who garden above ground level can allow themselves to feel smug; they literally do look down on everybody else! Having a garden way up there always feels special because we don't expect to find plants growing above our heads! These gardens might be exposed to the elements, but they also have the potential to become sky-high oases.

ACCESSORIZE

Following on from the temporary display idea, you can also decorate your steps with amusing bits and bobs, such as rows of huge church candles, tea lights in coloured jars, pots filled with glass, pebbles or beach finds, or baskets of fir cones.

Salix viminifera **has lovely red wood, and can be woven between balustrades. You can also wind fairy lights through balustrades for a summer step-party. Anything goes; make the area as creatively productive as any other part of the garden, as long as it doesn't hamper progress up or down.**

ABOVE **A little grand for most city gardens, but breathtaking nonetheless.**

UP HIGH

Ok, so you live in a flat, and you don't have a typical 'garden'. All you have is a balcony or roof terrace which is home to a couple of white plastic chairs, an unused parasol stuck in a corner, and a couple of cheap empty planters lying on their sides. The dream that never made it. Garden? What garden? But this little bit of space overlooking the city is, in fact, prime real estate and has just as much, if not more, potential than ground-level gardens. Gardening amongst the clouds, my young nephew calls it. Well, not quite, but it's getting there!

Skyscape gardeners have something that precious few of us ground-dwellers have – views. In the country views are fought over and will increase the price of a house; a sea view can add fifty grand to the asking price even if all you see is just the merest sliver of blue. Somehow having a view means we are part of the bigger picture and you can pretend-play that you own all that you survey. Well, visually, you do!

But what about views in the city? Aren't they just 'all buildings'? Come on . . . ! The view from a roof terrace on a summer night over the Thames or the Tyne is pretty amazing, and in some ways being above all the buildings makes you appreciate city living more than anything else. All the architecture, the way the shapes of buildings juxtapose, the banks of greenery, the sun glinting off the river . . . steady on, it makes me feel poetic.

In some cities the rooftops alone are worthy of a night on the tiles, being made up of all sorts of levels, pitches and angles. It's a veritable modernist backdrop, and one which can only be seen from up high. Our northerly cities might not be graced with the pantiles of Florence, but even here the views across the rooftops can be stunning. Views over grim industrial cityscapes can also take on an interesting character, and can be unbelievably dramatic at sunset or on dark stormy days.

So there is something wildly exotic about owning a balcony or roof terrace you can sit out on: you can look down on the city going about its business below, you can dine out while the world rushes past or you can sunbathe while office-workers beneath you trudge to the tube. On the other hand, if you are the office-worker who has just hiked home from work, you can sip chilled wine in the still-warm air of the evening, nibble some tapas, enjoy the sunset – and watch the moon rise and the city go to sleep.

WEIGHT MATTERS

Sorry to start off with the boring stuff, but before you get too excited with grandiose plans of a sheltered hot tub and gigantic palms screening you from the outside world, you should first think about the practicalities of gardening up high, for it's a garden like no other. Weight is the most important consideration. With tiny balconies tacked on to the sides of flats or townhouses you won't need to fret too much, as they would usually have been designed with the knowledge they'll have to take a few pots, a bistro table and chairs and you and your partner milling about, glass of wine in hand. Chances are you'll never overload it – if only because the space isn't big enough to accommodate giant planters or fifty guests. However, when it comes to roof terraces it's a different story. With flats or apartments built within the last twenty years, finding the load-bearing capacity of the roof is thankfully relatively straightforward. Look through the deeds of your house and, because the terrace will have been built with a sky-high garden in mind, the info should be easy to find. Problems arise when it's a roof terrace built on top of a Victorian or Edwardian building, because in those days it was either designed as a place to hang out the washing or to gain access to the roof, and not somewhere for a full-blown garden. Here you *must* get an inspection done by a surveyor before you get going and he will work out exactly what you can and can't do. It's a straightforward calculation: planters + soil + water + mature plants + paving + foundations + dining table and chairs + happily replete adults = heavy weight!

It is possible to strengthen joists and reinforce some roofs, but as this will be costly it's often better to simply work with what you've got. I know what you're thinking: that's all well and good, but a surveyor will charge a fortune and I don't need one because my plans are simple. But what if you get bitten by the gardening bug or your circumstances change? Bringing up 'just a few pots at a time' until there's quite a collection can spell disaster because you have no idea how much weight the terrace will support. And one day that one extra pot will cause the roof to sag and cave in. Compare the cost of a proper structural survey to having your roof rebuilt and it pales into insignificance. Knowing the load-bearing characteristics of your roof right from the start is immensely freeing: it'll help you plan confidently as you'll have all the facts to hand and those tentative, apprehensive thoughts will be a thing of the past.

Some potential problems are obvious: plastic planters, along with fibreglass and fake-stone imitations weigh much less than concrete, stone or terracotta. Think about where you are putting the weight and avoid placing pots in the centre of the roof terrace – which doesn't look good anyway – and restrict their numbers. Fixing pots to surrounding walls or placing them on cantilevered shelves will help to stagger the weight, as the walls will be bearing the load and not the roof itself. Peat- and coir-based composts are lighter when wet than soil-based composts, and use polystyrene granules in containers for drainage rather than terracotta crocks. For screening purposes, bamboo on a roll is much lighter than a stand of tall birch trees.

RULES AND REGULATIONS

Planning considerations are important when it comes to roof terraces and balconies, too, as flats are subject to strict regulations and covenants. New roof gardens are often considered to be an extra floor, and if you live in a conservation area or it's a listed building then you'll need to check your plans with the local council. Even if it's a roof terrace which has already been authorized for garden use, many structures like glass conservatories need a permitted development certificate. Your roof terrace is highly visible, and you shouldn't underestimate the visual impact your garden will have on the building and its surroundings; you don't want your finished design to be considered an eyesore by a suit from the local authority and subsequently have to be ripped out!

Balconies also come under strict controls; some local councils won't even let you paint the walls or railings a different colour, so check your title deeds or talk to the freeholder for clarification. Apart from this, most balconies are simply not big enough for designs that may cause offence, so you needn't worry too much. However, even up high you have neighbours, so always take them into account before recreating your vision of the Hanging Gardens of Babylon and blocking all light from the windows of the flat below!

Safety is, of course, paramount, so if you plan to put pots on ledges do make sure they are firmly secured. (Although it might be worth checking with the local council, as many don't permit this.) Pergolas, trelliswork, wire systems and glass panels must be well secured and fixings need to be easily accessible so that you can check or tighten them periodically. Also, make sure that railings or surrounding walls are study and strong enough to cater for a throng (or do I mean thong!?) of sumo wrestlers leaning against them. Legally they should be a minimum height of 1.1m (3½ft) from the surface of the terrace or balcony, so if you come up short then remedy the problem before you start work on the design-proper.

DESIGN RULES

Strong and simple is the key to designing for a roof terrace or balcony, as it stops them from being snowed under by their backdrop. Clean lines and minimal features work best and a small space should be as multifunctional as possible; plus this approach creates a calm peaceful atmosphere.

BELOW Borrow the landscape or create your own – the choice is yours.

Where space (and weight) permits, choose large bold planters rather than lots of little fussy ones because not only will they be easier to water but you can also choose big plants for real drama. On a roof terrace or balcony less is most definitely more and a more formal urban style is usually the most successful. Cottage garden replicas need careful consideration and often don't work because roof gardens and balconies are an urban phenomenon, and for the same reason profuse free- flowing beds and borders, eclectic objets d'art and rustic furniture can look too out of place.

If your balcony or roof terrace adjoins a room inside then repeating certain materials, colours or shapes will help to bring both spaces together. But if it's a roof terrace that you have to climb a flight of stairs to get to, it isn't always necessary to somehow link it to the interior. Here you can create a design safe in the knowledge that it's not going to jar with your home. At the time of writing I'm about to start a roof terrace in west London, and without a doubt the most exciting feature is that the space is up three flights of stairs and away from the flat, so I can try something different.

Whatever design you go for, don't forget to manipulate your view. Sure, some eyesores like gas towers and motorways may need screening, but a fine cityscape is a picture and you can create distant focal points by framing it with plants or other uprights. A fantastic view is something to be cherished and will enhance any design, so don't be too quick to hem yourself in. Echoing the square windows of nearby office blocks by using trelliswork, or mirroring church steeples with wire cones will tie the space into its surroundings, but don't go mad; your balcony or roof terrace is supposed to be a green haven amongst a concrete and brick skyline, after all.

In a long narrow space, as always, you don't want to be able to look or walk straight down it; some terraces and bigger balconies hug the building and resemble airport runways unless they're broken up. Delay the journey to the end of the space by having planters containing bushy *Pittosporum* or *Aucuba* jutting out so that you have to walk around them. Being guided along a gentle zig-zag as you travel through the space will foster the illusion that the whole area is bigger than it really is, because you have to cover a greater distance from one end to the other. Creating subtle diversions also helps generate the good-design threesome of tension, mystery and surprise. I realize there's usually a vast landscape beyond the perimeter– something you often can't escape from – but even on the tiniest balcony the careful siting of a screen or just one large plant half-way along makes things more interesting.

Most importantly, plan what you want to use the balcony or roof for before you start filling it up. This might seem silly when you have such a small space, but it's easy for a simple stylish design to start looking like a dog's dinner. Do you want to dine out on the balcony and/or entertain your friends? Is it to be used for a children's play area? Are you a frustrated gardener and do you have the room and inclination to create a green oasis high up in the sky? Or do you just want to sit out with a drink in the lingering warmth of a summer's evening, looking over the city?

Access is always a key factor that affects what you can do in a garden, but it is especially so on a roof terrace or balcony. Hoists and cranes to lift things up the outside of the building are a fantasy for most of us on modest budgets, therefore it's the dimensions of the lift, stairwells, doorways and corridors which will determine the size of pots, materials and plants you can use. Trellis panels and decking planks may have to be cut down and reassembled once they're through the building, and that huge glass table you've got your eye on may have to be substituted for a collapsible one.

ABOVE Open and functional this roof terrace looks like it could seat a whole rugby team!

SKY-DINING

A place to eat will undoubtedly come high on most people's lists for how they want to use their outside space, but dining out on a balcony or roof terrace (or in any garden, for that matter) needs a lot more space than is required simply by the table and chairs alone. Diners need elbow room, to be able to stretch their legs, and to get in and down from the table easily. You also need sufficient room to serve your guests without spilling food in their laps. If space is tight, know your limitations and opt for more elbow room per person rather than trying to cram in too many people. You can always squeeze up when you have to, but for general use the experience is much more relaxing and expansive when you have more individual space.

Dining out in a cramped space overlooking the rest of the city can feel unsafe, even dangerous, and this is especially so when the outside edge is open, as with iron railings. Where you have see-through railings it often makes people feel more secure if you have planters or willow screening up to at least waist-height. If this isn't your style, you could string wire between the uprights and let plants trail through it, visually making the barrier more substantial than it really is. Even window boxes firmly fixed to the top of the railings and planted up with trailing flowers will lend a more protective feel to that barrier.

Where space for free-standing furniture is limited built-in benches work well, as do folding tables and chairs which can be hidden behind large planters when not in use. Stackable furniture is also useful; just promise me you won't get the horrible plastic junk you find in DIY stores. It's a garden eyesore! Hammocks are perfect for roof terraces as there are usually so many strong fixing points available, and when not in use they take up virtually no space. Do position a hammock with safety in mind, though, as the last thing you want is to be inadvertently dumped over the edge and onto the street below. Alternatively, you could just drag beanbags and cushions outside, or buy a couple of classic deckchairs. They're simple, stylish, flexible and so comfortable.

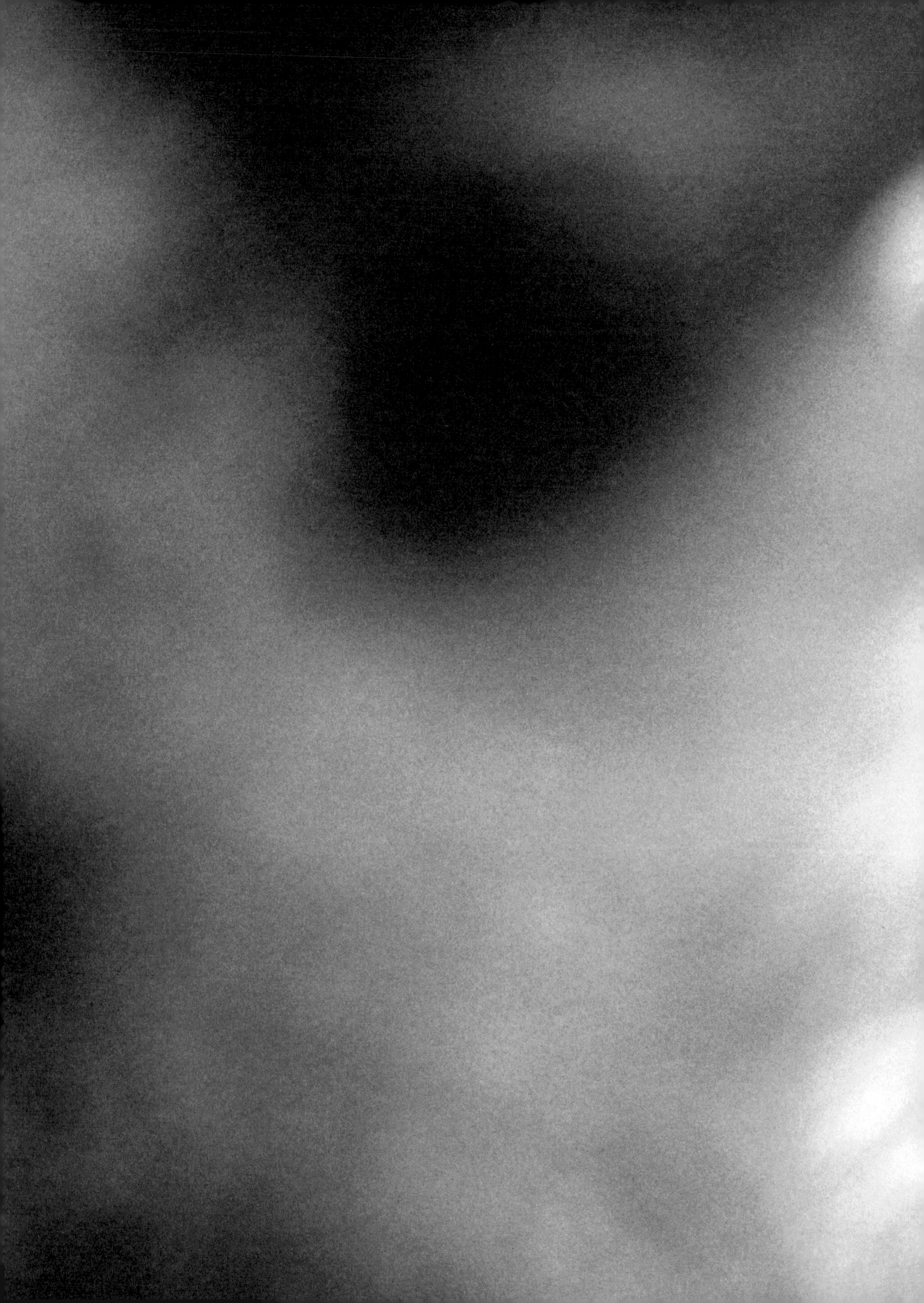

ABOVE Now unfairly considered passé, timber decking is still the most obvious choice for balconies where weight is an important consideration.

PRACTICAL NECESSITIES

A balcony or roof garden may have to fulfil some, if not all, of the more functional aspects of other garden spaces, especially if you have no other garden area. It would be nice if it could always look the biz and at the ready for a spot of intimate entertaining, but there are more mundane things to consider, too, such as storage and where to hang the washing. With everything on show in such a tiny space, these needs do have to be carefully incorporated if they aren't going to dominate.

Where the balcony or roof terrace has to provide storage space, whether for bins, bikes, DIY equipment, or whatever, then if it's possible try to build this storage space discretely. You can make simple benches which also double up as storage boxes, position a trellis to subtly screen off the bikes, and use retractable washing lines rather than permanent ones. If nothing else works, create features which distract the eye from the more down-to-earth aspects of your outdoor space, such as lush planting against the most visible side of the balcony; the bits and pieces which need to be stored can be put hard up against the house wall (or, preferably, tucked behind the door or in an 'invisible' corner).

At the early planning stage, don't forget to note where you're going to get water and power from. Routing new supplies to a roof terrace three floors up can be problematic and expensive, but both could dramatically affect the success of your garden in both its construction or even as part of the design.

FLOORING

Decking is often the preferred choice for roof terraces and balconies, primarily because it's warm underfoot, lighter than traditional paving and joists can be fixed to surrounding walls, therefore distributing the weight to them instead of the roof itself. It's a clean material too, one that dispenses with the need for mucky cement work. (The last thing you want to do is have workmen traipsing bucket-loads of mortar up from the ground floor!) But you needn't restrict yourself to just the green tanalized stuff you get from builders' merchants. Western red cedar, which smells of pineapples, is a stylish if more costly alternative. It is well worth the extra cash; the natural veining and colour of the wood is exquisite, especially when it's wet. However, the crème de la crème of the decking world are hardwoods like Ipe and Yellow Balau: both look beautiful, are incredibly long lasting and need minimal maintenance to keep them looking good. Every time I see them used properly it reminds me of chic Californian condominiums. The downside is the cost, but on a roof terrace where features are minimal you may be able to splash out. Or, for a modern rustic look, why not go for preserved reclaimed floorboards? They do start out being a little bit squeaky, but once the wood has settled in they're fine. If you're planning an out-and-out jungle then it might be worth having a few sections of decking that aren't fixed down, so you can easily clean out leaves and rubbish from underneath.

ABOVE Similar colours, shapes and materials means this balcony sits comfortably with the interior – a golden rule when gardening up high.

If your balcony comes off a room with wooden flooring, then consider using decking of a similar size or colour to blur the boundaries between inside and out and thus make both 'rooms' feel bigger. Decking can also be used to alter perspective: if the balcony or roof terrace is particularly narrow, place boards widthways across the space, or for squat balconies, down it – both of these methods create the illusion that the garden is larger than it actually is.

If you're passionately opposed to decking there are, of course, other options. Conventional sandstone paving is ok if the roof is strong enough, but up high and against most buildings I think it would look a little peculiar, whereas thin uniform limestone, slate or ceramic tiles usually fit perfectly. Gravel is always a cheap and effective surface and surprisingly isn't too heavy either, so it's great for a roof terrace or balcony. A standard 25kg bag will

ABOVE **Weight-wise concrete flooring and these giant planters will certainly need a strong roof!**

If you are thinking about including some lighting in your roof garden, decking affords the opportunity to use fantastic LED spotlights. LEDS, or 'light emitting diodes', have come a long way and buying them nowadays isn't difficult; you can get cheap low voltage sets for the price of the weekly shopping. LEDs are particularly suitable for roof terraces as they either shine a very precise light or, if it's a low wattage bulb, they simply glow. Both are ideal as they don't dominate a space (or the skyline) and you can still lie back and see the stars.

cover 0.4–0.5 sq m (4–5sq ft) at 40mm (1½in) deep. I wouldn't promote gravelling all the way through, as it's uncomfortable to sit on and it gets stuck on your shoes and dragged into the house, but the occasional square or border running round the outside of the space with pots in the middle is a good way to keep the cost down. At the height of most roof terraces and balconies, of course, the neighbourhood cats shouldn't be a problem either!

Be aware that most flat roofs tend to be covered in black asphalt to make them waterproof. This is fine, but not only is it ugly to look at (especially when painted with silver, solar-reflective paint), it also starts to melt when it gets very hot. Temporary reed or rush matting does make a comfortable and very cheap surface underfoot, but plonking it directly onto a blistering asphalt floor is asking for trouble. Better to lay paving, gravel or decking if you plan to sunbathe on your roof terrace all the time. One last thing – don't puncture existing asphalt if at all possible; repair work to a waterlogged home is expensive to say the least!

OVER-EXPOSED

Wind is one of the major challenges facing balconies and roof terraces. You could, of course, just accept it and do nothing to mitigate the wind and instead use plants that naturally thrive in these conditions: a sort of 'plant it and forget it' approach. But in most cases where protection isn't afforded by surrounding buildings, you'll need to provide some degree of shelter. Why have wonderful views and a collection of your favourite plants if you can't sit out and enjoy them because you're constantly battered by strong winds?

It's important that up-high windbreaks are fit for the job; don't go for something solid, such as fencing (well, would you? It'd block that view), because windbreaks need to be porous. This means that it should let some wind through rather than blocking it entirely, which negates the problem of turbulence on the leeward side. The ideal is about 50 per cent porosity and,

ABOVE **Suitable protection like the walls and timber planks in this garden mean you can grow almost anything.**

surprisingly, if you're sitting next to such a windbreak you won't be aware that there's such a gale blowing on the other side of it – there'll just be a gentle breeze on your cheek. Specialist wind-filtering gauzes and perforated vinyl sheets can be bought off the internet, but do tell them what you want to use it for so that the supplier can help you find the right one.

Glass is a commonly used wind buffer for roof terraces as it provides uninterrupted views, but do be careful that you don't site it across prevailing winds unless it has a few holes in it, or turbulence will hurl itself over the top with great force. Trellis, whether bought-in or homemade, is an excellent windbreak as it provides a partial rather than a complete screen; steel wire tensioned between firmly fixed steel uprights or galvanized scaffold poles is equally lightweight and wind porous, but has a more modern feel. Both can be softened using suitable plants like *Clematis* 'Elizabeth', or you could even have a grapevine rambling over a south-facing balcony. How about home-grown stuffed vine leaves ('dolmades') for an appetizer, followed by grapes for dessert?

If you don't trust your own skills to put up screening (and it isn't quite the same as DIY in ground-level gardens), get a specialist builder or rope access company to do it for you. Don't chance it yourself just to save a few hundred quid – it's not worth it!

Taller wind-tolerant shrubs will also offer protection for tender plants and softie humans alike. Think of them as a living screen. Tough evergreens such as *Phormium*, *Pittosporum*, *Choisya ternata* Sundance, spotted laurel, *Osmanthus* and *Elaeagnus* won't mind the exposure. Or you could choose acid-lovers like camellias and *Pieris*, as growing them in containers means you can easily get the soil right. Bamboo is worth trying on all but the most windswept roof gardens; both the black bamboo *Phyllostachys nigra* and the golden bamboo *Phyllostachys aurea* grow tall and strong and will thrive in containers.

A balcony or roof terrace is the urban equivalent of an exposed clifftop garden. So it's well worth noting the plants that thrive in similar inhospitable conditions down by the sea and that way you can pick plants safe in the knowledge that they will tolerate a little overexposure to the elements.

SUN HITS THE SKY

Humans and plants alike need some overhead shelter from the hot sun. Whereas balconies do at least get some variation in light and shade (the sun might heat up the south side of your flat but as it moves round it brings some welcome shade), the roof garden is totally different and will nearly always suffer from full sun. Trellis is a cheap, easy-to-assemble option, but for something a little more classy you could use rolls of bamboo or heather instead. Affix a pole to one end and you can wind it back and forth over a steel frame when you need to. Permanent shade sails are also good and, again, wind-porous materials work best for these because you don't want to create too much of a solid barrier so that the fabric rips or flies away. You can buy bespoke or off-the-peg sails on the internet, but cheaper options are parasols or umbrellas bought from DIY superstores and garden centres. For an even cheaper overhead cover, use cotton sheeting. But do be wary of gusty days, or your Bedouin-style shelter will end up in another county!

Being up and open to the elements does have its advantages: in the height of summer, while the rest of the city swelters away, these exposed areas catch whatever breeze there is. If you've had the forethought to build some shade into your garden you've got the perfect retreat to chill out in. On particularly steamy nights you could even sleep out on the balcony or terrace. (A bonus probably exploited more often in hotter climates than ours!)

PRIVACY

On my balcony sunshine would be a fine thing. It faces north-east, which is a real pain when it comes to growing plants as I get little sun in the morning and come midday, once the sun has moved round, I get none. Not a sausage. By then the sun has been eclipsed by my block of flats. I'll be honest and admit that if I had known when I first moved in how difficult it was going to be to garden successfully in such an inhospitable space I might well have chosen somewhere else. But (and with gardening there's always a 'but'), as I said

in Chapter One, I cope – and then some! I'm in no doubt that I have more failures than most – if only because I'm constantly challenging the rulebook – but what really frustrates me is the lack of privacy, as I'm naked to the balconies opposite.

Some of my neighbours feel the same way and they've erected a variety of weird and wonderful contraptions to deal with the problem. Calico sheets suspended from wires, umbrellas with swivel heads, trellis panels, plants which look like they eclipse all the sunlight in the living room – all manner of ingenious things. Some of these look like they work, and some like they don't. In tiny balconies like these much is owed to trial and error, and you'd be amazed at what works. I myself have done nothing, for I'm frightened that any structure used to obtain privacy will block out the limited sunlight I already get and subsequently all my plants would suffer. I've resigned myself to the fact that my balcony is a picture and not somewhere for down-sized dinner parties. It's a hefty compromise, but for me it's just a space for plants and somewhere that I can potter.

ABOVE High walls are one way of creating privacy in a rooftop garden but, admittedly, it's a bit of rarity in most cityscapes.

PLANTS

Whether you go for a minimalist retreat or a tree-top jungle, you will still have to choose plants to suit the rather inhospitable conditions. Aspect is an important consideration. A shaded, north-facing balcony will be able to support a very different range of plants to an exposed, south-facing one where anything which requires cool, shade, or lots of moisture is a complete no-no. Whatever the aspect of your space, most high-rise plants will need to be wind-tolerant, although you can make room for the more tender specimens by careful screening and a bit of TLC.

ALL-WEATHER PLANTS

The problem with wind is that it wicks moisture away from plants even more than exposure to fierce sunlight. Evergreen plants, those that commonly survive on our coasts, are good choices and most have thick glossy leaves which prevent them from drying out too quickly. *Griselinia*, *Garrya*, *Viburnum tinus*, *Escallonia*, *Euonymus japonicus*, *Carpenteria californica*, *Fatsia japonica*, *Mahonia* and the European fan palm, *Chamaerops humilis,* are ideal. Evergreens also importantly provide the year-round framework for transient bulbs and perennials, so they should be considered the core of any rooftop planting scheme. Even in winter the bleak roof terrace or balcony is a picture to be enjoyed from the confines of the home; you won't want to look out on a few naked twigs, would you?

ABOVE **Mounding grasses and alpines are the perfect choice for exposed gardens up high.**

SOME LIKE IT HOT

On open roof terraces plants must be able to cope with the blazing sunshine too. Consider plants like *Potentilla*, *Phlomis*, *Olearia*, *Lavender*, *Caryopteris*, *Helianthemum*, *Lithospermum*, *Convolvulus cneorum*, *Astelia*, *Ceanothus*, *Euphorbia*, *Abelia* and *Hibiscus*: those that originate from hotter climates like California, Australia, the Mediterranean, South America and the Middle East. For real drama use spiky yuccas, agaves or cordylines spaced equidistantly apart in tall, vase-shaped containers against a clean neutral backdrop. An arrangement like this looks so much more effective than a random collection of plants, and it leaves plenty of space for you, too.

Grasses like it hot, add subtle texture and will rustle soothingly in a breeze. *Miscanthus* are the most popular as they stay tall and don't collapse easily. Choose *Miscanthus* 'Morning Light', 'Rotsilber', 'Flamingo', 'Gracillimus' or the zebra grass, *Miscanthus sinensis* 'Zebrinus' . This grass definitely lives up to its name as it has odd pale-yellow horizontal markings on the leaves – just like a zebra. Unlike dense evergreens which can leave you feeling hemmed in, taller grasses are helpful in that they allow privileged glimpses of what's beyond, therefore making the space seem bigger.

For very windswept sites choose evergreen grasses like *Pennisetum* 'Hameln', *Carex conica* 'Snowline' and *Festuca glauca* 'Harz', which are plants that form neat compact clumps; as they don't have a lot of 'sail area' they're less likely to get damaged or blown onto passers-by below. *Festuca glauca* 'Elijah Blue' is a commonly available ground-cover grass with fierce little clumps of bizarre glaucous-blue leaves. It's particularly at home in contemporary container schemes or modernist gardens featuring glass or steel. *Luzula nivea* (snowy woodrush) and *Luzula sylvatica* (greater woodrush) are priceless ground-cover grasses, which thrive absolutely everywhere (including the dry, shady pockets underneath trees), so they're well suited to dry roof terraces. Dwarf conifers like *Juniperus sabina* 'Tamariscifolia' and

ABOVE Silvery plants and those with thick leathery leaves won't mind a hot spot.

Pinus mugo 'Mops' tolerate hot, exposed sites too and are ideal for sun-trap roof terraces; you'll see many of them battling the elements on cliffs or in arid plains abroad. For tall, narrow, columnar shapes choose *Cupressus sempervirens*, which is the classic pencil-shaped tree you find throughout southern Spain and Italy. Or if that sounds a little too big, choose *Juniperus scopulorum* 'Springbank' or *J. communis* 'Hibernica'; both of these grow slowly and eventually reach a height of 3 metres after about twelve years or so.

Alpines, as the name suggests, originate from high up in mountainous regions, and are commonly used on roof terraces as they need little water and tolerate extreme exposure to both intense sunshine and strong winds. Picture rows of dark terrazzo bowls full of carpeting sedum, *Aloe pearsonii* and houseleeks lined up on classy decking – elegant and effortlessly simple.

HERBS UP HIGH

If you fancy a little bit of self-sufficiency, nothing is easier and more appealing than growing your own herbs. Imagine plucking fistfuls of coriander or parsley that you've nurtured in your own sky-high garden. The Mediterranean herbs sage, oregano and rosemary love lots of sun, but even in shady spots you can grow the real perennial toughies such as lemon balm, chives, mint, parsley, marjoram and thyme. Many come in different colours so you can grow them for their looks as well as their flavour.

Plant them together in mixed groups, arranging them with height and shape in mind or, for a minimalist look, go it alone with some bold mono planting – a smart steel cylinder spilling with purple sage or prostrate rosemary. Many herbs are what I call 'touchy-feely' scents; you have to grab 'em to smell 'em! Unless you have provided a wind-still and significantly sheltered environment they should take dominance over free-scented ones.

SHOE-BOXES!

Admittedly, if your balcony is nothing more than a deep window ledge sticking out into space, then you can't opt for a grand plan à la Versailles, but you can plant a couple of climbers in deep planters positioned one at each end. Let them ramble up trellises on either side of your window so that their foliage and flowers gently overflow into your line of sight. This not only frames your view of the city, giving the impression that something grander is going on outside, but it looks really attractive from the street, too.

Where space really is tight, try fixing window boxes all along the edge of the balcony – either to the metal railings or the supporting struts – and then plant them up. It doesn't take much effort to plonk some *Euryops pectinatus* in the centre and a few ivies, *Bidens* and nasturtiums to trail over the sides. All these will thrive in an exposed spot. You could even opt for some sculptured topiary: box is a toughie and will provide all-year-round greenery. Imagine a balcony seen from below, or opposite, that has a row of small, neatly-clipped balls, cones or even tiny chickens marching along in a line. Smart, eh?

Just think, the idyllic chocolate-box view of Bavarian villages is characterized by that proliferation of window boxes overflowing with colourful annuals on every house. We can do that here. If more city dwellers planted up their unused balconies, grey cities would be transformed.

IRRIGATION

On roof terraces, where you can generally fit in larger planting schemes, drip irrigation systems are vital – especially if you've gone for plants that aren't drought-tolerant. The piping can be fixed to the wall with the drippers hidden behind the containers. For peace of mind the whole thing can be controlled via a simple battery-operated timer, but it's important to emphasize that automated irrigation is not a substitute for watering by hand, as this gives you the opportunity to get up close and personal with your plants and check them thoroughly for drying out and signs of pests and diseases. Where it's impossible to route a new water supply from the mains, consider having a water butt or two. Admittedly, it's not the most attractive feature in your garden but you can of course hide it with heather panels or timber shingles. Mulching round the tops of containers with bark, straw, coconut-fibre, gravel, pumice, or extruded lightweight 'pebbles' will help restrict evaporation from the planting medium. Using water-retentive granules in the compost will also help the soil retain its moisture for longer. Drip trays and self-watering containers (i.e. those with an in-built water reservoir) are very useful, but for more watering tips, check out Chapter Six.

Whatever garden you have, be it up high or down low there's bound to be one thing they all have in common: boundaries! The smaller the garden, the more you should take advantage of growing on the vertical plane. There are so many possibilities – not least covering a wall or sturdy fence with plants doubles your growing space. No more blank walls, please!

WALLS

Walls – blank walls – don't have good press, as they suggest a barrier rather than anything positive. But there are ways in which you can use your wall or fence to significantly increase the size of your garden: simply think vertical.

With a small outdoor space every bit of it needs to stand up and be counted, including the boundary. (This is especially so in city gardens where walls and fences can easily dominate.) Because walls are so obvious they can seem huge and often ugly. Imagine a 6-foot-high larch-lap fence surrounding a tiny garden. A lot of new homeowners are faced with exactly this overly intrusive orange monster and some city gardens, such as basements and enclosed courtyards, tend to be wall-focused. In these scenarios the boundaries almost become a more important consideration than what's on the ground; remember you tend to notice what's directly in front of your face rather than what's a couple of feet in front of your toes. The key is to imagine your boundary laid flat; then you can see immediately how the overall size of the garden is increased. So if you have all this extra space, why not use it to its full potential? Claim your boundaries. If it's yours, if you look at it daily and it resembles a prison perimeter, then something needs to be done.

ABOVE This beautiful sculpture decorates the wall behind wonderfully.

BOUNDARY BLUES?

The problem with boundaries is that they seem to emphasize what we haven't got: they're a full stop, reminding the gardener that he or she doesn't have a vast country estate that goes on for miles. This is the first hurdle to get over. So, rather than regarding them as a restriction to our domain, let's think of them as a container for everything we own, and let's make the sides of that container as attractive as possible.

Walls and fences might be a constant reminder of where our property ends and someone else's begins, but they also have an upside; a small city garden with high walls is a God-given enclosure and enclosures make for the creation of a unique atmosphere. If you don't believe this and always think that bigger is better, then visit some National Trust gardens. Although the acreage of these places might be considerable, you'll notice immediately that closer to the house the garden is usually divided up into a series of outdoor rooms, and this is where you find most of the visitors congregating. It's those blessed walls that do the trick; creating spaces that are human-sized, where we feel we can hide ourselves away. Think of your small city garden with its close boundaries as one of those garden rooms in the big country estates and make use of its verticals to create a little green duvet.

Take time to look at the walls that surround you: house walls, garage walls, those that frame your back and front gardens. Everybody has them, yet few make use of them. I hope to make you think differently.

WALLS AND THE ELEMENTS

If you already have solid walls around your boundaries, be grateful for them, work with them, and don't even think of taking them down. But, if you have any choice, and you are starting from scratch in a windswept garden, think about building boundaries that aren't entirely solid. Wattle, reed and slatted fences do a far better job, as they are permeable and filter rather than stop the wind in its tracks. Plus they're cheaper to build.

Solid vertical structures (including house walls) have a unique microclimate and the biggest thing that affects this, apart from their orientation, is wind. Verticals markedly affect whether air flows freely or whether it is impeded and tunnelled.

The prevailing wind hits a solid structure, creating a wind-blasted side and a sheltered side. Simple, you might think, what's the fuss? But it isn't quite as straightforward as that. Prevailing wind isn't stopped in its tracks when it hits a wall, it has to go somewhere, so it swoops over the top and down the other side with force. If most of the wind affecting your garden comes from the east or north, then the leeward side of any wall crossing it is not the place for delicate plants that require cosseting. Walls which cut across a prevailing wind need tough plants on the leeward side because the turbulence hits them like a smack in the face! When wind hits a wall that runs with the prevailing wind it will be forced to one end of that wall in a funnel-like effect. Don't plant tender or wind-sensitive plants there either, because they'll also get a battering.

Rain shadow is another factor that affects many walls, as does shadow from the overhanging eaves of the house. When it rains, the soil at the bottom of the wall, for about a foot or so out, stays dry as rain generally falls straight down, not at an angle. Add to this wind howling round a house, plus the radiator effect of brick and stone, and no wonder hanging baskets need watering two to three times a day in hot weather.

DRY ZONES

Always treat the base of house walls, as well as areas under eaves, as dry zones and choose plants for these places that tolerate these conditions. Another factor which adds to the problematical mix here is that house footings usually extend out for a considerable distance, which means that you can't plant right up against the wall because if you do, plants will struggle to anchor themselves and get water. For this reason, always plant at least a foot away from the base of the wall and, to be extra safe, excavate down or carefully hammer in a wooden stake where you want to plant, just to make sure there isn't any concrete below the topsoil.

Equally, because the soil at the base of a wall is very dry and has little structure it is often very poor quality. As always, the key is to dig in loads of compost, homemade or bought, because this will help retain moisture as well as provide nourishment for the plants. Sometimes you'll come across a lot of rubble buried at the base of walls, too (a problem frequently found in new-build gardens), and the only way to deal with it is to dig it all out and replace the soil with decent stuff.

OUTDOOR HEATING

All this makes it sound as if walls aren't such a desirable thing, but this isn't true as many city gardens are protected from prevailing winds by surrounding buildings. Here walls provide shelter, which means you can grow Mediterranean plants such as bananas, cannas and figs within them, despite the fact that beyond them there might be a pretty inhospitable climate. Walls hold heat in and then release it at night just like storage radiators, so they are considered priceless for growing tender and sensitive specialities like peaches, apricots and tropical climbers. Don't waste that hot and sheltered south- or west-facing wall space on something tough that'll grow almost anywhere; think of this area as a place reserved for your tender treasures. As with everything, there are positives and negatives, and once you've worked out the limitations, you can go with the flow!

BELOW Neutral colours work best on walls and allow the plants to stand out better.

COLOUR UP

I'm a huge fan of traditional old brick walls as they have a certain in-built charm: they are so texturally beautiful to look at, and their character is only enhanced by all the little ferns and mosses which often appear in the cracks. But, as always, it's a matter of opinion: to many people old walls seem gloomy and oppressive and increase the sense of being hemmed into a small space. Cleaning these walls off with a pressure washer will brighten them up, but it is only a temporary solution, for city pollution will soon dirty them again. The easiest and cheapest way to transform the appearance of an old wall is to paint it.

In many instances this method is preferential to concrete render as the paint adds to the textural quality by accentuating every single brick. The trouble is, you can't just slap on the stuff; there's quite a bit of laborious preparation involved, otherwise the paint will flake off in a season. So you need to scrub the whole surface with hot soapy water and then rinse it down. After repairing any defects, paint the whole wall with a fungicidal wash to rid yourself of troublesome algae, followed by a stabilizing solution or primer. This will help seal the surface so you won't get powdering or flaking later. Some paints will need a basecoat; and this is well worth using as it will ensure that the colour both lasts longer and is as close as possible to the sample on the paint chart.

To make the wall itself into a feature it can be painted any colour you fancy, and you can often get away with far brighter colours than you would use inside. But those shades that work best with plants usually come from a subtle low-key palette: pale blues, light violets and silver greys are like green in that they recede into the distance and make a small space feel bigger, especially in the evening. Earthy Indian reds, warm yellows and golden

'To make the wall itself into a feature it can be painted any colour you fancy, and you can often get away with far brighter colours than you would use inside.'

Do a bit of colour research before you pull out a paintbrush. White is usually the first choice to brighten up shady corners, but it isn't always the best. White gets mucky easily and too much of it can overwhelm a small space. In hot gardens it reflects a lot of light, too, making it uncomfortable to look at without sunglasses. Better to choose a subtle, distempered off-white colour with hints of grey or cream (which are the colours that white will turn into after twenty to thirty years or so, anyway), as this blends in effortlessly and isn't so dramatic. Dull green in all it's various shades and hues is the perfect colour to make ugly walls and fences almost disappear into the background and also makes a small space feel bigger. However, painting a large boundary wall or fence green can 'muddy' a border, as it doesn't provide sufficient contrast with the plants, so pick the colour with your planting scheme in mind.

browns will make a cold space feel more inviting, but will also make a small space feel even smaller – which works in your favour if it's an intimate atmosphere that you're after.

It's unlikely that the colour you choose will be exactly the same as on the tester card, even with the best of preparation. Light affects colour in strange ways; in full sun, dark colours will appear lighter when applied over a large area and, on the flip side, light blues can appear very cold and unwelcoming in shady corners. I often paint a large plywood sheet the colour I've got in mind and then lean it against the wall I want to paint, which gives me the chance to change my mind if the colour alters dramatically as the sun moves round during the day. Of course, in most cases repainting a wall if the colour turns out to be wrong isn't too difficult, so you could just go for it and hope for a 'happy accident!'

SPECIAL EFFECTS

Solid paint colours will almost always need breaking up with planting, trelliswork or containers – if only because whatever colour you choose will appear monotonous over a large area. It might even be worth painting different walls in different hues of the same colour, or another similar one, to break up the monotony.

If you're feeling artistic, a trompe l'oeil mural is a clever way of messing with perspective. This usually involves paintings of landscapes to trick the eye into thinking that the garden is bigger than it actually is. In my opinion this usually works best in classical designs because in modern gardens, with their hard lines and up-to-the-minute materials, these images often appear out of place and so somewhat shatter the illusion. If you feel like having a go, then practice, practice, practice, or get a professional in to do it for you (which will be expensive). Trompe l'oeil needs to done well for it to be effective and there are a few golden rules: keep it simple, limit yourself to only one or maybe two panels (depending on the size of the wall), place it in a shady spot so shadows don't ruin the fantasy and, lastly, use plants to cover its edges.

To get the best effect always use the specified paint: masonry, acrylic or lime wash for walls, oil-based paints for timber and metal, and water-based stains for wood. It sounds obvious, but choosing the wrong type of paint will dramatically affect the colour itself, the application rate and also the durability of the finish.

Whatever you opt for, take note that this will probably need to be re-done every few years, so anything you plant in front will get in the way. Also remember that once applied, paint is the very devil to get off brickwork and natural stone without expensive sandblasting and re-pointing, so be confident that you're making the right choice.

ABOVE **On their own concrete walls can appear stark and ugly, but not when they provide the perfect foil for colourful planting.**

CONCRETE COVER-UP

Walls that are structurally sound but ugly can be clad in a variety of materials – such as bamboo, heather or reed screens – without you having to do a demolition job or reaching for the paint. This method is ideal for hiding an ugly

ABOVE **Delightfully different colourful panels make the end wall of this garden a prominent focal point.**

breeze-block wall and it's the easiest way to bring some texture to a boring flat surface – I look at screens as being just like an instant hedge. And they are easy enough to do yourself. Simply fix pre-treated roofing battens to the wall and, using thick staples, attach your chosen screening material to them. Most screens will only last for seven to ten years or so, but as they're relatively inexpensive it doesn't cost too much to replace them.

In contemporary gardens, copper, aluminium or steel sheets can be screwed onto the wall and will not only camouflage unsightly surfaces, but will also inject some light into the garden with their reflective properties. Unlike a mirror, these won't reflect you (or the compost bin), either.

Trelliswork will also screen unattractive walls a little more subtly; treat it like outdoor wallpaper. Painted the same colour as the wall, trellis will retreat into the background, or you can paint it a different colour to make it a focal point – but do be careful that this doesn't defeat the object of the exercise and cause the boundary to 'jump out' and dominate. False perspective trellis is fun, and even though it deceives nobody, a bit of trickery in the garden is always a talking point!

The key to using trellis in the garden is keeping it simple; elaborate convoluted designs often look out of place or messy. Pick a sturdy one too, a trellis that won't crumble with age and will stand up to nasty British weather; some of the ones I've seen offered for sale look like they'd collapse before you'd even put them up! I often make my own trellis using pre-treated softwood or western red cedar battens; that way I can play about with different designs, safe in the knowledge it's been constructed properly and will last.

A favourite and trendy style of wall at the moment is the rendered wall – painted or not – which is then lit up with sharp shafts of light to make it a feature. Whilst it's the perfect surface for contemporary gardens it does mean having a lot of vertical concrete, which might be something you'd think was too much of a good thing in the city. But once a wall is rendered you do have the perfect surface on which to splash some paint and inject a touch of colour into the garden.

BUILDING A WALL

Obviously building a wall or two is a big job, and one that is best tackled by a professional – especially if you're after something complicated with plinths, buttresses, piers or tricky bonds. Wall-building is like laying a patio: there's an awful lot of stuff you don't see, but which is absolutely vital if you want it to stay up! Even to build a simple wall of up to three or four courses high (which is possible for a competent DIY-er) is quite a job: trenches for the footings have to be dug, hardcore and concrete needs pouring in and levelling, not to mention the need for decent bricklaying skills.

Many people only think of brick when building a wall, but there are numerous other potential materials, too. Stone walls made from the real thing (especially local stone) are hideously expensive but, if you can afford it, are so worthwhile. After all, you're not going to replace such a wall in a hurry, are you? So it makes sense to splash out on the best wherever you can. Brick walls with flint panels or cobble blocks are perfect for period gardens, whereas those built using rendered breeze blocks, glass blocks or gabion cages and filled with stone, logs, tiles, knapped flint, limestone chunks – whatever you like, really – are best used in modern designs.

Whatever material you choose, remember that a wall is a pretty dominant statement in a garden, so it must blend in with the house and its surroundings. Don't worry about the sheer newness of bricks or stone; these will weather if they're natural materials. If your choice is reconstituted stone or concrete imitations, however, think carefully because these materials have the uncanny characteristic of looking the same ten years after the day the wall was built.

A good idea is to make a timber and cardboard mock-up of the height of the wall you're after and fix it temporarily into position. It sounds daft, but it really is worth doing because this way you can see how the wall will fit in, whether it casts too much shade, whether it is the perfect height for screening or whether it's in the right place. It'll also help ascertain whether the wall is in proportion to the garden as a whole. If you can, leave it in place for a while because time will allow you to see its limitations and its suitability and will probably help spark off other creative ideas, too.

WHEN IS A WALL NOT A WALL?

If you haven't got a beautiful brick wall, or even an old has-been wall that would benefit from some rendering, don't feel left out – there are other good alternatives that are just as stylish and just as plant-friendly.

FENCES

Fencing is the cheapest alternative to solid brick walls and comes in many styles – other than the common larch-lap with its hippie orange colour. Fencing can have a good long life if it's erected properly, and if you use a quality manufacturer you won't need to go over it with a plant-friendly preservative every few years. I prefer to leave fencing unpainted. True, it doesn't last as long, but slapping on coloured preservative only ruins the unobtrusive weathered colour. If you've got new larch-lap fences, I confess I can't think of a single plant that looks good against an orange background but, fortunately, this factory finish does fade fairly quickly. If you're truly disgusted and really can't wait for it fade you can always paint over it. Brown shades are best because they don't draw attention to themselves, but never use cobalt blue; it might be a lovely colour, but for fences it should be banned.

What generally happens, though, is that the border gets planted, matures, and completely hides the fence and any remedial work that might need doing. It's not an easy job to take down an old fence and put up a new one when there are a lot of mature plants in the way so the best option, if you have the choice, is to assess the life of an existing fence and, if appropriate, replace it before planting up a border in front.

Front gardens – especially those with a more relaxed country feel and where privacy isn't an issue – suit low picket fencing, but it needs to be substantial in appearance, made of good solid wood (which you can paint white if you're into the New England look) and fixed firmly to posts set in concrete. Nothing looks worse than a fence that has a section which has wobbled out of line and come loose!

HEDGES

Hedges are living fences and form the perfect natural backdrop to planting. Although their effect isn't as immediate as a fence or wall they are cheaper in the long run, even if you have to erect a temporary fence until the hedge is established. There's a wealth of suitable plants from tough rugosa roses to apple-green *Griselinia*– a fast-growing evergreen shrub. Yew is wonderful: it always looks expensive and adds an air of formality to any garden but, although it's not as slow-growing as you might be told, compared to other hedging plants it does drag its feet. Planting holly has the added attraction of winter berries (however, you will need both male and female plants to get berries, unless you use the variety 'J.C. van Tol'), and it comes in variegated forms as well as smaller-leafed cultivars.

Of all the plants that can be used for deciduous hedges, beech is my favourite. It can be trained and clipped to make a wonderful hedge – and not necessarily a very tall one, either – and in autumn and winter it often retains the old copper-coloured leaves until the gorgeous translucent new foliage starts afresh in spring. It is a particularly useful hedging plant for frost pockets where many evergreens would suffer frost scorch and die back.

One drawback with hedges is that they tend to be wider than walls or fences, so they're not suitable where space is at a premium, but they are fantastic at mitigating the effect of wind: filtering rather than blocking it. In such situations, though, watch out for wind scorch. Whatever plant you use, remember that the hedge will need annual clipping/trimming. If you already have a hedge, think very, very, *very* carefully before ripping it up as it takes years to grow another. Plus, what wall flowers and changes colour throughout the year?

CLIMBERS

Of course, the ultimate way to brighten up any boundary and make it a bit more interesting is by using plants. If you don't have room for a hedge, climbers can be great space-savers in a small garden as they climb vertically and, with a little judicious pruning, won't protrude into the garden too much. Most people will automatically think of four of five climbers when it comes to walls: ivy, jasmine, clematis, honeysuckle and cottagey roses, but actually the choice is far, far greater. There are so many more unusual plants for any boundary, whether it is one that faces north, south, east or west. Don't restrict yourself just to the range that is offered at your local DIY store or garden centre; specialist nurseries will have all manner of weird and wonderful things. For a hot south or west-facing wall, why not choose a passionflower, kiwi, *Eccremocarpus scaber* (the Chilean glory flower) or a fragrant star jasmine, *Trachelospermum jasminoides*. For shady north and east walls, nothing beats the golden hop (*Humulus lupulus* 'Aureus'), or *Vitis coignetiae* – a giant-leaved grape vine which, admittedly, grows very big so it will need some space to spread out.

FREE CLIMBERS

Ivy seems to have become the villain of the plant world, with people ripping it off walls as if it would eat them! Ivy has an undeserved bad press: it is NOT a destroyer of walls, and it will not tear your house down or cause your wall to crumble on passers-by (unless your wall is in a pretty poor state of repair anyway, in which case it will simply take over and finish the job!).

Ivy climbs by means of aerial roots – these are roots which appear along the stems and which attach to the surface of the wall and to any natural little cracks. If your walls have any mortar which is loose and falling out, ivy will root into it and in time will force the stones or bricks further apart until eventually the whole fabric of the wall will become unsafe and water will seep in through the cracks. This might take years, but it won't happen at all if the wall is kept in a good state of repair. In fact, ivy and walls make a perfect marriage: ivy provides nesting-sites for birds and its flowers are a late source of nectar for bees and other insects. And it always looks good, no matter how wet or dry the climate. What's more, there are loads of different leaf colours and leaf shapes to choose from: 'Green Ripple', 'Ivalace', 'Buttercup', 'Pedata', 'White Knight' and 'Elegantissima' are favourites.

For covering large expanses of ugly walls, the gable end of an adjacent house or the back of a factory, nothing beats parthenocissus for sheer smothering power! A free climber like ivy, the Virginia creeper attaches itself to a surface using aerial suckers and would cover a skyscraper if you let it! I love *Parthenocissus tricuspidata* 'Veitchii' (commonly called the Boston ivy)

which, like all Virginia creepers, has spectacular autumn colour when the leaves turn an incredible dark reddy-purple. Of course the downside of using *Parthenocissus* is that it's not evergreen, so when the leaves fall what you're trying to hide comes into full view. Instead of ivy for a shady north-facing wall, why not go for *Hydrangea anomala* subsp. *petiolaris* or *Schizophragma hydrangeoides* 'Roseum' for some all-year-round cover? Although they're not as fast growing, both are tough free climbers, too.

CLINGY CLIMBERS

Climbers like clematis, sweet peas, hops, runner beans, wisteria and passionflower need something to climb up as they have no means of clinging to the wall without support. The simplest solution is to make them a climbing frame.

Trellis is traditionally the support of choice for climbers, but don't fix it close up to the wall or your plants won't be able to climb up it. This might sound obvious but it happens all the time. Trellis has to be fixed *away* from the wall with a gap behind it so the climbers can weave in and out, back and front. Just put spacers or a batten between it and the wall or fence to give the necessary space. (This also functions as an air-gap which helps stop moulds and diseases from becoming a problem.)

If you don't want to use trellis, fix eye screws, or vine eyes, into the wall or fence and stretch stout galvanized wires horizontally between them. Done a foot or so apart this will give twiners, or those plants which climb using tendrils, something to get a grip on. You won't really notice the wires, as they soon become invisible under the mass of growth. Bear in mind, though, that wire supports do need to be heavy-duty, and should look as if they're almost too substantial for the job; believe me, there's nothing worse than flimsy wires breaking or sagging under the strain of an eager climber.

'The ultimate way to brighten up any boundary and make it a bit more interesting is by using plants. If you don't have room for a hedge, climbers can be great space-savers in a small garden as they climb vertically and, with a little judicious pruning, won't protrude into the garden too much. '

When climbers are at the baby stage, it's worth gently teasing out the young shoots and very loosely tying them in to colonize the lowest wires first. Clematis is a good example of a climber that will look all the better for this treatment. For jasmine this is vital as it's a rocket of a plant – left to its own devices it just shoots up, and the bottom half of the wall is left bare with just the main stem showing. In fact, clematis always seem to look better from your neighbour's garden – have you noticed how they seem to froth themselves prettily over the top of the wall and flop down the other side, while you're still waiting for the flowers to show on your side of the wall?

WALL SHRUBS

If you've got enough space, why not grow a few wall shrubs? *Cotoneaster horizontalis*, and dwarf *Pyracantha* are traditional favourites, their flowers followed by sparkling berries. Usefully evergreen, they can be a bit dull once the flowers have gone so to keep interest going plant them with summer-flowering clematis which will use the limbs of the shrub as support. That way you get double your money; flowers at two different times of year.

Roses make excellent wall shrubs, especially when tied onto arbours, pergolas, metal railings or trelliswork. You'll need stout gloves for the job and, to get the best flowering out of them, tie in the arching stems laterally to the framework. For a little additional colour, clematis like *C.* 'Miss Bateman', 'Niobe' and 'Mrs George Jackman' are classic accompaniments.

More tender shrubs like *Lonicera* x *purpusii* and *Chimonathus praecox* 'Luteus' will repay being grown against a south-facing wall. This couple flower in winter: the *Lonicera*, known as the winter-flowering shrubby honeysuckle, bursts forth with the most amazing fragrant flowers in early spring. The wintersweet will reward a little TLC with a smothering of delicate, pale-yellow, bell-shaped flowers from January onwards which will last a long time, and the scent of the flowers has to be breathed in to be believed! Once the flowers have gone, however, it does look rather dull, so here's another candidate for adding a *Clematis* 'Mrs Cholmondeley' or an annual nasturtium, which can use the branches as a climbing frame.

Bear in mind that wall shrubs might also need some support, as many quickly become top heavy. If you are planting shrub/climber combinations make sure, too, that the climber isn't be too vigorous otherwise it will overwhelm the shrub completely. The effect you're after is a sprinkling of flowers peeping through the bush, not a smothering! Do make sure that you pick a climber that won't mind being accidentally trimmed a little, as many wall shrubs need regular training and pruning to maintain their shape.

VERTICAL TOPIARY

If you're lucky enough to have a large expanse of high wall or fence, you could consider growing some fruit along it. Fan-trained and espaliered apples and pears (pears love walls, and fruit much better when grown against them) might be more expensive than shrubs or standard trees, but they are designed to be grown tight to a wall; all you have to do is keep up the training. For shady north walls, grow Morello cherries – you may not get a bumper crop every year but even a smattering is cause to brag! With a sheltered south-facing wall you do, of course, have many more options, so try growing an apricot or peach, or even a fig. The fig will need its roots restricted otherwise you'll have a monster on your hands, so grow it in a large tub or in a hole lined with perforated plastic.

DIVISIONS . . . DIVERSIONS!

Design-wise, walls help create divisions in the garden by chopping up the area into a number of smaller spaces. Don't be frightened to add a free-standing wall to a little garden: you might think it will make the garden even smaller, but if the proportions are right it usually won't. What actually makes a garden seem small is seeing all of it at once; where everything isn't immediately obvious, and where you have to go round the other side of a wall or some planting to see more garden, your mind will trick you into thinking that the entire space is bigger than it actually is. A design feature in their own right, free-standing walls are appearing in small city gardens all over. If you have a small area and you divide it up – the result? Two rooms instead of one. And, if you can't see what's on the other side of the wall, a sense of anticipation is created, too – what *is* on the other side?

Slatted fencing, trellis, wattle and osier hurdles also replicate the wall-as-division concept and not only are they cheaper to build, but they're useful if you have a shady garden because of their light-porous nature. They also help to delineate areas with different themes without screening them off completely. If your garden is big enough and you have eclectic tastes in design and planting (and you want to incorporate every conceivable garden style!), then repeating the same vertical throughout the garden will provide the necessary link between each area.

Low twin-walls can be used as narrow planters, either to bring up small plants to a decent viewing height, or to act as scented seats. In-fill the space between the two sides with decent soil, plant lawn chamomile on top, and whenever you plonk yourself on it you'll get a wonderful whiff. Or you can grow rockery plants and alpines along the top, plants that would otherwise get lost in many beds and borders. Twin-walls can double up as storage, too; build each side wide enough apart to take plastic storage containers, and then top it all off with a treated timber lid which can be lifted off or hinged back. You can use the top as seating, or as space for elevated planters. This gives you twice the value from a single feature!

WALLS OF WATER

If you want to really make a statement, plan a water-wall; this is so lovely in a small space you'll wonder why you didn't think of it before! You can have the water cascade down from the top of a new or existing brick wall and fall like a sheet of water, or gently shimmer down an aluminium façade fixed to the front. If such a cascade of water is carefully sited you can use it to reflect light into those darker parts of the garden. Long gone are the days when you had to have something like this fabricated from scratch, just search on the internet for a myriad different styles; there's one to suit every garden. Simple copper spouts or quirky lions' heads are perfect for more traditional designs, and when enveloped in planting they can be a wonderful surprise as you come across them.

Most wall lights need cables and sometimes conduit which, when snaking across the surface, can detract from the beauty of the wall or the light cast by the fitting. Ideally, chase them into the wall and render over the top, or hide them with climbers or strategically positioned planting if rendering will spoil the look of a brick wall.

LIGHTING

Walls are excellent places to play about with lighting because the results are quite distinct. You don't need masses of lights; the glow from just one 50-watt spot will travel some way, giving different effects the further it gets from the source. A big wall is a sleeping giant in the day, but it comes to life when lit up at night. Something magical happens after dark, especially when you graze light up walls that have bumps and shadows; you might not notice the wall in the day, but lit up with a row of spotlights you'll think you're in another garden! I love seeing walls used as projector screens, with spotlights angled through architectural planting to cast theatrical shadows on the surface behind.

The combination of wall, water and lighting has got to be one of the most exciting possibilities in garden design, and it's ideal for the tiny back garden. Water from a spout is one thing, but having a sheet of water falling from a lip at the top of the wall is a fantastic statement. Lining the wall behind the flow with shiny aluminium, and uplighting this with tiny, water-resistant LEDs shining up from a pool beneath will have you giving up TV!

What happens if your garden's the size of a shoe-box or you've no garden at all! Why not simply decorate the inside of your house with green? Don't think you're a poor relation; indoor gardening gives you the wonderful opportunity to grow exotics, plants which are too chicken to survive our harsh winters. Plus even if you've the biggest city garden in the world, houseplants are an important element of interior design, and the easiest way to link both inside and out.

ABOVE Grazing walls with sharp shafts of light is a favourite on alley walls – it's drama without taking up precious space.

BRING THE OUTSIDE IN!

For those with a tiny shoe-box or no garden-proper at all, houseplants give you the opportunity to have a garden – it just happens to be inside! I must confess to having a passion for houseplants; and before you scoff and think of elderly relatives with their spider plants and poinsettias, think again. There's now a huge range of exciting houseplants available: there's *Gardenia* and *Mimosa* for the enthusiast, *Medinilla* and *Sanchezia* for the connoisseur, asparagus ferns and *Aeonium* for novices and even indestructible gems such as *Sansevieria* (mother-in-law's-tongue) for true beginners.

If you need a little more encouragement, just look at the recent interior design boom and you'll see that no longer are houseplants a token gesture. Gigantic palms, orchids, bromeliads and *Strelitzia reginae* (bird of paradise) are commonly used to make theatrical design statements indoors, and even humble ferns, *Selaginella*, *Tradescantia*, *Maranta*, *Manettia* and mind-your-own-business will soon turn a humid bathroom into a steamy oasis when grouped together carefully. I noticed the powerful effect that indoor plants have when a friend who had a living room decked out like a jungle decided to redecorate. One day I arrived to find everything in place except her plants and I was stunned at how utterly soulless the room was without them.

The term 'houseplant' seems to put many people off as it inspires memories of kitsch 60s wicker chairs and dusty Swiss-cheese plants abandoned in a corner. But think again: houseplants are so-called purely because they are plants that need to be grown undercover in Britain throughout the winter when temperatures drop and frosts occur. A houseplant is really just a plant that we want to grow here even though it actually originates from a hotter climate. This opens the door to a world of exotic, tropical and sub-tropical beauties – many of which grow to gigantic trees and enormous climbers in their natural habitats. Now that's exciting. What an opportunity for a slice of distant lands!

If you're lucky enough to have a conservatory where you can grow citrus fruits and bananas, or even if you only have an uncluttered windowsill, go for it with gusto. Decorate your interior with green and you'll see that it's the easiest way to create a link between you and the outside world – in more ways than one.

HEALTH BENEFITS

ABOVE Repeating shapes and materials helps tie inside and out together.

A few plants indoors keep us sane when we can't get outside; just to have something green and alive in the room keeps us in touch with nature. It's actually been proved that plants are good for the soul (not that you need much proof!), and studies have been done in offices where living plant displays have undoubtedly affected the mood of the employees, cheering the spirits and reducing absenteeism by creating a calming, pleasant place to work. Not so long ago imitation plants were all the rage but, not surprisingly, they didn't have the same effect and now the real thing is taking over. Looking at living green – whether it's a towering beech tree in a country park or the little cyclamen next to your computer – is incredibly calming. When I'm working and stuck-in-a-rut I always look over to the windowsill at my favourite *Tradescantia* in the hope that it raises a smile and lifts my gloom. On many occasions I'll grab the watering can, and before long I'm taking cuttings from all the plants in the flat. Invariably this frenetic activity leads to a cup of tea, and then finally I can get back to work with a renewed sense of enthusiasm.

Having plants inside also has proven health benefits. As they photosynthesize they replenish the oxygen we breathe in from the air, but they also help to purify the air by taking in carbon monoxide and carbon dioxide from the atmosphere and breaking it down. How's that for a no-effort detox?

IN DAYS OF OLD

The Victorians were the first to become fanatical about growing plants indoors. Being great collectors of anything new, the Victorian middle classes loved to boast about rare acquisitions from dangerous plant-hunting expeditions and, because they held indoor plants in such high esteem, they were prepared to spend vast sums of money on furniture specifically designed for displaying them. True craftsmen created the 'Wardian case', the 'armoire', 'plant windows' and even whole closets so that plants could be proudly shown off like fine china.

In recent times, these sorts of displays are restricted to classic 'terrariums' or bottle gardens. These open-topped, or sometimes sealed, glass 'aquariums' have been popular since the 1850s, mainly for growing ferns or small sub-tropical and tropical species that require a moist, draught-free microclimate. Plants were found to thrive in glass cases for many years, as the water was continuously recycled and so the atmosphere remained balanced. You can find drawing-room Wardian cases in antique shops and because of their intricate detailing many of them are highly prized. If you've got a period house it can only add to the ambience, so if you can, snap one up.

Today, indoor plants are typically displayed as specimens or grouped together in their individual containers. Sometimes they might be grown collectively, and usually in all manner of modern planters, bowls, dishes, baskets and window boxes.

BIG AND BOLD

Specimen plants usually have one thing in common – dramatic form! Rubber plants, *Schefflera actinophylla* (umbrella tree), Bengal figs, philodendrons, *Beaucarnea recurvata* (pony-tail palm), Kentia palms, *Schefflera* (finger aralia) and *Dracaena* (dragon tree) are architectural monsters with distinctive leaves perfect for that striking indoor focal point. In contemporary interiors a few chunky specimens like these can be treated as choice bits of furniture and they are all you need to create a real impression. The key to displaying them with maximum impact is to put them against a neutral backdrop because, as always, focal points need to be noticeably different from their surroundings for them to stand out. Walls painted in off-whites, soft greys, mellow yellows, stone and light cream colours usually work best. Ornate, heavily-patterned wallpaper doesn't work at all because there just isn't enough contrast between the plant and its background.

For additional drama and a sensational night-time effect, why not illuminate your favourite plants? Uplights placed at the base of the plant will cast

Marvellous
Marvin
'84
FIGHT NIGHT
Madison Square Garden, NYC.

dancing shadows on a ceiling or, where there's space, try backlighting plants to cast the leaves into relief and create a silhouette on the wall behind.

GET TOGETHER

Many breathtaking flowering houseplants like *Gloxinia*, *Ixora* and orchids also make wonderful focal points as solitary specimens. However, unless it's the 'vase of flowers' type of effect that you're after, most normal indoor plants such as *Begonia*, *Anthurium*, *Caladium* and *Kalanchoe* usually look better when grouped together. The result is more impressive and by presenting them en masse smaller plants such as *Ficus pumila* don't get lost. View them with an artistic eye in much the same way that you'd consider where to place treasured ornaments for best effect. If you're grouping plants together, layer small plants in the foreground and larger ones in the background – just as they would be in nature. Think about shape, form, colour, texture and the inter-relationship between each plant and the pot, too. And, importantly, don't mix sun- and shade-lovers together, as not only does it look odd (picture a cactus next to a fern), but the plants won't appreciate it either as they require different growing conditions.

Collections of plants in individual pots are best for flexibility, but growing them together in a single container is a common alternative. This is advantageous because most plants grow better when their roots can expand and also because the close spacing raises the humidity around them. The downside is poor ventilation, which means pests and diseases can soon cause trouble if you're not vigilant. Instead of actually planting direct into the compost you can leave each plant in its pot and sink that into the soil. This is handy because as the plants grow you can remove a couple to prevent overcrowding, plus you can change the composition whenever the whim takes you.

Arranging houseplants is very much down to personal taste, although if there was a rule, it's going to be the obvious one of 'keep it simple' – you don't always need a riot of colourful flowers, sometimes a subtle collection of foliage plants is more attractive.

THE GARDEN ROOM

Conservatories are 'garden rooms' in the real sense of the word; with their comfortable seating and central heating (essential for all-year-round use), they are the perfect transition between house and garden. A conservatory is often the favourite room in the house: somewhere for plants like *Brugmansia* and *Plumbago* to flourish, yet also a space for us to relax and enjoy as though we're outside. Garden rooms are a possibility not only as a ground level

extension to the home, but also up high on a flat roof or a wide balcony. Just be sure to check with the local authority if you want to build one, because it'll probably need planning permission.

Conservatories and summerhouses are fast gaining popularity amongst those wanting to escape the rat-race. With wireless technology and sophisticated communications, people are no longer chained to their desks. Why be stuck in a stuffy office when you could work in the garden, whatever the weather?

ABOVE Indoors? Outdoors? Who knows!

ALLOCATE SPACE

Work out how much space you want to devote to your indoor plant displays. Why? Because the bug will bite you, I guarantee it! I have been in houses that are literally bursting at the seams with plants, as if the owners were trying to bring the whole outside world into their homes. The problem is that even with a master plan, you'll still find that houseplant land is impulse-buy territory, and I for one am guilty of lugging purchases back from the garden centre only to find that I have to move the furniture around in order to accommodate them. One infamous gift to myself was a 7-foot-high banana plant I bought while in Leicester. I arrived home, put it in position – and then my girlfriend walked in . . . Without going into too much detail, it now lives at my dad's!

CONSERVATORY CONSIDERATIONS

- Be sensitive to external decorations. A period house will need a Victorian-style conservatory to gel, whereas for contemporary houses all-glass frameless houses often work better.
- Conservatories are either made of wood, metal or PVC. A natural hardwood version is undoubtedly preferred by most, but the cost can be prohibitive. PVC is a cheaper alternative and more than adequate if a painted finish is desired, plus it needs far less maintenance. Frameless glass conservatories need virtually no maintenance – just a good window cleaner!
- With scale and proportion in mind, go for the largest conservatory you can afford. Once you add a table and chairs the space shrinks dramatically and what can happen is an unhappy compromise: you end up having less furniture than you wanted, and also fewer plants.
- Ask yourself how a conservatory will look from the both the garden and the house. For example, large panes of glass have a cleaner look and offer uninterrupted views, whereas elaborate lead-work, stained glass and loads of small panes look fussy.
- Position it carefully. Avoid positioning a conservatory against a south-facing wall as it's going to be hot, hot, hot – especially in high summer. That said, sauna-like conservatories can be easily cooled with plenty of blinds and windows. Under trees isn't the best option, either – especially sycamores which have a heavy leaf fall, or ash which is known for its brittle branches. My dad's conservatory is north-west facing, and whatever time of day sitting (or snoozing!) in it is idyllic. Shady conservatories also let you grow a wider range of plants than one that's constantly sunny.
- Make sure that the floor surface is easy to clean. Ceramic floor tiles come in numerous styles and colours and suit modest budgets perfectly. (You can even use linoleum or cork tiles, sealed with a waterproof varnish.) If you can, link the conservatory with the patio outside. Granite, limestone and polyophry slabs are hard-wearing options and can be used inside and out.
- The temperature in the conservatory can fluctuate a great deal, especially at night. That is the main reason why most traditional houseplants sulk and ultimately die. But even for conservatory favourites like bougainvillea, which will tolerate dramatic temperature changes, it might be a good idea to install underfloor heating, or simple electric heaters on timers. This will make it comfortable for plants and softie-humans alike, especially in winter.
- Most importantly: seek advice! Building a conservatory is for professionals only. There are many specialist firms who will give you advice and help you pick the best one for your home (and garden).

GETTING THE RIGHT ENVIRONMENT

Whether you have a conservatory or just want to put a few pots around the house, to get the best from houseplants you need to look at them in exactly the same way as you would plants for the garden. The same factors for plants growing outdoors are vital for healthy, happy plants indoors. Plants must be placed where they will receive the appropriate amount of light, heat and humidity, and this will need some detective work on your part. Some areas in the house might get morning sun, afternoon sun or perhaps no sun at all. Other places will have the central heating turned up high and the air will be dry, or they might be steamy and moist for part of the day, or draughty and cold. You must suss this out right from the off and pick your plants accordingly.

LET THERE BE LIGHT

Aspect is an important consideration for plants being grown inside the house. Every plant needs light to photosynthesize and grow healthily, but not all houseplants have the same light requirements. You won't go far wrong thinking that south-facing rooms receive more sunlight than north-facing ones, but proximity to a window also has a marked effect. The further away from the window you position a plant, the less available light there is for it to absorb. In a typical-sized living room, next to a window will be bright, whereas the wall opposite will be shady and the middle of the room will be in semi-shade. Even if you have chosen your plants with this in mind, those in shady spots will lean towards the nearest light source, making them lopsided. You'll have to turn them regularly, or you'll end up with a funny-shaped plant. Get this right, as plants that don't get enough light will inevitably perform badly; small yellow leaves, little or no flowers and stunted growth are all bad signs.

Bear in mind that light doesn't necessarily mean sun. A sweltering, south-facing windowsill is often too hot for most houseplants – except those like cacti, which originate from arid desert regions. You can use blinds to protect timid plants from blazing midday sunshine by pulling them down to cast welcome shade on particularly hot days, but in many cases it's simply easier to work with what you've got.

If you are living somewhere with very limited natural light but you really want to grow sun-loving aloes or orchids, for example, you could try using some artificial lighting to keep them happy. Commercial growers use mercury-tungsten and metal halide lights in their glasshouses to grow plants and also to manipulate them into flowering out of season, whatever the weather's like outside. But this is a specialist domain and this kind of lighting is quite obtrusive, even ugly, in most homes.

HOT STUFF

As I've already said, houseplants are plants that we want to grow here which generally originate from the tropics. The main reasons that most houseplants are grown inside in Britain is to protect them from frost and keep them at a favourable temperature, and with insulation and heating, most of our houses mimic these warm, tropical temperatures. Ideally, the temperature should always remain constant and no higher than 24°C; which isn't always an easy thing to do, especially with central heating. Of course, many species do have specific temperature requirements and this is where looking at the label before you buy the plant becomes so important. Any really tender and sensitive plants might need a little extra protection from draughts or on cold, frosty nights, which can be as simple as moving them inside the curtains rather than leaving them in a cold no-man's land between the curtains and the glass.

Temperature is also an important consideration when growing plants in the conservatory. The most notable cause of failure is picking plants that require a minimum temperature that you can't maintain during the night, especially in winter. With a cool conservatory it's relatively easy to maintain a night-time temperature of 2°C, but in a hot house trying to maintain a mean temperature of 20°C can be tricky to say the least!

Tubular heaters fixed to the wall will help, but they will cost. Electric fans heaters on timer switches are a cheaper alternative, but they may have an adverse effect in that plants can dry out. It's often better to recognize the minimum temperature you can realistically maintain and choose plants accordingly. You may not be able to grow certain palms, for example, but there are masses of others which will thrive in lower temperatures.

HUMIDITY

Central heating also dramatically affects humidity, which is undoubtedly the most difficult environmental factor to get right. Radiators dry out the air and decrease the moisture levels, which causes flowers to drop and leaf tips to turn brown as if they have been scorched. At worst the leaves will drop off completely and the plant will die.

Fortunately, raising the humidity around houseplants is reasonably straightforward. Humidifiers will help, but as they can raise the humidity to uncomfortable levels for humans it's better to use a water sprayer (but you have to be dedicated and mist every day!). Alternatively, putting a 4–5cm (1½-2in) layer of pebbles in the bottom of a tray and partly covering them with water will keep humidity high, especially if the tray is placed above a radiator, which causes the water to evaporate. This much less labour-intensive method works wonders for plants like *Mikania*, *Calathea* and African violets which all detest central heating. If you haven't got any pebbles, look in the houseplant section of your garden centre for expanded clay granules, or 'Hydroleca' as it's commonly known. Grouping plants closely together and plunging them into larger containers filled with compost will help, too.

'Temperature is also an important consideration when growing plants in the conservatory. The most notable cause of failure is picking plants that require a minimum temperature that you can't maintain during the night, especially in winter.'

GIVE ME A BREAK!
Keeping houseplants alive in summer is a doddle; you can even put them outside on the patio (which they love!), but getting them to go through the winter satisfactorily is when most trouble occurs. Radiators and central heating mess about with a plant's natural resting period, which usually occurs over winter when the temperature drops and light levels are too low for active growth. Call it hibernation. During this time watering and feeding should be kept to a minimum, as watering at the same rate during winter and summer is asking for trouble! The problem is that, just when this dormant period has arrived – wham! – on goes the central heating, and the plants are either forced to continue growing (when they need a rest) or they dry out. Result: exhausted plants. In some cases, moving those which really do need a winter rest into a cooler room – perhaps a spare bedroom – is the answer. The only exceptions to this rule are winter-flowering plants like heather and cyclamen. These are still actively growing at this time and therefore they must be fed and watered as long as they are on display.

ROOM INSIDE

All the rooms inside your house have a different microclimate, which suits some plants and not others. What follows is an over-simplification (since some houses break all conventions), but it will give you a starting point and help in the selection process.

Living rooms are generally warm and have high light levels but low humidity, due to central heating. The kitchen is warm, has lots of light and at times high humidity, followed by draughts when you open the window to let out the steam. The kitchen is often the best place for plants that need constant care and attention as they're in view every time you do the washing up. Hallways are generally cool and shady, often because there are no windows and therefore no natural light, and humidity is typically low. The dining room is often left unused for most of the time, so it's usually cool. Again, it has low humidity. Bedrooms vary enormously. Some resemble living rooms, being warm, with good light and low humidity, but they can also cool down rapidly at night if you have the windows open. The bathroom can resemble a sauna or a tropical rainforest at times, but generally the temperature is kept constantly warm, especially if you have a towel rail which operates independently of the main thermostat. Windows opened to let out steam do create nasty draughts, but for a limited time only. The porch is often very draughty and usually cool, but it does, however, get lots of light.

ABOVE **Even your windowsill can be home to your own cottage industry. (Not so sure about the pots, though!)**

INDOOR EDIBLES

Decorative plants aren't the only ones you can use to create an indoor garden. What about growing your own fruit and vegetables? It's amazing how many herbs and edibles you can slot in on windowsills or sunny kitchen worktops. Whatever you grow, the key is to keep them moist and not allow them to bolt. (Bolting just means flowering too soon.)

Herbs are best grown as short-lived plants, so you will need to replace them from time to time. You can also grow pots of rocket and other small 'cut-and come-again' salads – 'Saladisi' is a good variety. Now, these really are worth growing as they're so expensive in the supermarket, but the real reason to grow your own is because picked-fresh salad leaves are going to taste fabulous – much better than the ones you buy.

GOOD INDOOR EDIBLES

- Herbs – particularly basil and coriander (you'll have more success in summer with these because they really need good light and heat), parsley, chives, mint. If you're cunning, buy some small pots of herbs from the supermarket and split these up immediately, potting them on into bigger pots with new compost: four for the price of one! Picking herbs when you need them is much more cost-effective than forking out for packets of cut herbs that go off in the fridge before you get round to using them.
- Beansprouts – mung beans. Soak them overnight in warm water (use a thermos if you have one), drain off the water, transfer to a large glass jar and rinse them daily. They do well with moist muslin over the top of the jar, and in the airing cupboard. Keep them rinsed and a week later, once they have sprouted and made a root half an inch long, you can eat them.
- Tomato plants and small varieties of pepper in summer – these need a hot, sunny windowsill and you'll need to choose the smaller varieties like Tomato 'Cherry Belle' or 'Tumbler' because some tomato plants can reach 2 metres or more.
- Cucumber – a porch that bakes in summer would grow you so many indoor cukes you'll be giving armloads away. 'Fembaby' is the most popular indoor variety.
- Aubergines – a little more tricky to grow well, but in a good summer these will crop in your sunniest spot.
- Watercress – this one's a winner. Buy a bunch from your local greengrocer and just pop several stems in water and watch them root. Pot them up, keep them well watered and then continue to pick fresh, tangy leaves as and when you want to!
- Citrus plants – not the easiest to grow, but they have wonderful scent when in blossom and there's nothing better than plucking a lemon off your own tree for that G&T! The ideal spot would be a sunny porch that's cool but frost-free in winter. Do undertake some research before buying citrus plants, as they require lots of specialist care and attention.

In summer your houseplants will positively love you if you put them outside in the real world where they are open to the elements and can feel like they're back home again. It also means you don't have to worry so much about watering and pest and disease control, plus they can decorate your patio as a temporay seasonal display.

CARE AND MAINTENANCE

As houseplants are living in an unnatural environment, it really is up to you to meet their needs and keep them happy and healthy. If you follow a few basics, they're not that demanding!

WATERING

Contrary to popular belief, the commonest cause of unhealthy houseplants is actually watering too much, rather than not giving enough. (Most houseplants actually prefer neglect as opposed to overwhelming care and attention when it comes to watering – but don't use that as an excuse!)

How much and when varies according to the species of the plant and also where it is positioned – if it's in a warm room, sunny window or a conservatory, it will obviously need more water than it would in a shady, cooler room. Plants also require more water during their growing season (which is usually mid-spring to early-autumn), but other than that they will need watering only sparingly. If in doubt, shove a finger quite deeply into the compost and see how wet it feels. If it's soggy, hold back on the watering, if it's dry or slightly damp it could probably benefit from a drink. Keep an eye on plants in the winter – although they won't need water for growth, central heating can dry the compost, so you might need to give them a top-up. The key thing to remember is that plants are more likely to survive under-watering than over-watering – too much water waterlogs the soil and deprives the roots of oxygen, thereby eventually causing the roots to rot.

Fortunately it's easy to spot if you're over- or under-watering. Plants that are parched will have limp or wilted leaves, poor flowers and older leaves might turn yellow and drop off. Plants that are waterlogged often look mouldy: the leaves and flowers will be rotten and the roots will probably be mushy and smell horrible.

How much and when to water are both really important considerations, but you should watch the temperature of the water, too. Although tap water is more than adequate for most plants, just make sure it's not too cold.

If you're going away on holiday during the summer and don't have anyone in mind to water your plants, stick them in the bath or on the draining board on a damp tea towel trailing down into water in the sink. The plants can draw up water through the drainage holes in the base as and when they need to. It's worth removing any flower buds, too, and be sure to pull off any dead or dying leaves before you go, as these will rot and go mouldy. In a conservatory, consider installing an irrigation system on an automated timer. That way you can ski or sunbathe safe in the knowledge that your plants' water requirements are being met.

FEEDING

There should be enough fertilizer in ordinary compost to feed a new plant for about 6 weeks, and after this (during the growing season only), you will need to feed them regularly. The most effective way to feed is to use a liquid fertilizer, which you can apply every time you water. I'm a big fan of pills and sticks, too, as they take away all the hassle and you know that for a set time the plants are being properly fed. But, do note how long they last and try to work it so that plants aren't being fed excessively over winter. If you're unsure, hold back on popping a pill in from September onwards.

The easiest way to determine how much and when to feed is to look at the label! Some plants have specific requirements. Flowering plants might need extra potassium when they are doing their stuff to keep the display going, so give them a boost with a high-potash feed or some tomato fertilizer.

PESTS AND DISEASES

Of course, houseplants aren't really designed to grow in our hot, dry homes, so pests and diseases can be rife as they take advantage of the plants being a little stressed out. Vigilance is the key. Get up close and personal with your plants daily: finger the leaves and prod the compost to check for obvious signs. If you spot anything, use an insecticide or fungicide quickly and isolate any sick plant if you think it's necessary. Pest-wise, the common ones to watch out for are: red spider mite, aphids, mealy bugs and scale insects. The easiest way to prevent fungal diseases, such as rots and powdery mildew, is fresh air. On warm days open the windows; not only will it cool down a hot room or conservatory but it'll stop potential diseases from taking hold.

Biological controls

Until ten years ago biological control methods for dealing with pests were uncommon. Now, because we all want to reduce the amount of pesticides in our environment, they are much more popular. A bio-control agent is a natural predator which works on your specific pest and is available by mail order or at garden centres – you'll find them in a fridge! Bio-control works best in an enclosed space, rather than outdoors, and is particularly effective in conservatories. *Encarsia formosa* is a parasitic wasp of whitefly and has been used with great success in the food industry. *Phytoseiulus persimilis* is a predatory mite which devours both the adults and the eggs of the red spider mite. And *Cryptolaemus montrouzieri* is a predatory ladybird beetle which annihilates mealy bugs. But there are numerous others, too, and my favourite is *Steinernema kraussei*, a nematode (a parasitic worm) which kills vine weevil larvae. Like mercenaries on a seek-and-destroy mission, they hunt out their prey, puncture their bodies and infect them with a fatal disease! And before you get a little freaked that bio-controls will become a nuisance – once the food source has been used up, they either die or fly off to find more food.

POTTING ON

Plants inside the house will probably need to fit in with your décor and style – particularly the pots – so choose these carefully because they are going to be prominently on display. Terracotta-coloured or black plastic pots are ugly, but you can deal with this by slipping them into a more attractive 'shell', like a bamboo outer or a porcelain urn which does not have drainage holes at the base, thus protecting your floors as well as conserving water. If you are planting straight into other containers, make sure you have a saucer or tray underneath to catch excess water. I like to use the clear drip dishes you can buy – that way they don't detract from the plant or the pot.

Although you will be topping up their nutrients by regular feeding, it's still important to start your houseplants off well with a good compost. It doesn't matter if you use standard soil-less or soil-based multipurpose compost or specialist houseplant compost; most plants aren't fussy. That said, citrus plants, African violets and orchids are notable exceptions and you can buy tailor-made composts for these at the garden centre.

If your plant is looking a little sad in its pot, chances are it needs to move on. The best time to re-pot a houseplant is in spring just as the new growth starts to kick in. It does depend on the plant but generally you need to pot on your plants every 1–2 years. Choose a pot that fits the old root ball comfortably but which also gives you about a 5–10cm (2–4in) gap round the outside. A common mistake is to plant it into a huge pot, thinking that will avoid re-potting it for a few years; what actually happens is that the soil will slowly compact and go sour.

POTTING UP SPECIMENS OR COLLECTIONS

- Take a clean, suitable-sized container.
- Check for drainage holes and/or add a thin layer of crocks – for a 30cm-high (1ft-high) container a layer 4cm (1½in) thick is ideal.
- A third-fill it with compost, adding the appropriate amount of a slow- or controlled-release fertiliser to avoid having to feed regularly.
- Remove the pots from your purchases; check the roots and gently tease out those winding around the inside of the pot. If the plants are particularly dry, soak them in water and allow the excess to drain off before potting up.
- Arrange your chosen plants into the desired positions.
- Fill in between them with compost, covering the root ball of the plant by approximately 1cm (½in) and firm gently. Leave a 5cm (2in) gap down from the top of the pot for water.
- Water and place into position.

CHAPTER SIX
CONTAINERS

ABOVE Terracotta doesn't have to mean traditional – you can use it in contemporary arrangements too, such as with this colourful collection of grasses.

THE JOY OF CONTAINERS

In the gardening world 'container' is such a lovely word, isn't it? It has so much potential. There isn't a space that can't accommodate one or two pots and, at the opposite end of the spectrum, some gardens consist entirely of containers. If you have no garden, an all-concrete garden, or soil that's like concrete or if you live in a flat, on a canal-boat, or even in a mobile home, then the container is your gardening saviour!

POT FRENZY

In recent years the popularity of container gardening has increased ten-fold, primarily because they're so versatile and it's far easier to make a success of them than tackle a whole garden. As a result, the range of containers offered for sale in nurseries, on the internet and even at the local corner shop is astonishing, so you're sure to find one that'll suit any setting. For contemporary designs, choose chunky square concrete or terrazzo tubs, or for period or cottage gardens choose lead or reconstituted stone planters, oak boxes or weighty hardwood barrels. Don't forget that heavy pots are not a good idea on a roof terrace or balcony (see Chapter Five, Up High) because of the weight restriction – the last thing you want is for your garden to end up in somebody else's living room! So on these occasions choose pots that are made from lightweight materials. You might think all fibreglass and plastic pots are a bit naff, but I've seen imitations that have fooled me into thinking they were Cretan urns until I got close – and I mean very close – and some of the new moulded resin pots are true modern sculptures, with or without plants. Copper, zinc, aluminium or brushed steel containers are also light and easy to handle and for modern designs I really go a bundle on these. A row of shiny silver cubes on a simple glass stairwell looks ridiculously classy. These aren't just pots; when they're filled with some lavender or veronica they are design statements of the coolest order.

TERRACOTTA TALES

To many people, 'container' means the time-honoured terracotta. This is a great place to start, because there are so many different designs out there. Fluted bowls or Florentine urns will complete a classic courtyard, whereas smooth-glazed long toms are ideal for the ultra contemporary city balcony. If you are in any doubt about a new containerized addition to your garden, plumping for terracotta won't see you wrong. Why is this so? I like to think it's because terracotta is actually made from the good old earth that we grow our plants in, so it has a natural bond with them.

'There isn't a space that can't accommodate one or two pots. If you have no garden, an all-concrete garden, or if you live in a flat, on a canal-boat, or even a mobile home, then the container is your gardening saviour!'

Do shop around if you're going for terracotta, as prices can really vary. The cheap, slip-cast, plain-sided ones usually cost as much as a bag of sugar, but hand-thrown, ornamental heavyweights – those that would grace an Italian Count's garden – will break the bank. Always check the frost tolerance-of your potential purchases, too – chances are that the cheap ones may literally go to pieces the first time the temperature dips below freezing, whereas the more pricey ones won't – you get what you pay for.

For cold spots, go for clay every time as it keeps those roots insulated better than plastic or metal, but even if your clay pot is certified 'frost-proof' it's likely to sit in frozen water over winter, so put blocks of wood, old bricks or clay 'pot feet' underneath, to give it a chance to drain off and sit above a soaked surface, just to make sure.

THE AGEING PROCESS

The great thing about terracotta pots is that their looks improve with time. After a season or two, there's nothing to remind you of their brash orange newness. If you're an impatient gardener, it's easy to accelerate the ageing process. Mix up some live yoghurt into water, and add a dash of rotten organic matter then, using a paintbrush (or your hands!), liberally spread the mixture over the side of the pot and place it in a shady corner. The pot will soon have that been-there-for-ever look as, in a month or so, it will be covered in algae. I've tried the same technique on terracotta-coloured plastic pots too, admittedly with varied success.

ANYTHING GOES

You don't have to restrict yourself just to the collection of pots at your local garden centre; anything can be used as a container. I've seen some pretty weird things on my travels – talk about variety. Secondhand oil drums can hold pretty big trees that'll be happy for years. In Greece they use 5-litre olive-oil cans, which often have really nice painted designs on the outside, like Mucha-style art deco pictures. But that's not all; stacks of tyres can be used to grow potatoes (you get huge crops), or you can grow plants in wicker clothes baskets lined with plastic, coal scuttles, wine crates, rusty watering cans, tin baby baths (get down to a reclamation yard for these), old prams, chimney pots and Pither stoves. As long as the container is strong enough to retain some soil, it'll do. But don't get too carried away, as naff planters abound. Concrete welly-boots, miniature wheelbarrows, wells and other gnomish oddities like leather boots, pixie hats – well, what can I say about these? Better just to smile and move on.

Whatever you go for, always make sure there are good drainage holes in the base or your plants will struggle to breathe, or will rot in winter. If you don't see any holes, use a drill with the appropriate bit and plough some through the bottom – five or six will usually do, but, of course, it depends on the size of the container. A thin layer of broken terracotta 'crocks' or coarse grit placed in the base will help as well, or for those nervous about weight, use polystyrene chunks. I always place a semi-permeable horticultural membrane, fleece or thick layer of newspaper over the bottom, too. It helps stop dirty water running out and staining the patio.

MAKE YOUR OWN

If you really can't find anything that works for you, why not create something yourself? Containers allow the artist in you to come out, and without much outlay pots can be covered with broken tiles, mirror off-cuts, paint, stencils, gold leaf, cones, pebbles or mosaics. If it's just a simple tweak that you want to make, use modelling clay to add your own detail to cheap, plain planters. When planted up, you can cover the soil surface with textural finds like shells, small round pebbles or holey stones, or bits of broken china. This will serve the double purpose of adding a bit more interest while also acting as a barrier to reduce water evaporation from the soil. (See Pot Prowess, page 261.)

Making your own wooden planters is also a great idea if you've got an awkward space to fill, as they can be tailor-made. Use pre-treated timber for the frame and WBP (water- and boil-proof) or marine plywood for the sides and slap a coat of bitumen paint on the inside to stop water getting in. Don't forget to drill those all-important drainage holes, and then you can either stain it or go crazy and bring out the paint chart!

POTS TO THE RESCUE!

Containers can save any impulse buys: a useful trick is to pot up a plant that you've been seduced into buying as soon as it arrives home, so you don't worry about it while you work out where to put it. Many sale bargains are pot-bound and therefore need more room immediately. This emergency potting up gives you a bit of thinking time and allows the newbie to recover and grow a little before it has to compete with all the established fellas.

VERSATILITY

What I like most about containers is that they can be used in a design in so many different ways, not just for masking an ugly gas box or a cracked paving slab. A large urn packed with fragrant *Lilium regale* is the ideal focal point to 'pull' you along a path, or a huge tub filled with *Molinia caerulea*, *Heuchera* 'Palace Purple', long-lasting *Verbena bonariensis*, *Sedum* 'Matrona', *Gaura lindheimeri* 'Siskiyou Pink' and *Iberis sempervirens* is just the thing in a sunny position to soften hard landscaping. Topiary is a must: two standard bay balls, or similar, will perfectly frame your front door, and you can ring the changes by under-planting them with polyanthus in the spring and floriferous busy lizzies in the summer. Wow. Welcome home!

One major advantage of containers is that you can create environments to suit every type of plant in one garden (well, almost!): acid-loving azaleas or pieris can go in one tub, bog plants like bulrushes and yellow flag irises in another, small water lilies in whisky barrels (obviously those that are watertight!), and rock gardens in old butler sinks and farm troughs. Another advantage of container gardening is that you have a better chance of success with choice plants that might otherwise get lost or munched by pests if they were planted out in beds. A container allows you to keep tabs on particularly tasty or sensitive plants and provide suitable TLC. (See Pot-specific Pests, page 263.) Containers also allow you to grow tender plants that can live outside in summer but need protection in winter. Oranges and lemons, some grape vines, bananas and small palms can be grown in big containers with a wheeled saucer or base underneath, which enables you to push them under cover before early frosts hit.

BELOW These tall vases filled with lavender help frame the main view down the garden and their shape replicates the box cubes beyond.

PLANNING YOUR POT

All the spaces in this book have room for containers. Of course, they might have to be adapted – for example, in terms of weight in the case of roof terrace and balcony gardens – but elsewhere, anything goes. What's good about planting a container is that its size is reassuring; it's something that you can easily deal with. That can be a very freeing thought when you don't have to frown over how to plant up a gigantic border and wonder about the relationship between thirty different plants. With containers it's all downscaled, and therefore much less complicated.

ABOVE A classic tiered arrangement of *Cuphea*, *Molinia caerula* 'Variegata' and *Peperomia* hybrid.

WHAT GOES WHERE?

Because you are dealing with a much smaller area and one that will probably have fairly immediate impact, it's important to get the planting right. But don't panic, arranging plants in containers and hanging baskets is relatively easy, provided you always position each plant to complement and enhance the others. Basically, that means getting the balance right. The core of most traditional containers is a taller centrepiece, commonly with architectural form – perhaps a cordyline or canna lily, for example. Smaller bushy or prostrate plants like *Fuchsia* 'Love's Reward', *Isotoma*, sage and *Osteospermum* can then graduate down to the lip, or down to trailing *Helichrysum*, *Cuphea*, *Plectranthus*, *Diascia* and purple *Tradescantia*, which are perfect for planting tight to the edge of a pot to obscure the unsightly sides of hanging baskets or window boxes. If your container is going to be placed up against a boundary, move the central showpiece towards the back and plant downwards at the front. Remember that this time you only have to bother about the aspect from three sides.

Apart from 'taller plants at the back and smaller ones in front' there are no hard-and-fast rules about where plants should go, just make sure they're not screening one another and that each one is positioned so you can see it.

COLOUR

Colour-wise, should you choose a calm, harmonious scheme or go all out for some eye-socking colour? Well, the choice is yours! At different times you'll find me in both camps. I love vibrant summer tubs filled with cherry cannas, dark red pelargoniums, scarlet snapdragons and *Hordeum jubatum* (Squirrel-tail grass), yet the soft restraint of a weathered copper tub filled with white marguerites, purple verbena, blue petunias and silver helichrysum appeals too. On occasion I find that it's all about only one plant – nothing beats a barrel packed with huge yellow daffodils to herald in the spring.

The only word of caution when planting a container is do consider its colour, size and shape in relation to the plants. White planters work with almost anything, but green ones need a keener eye and more self-control. A tall vase often needs erect grasses or trailing fuchsias to balance it, and squat bowls call for mounding *Ophiopogon*, houseleeks or *Echeveria* – together they just work. I could preach about this all day, but knowing if the plants and the container are in harmony when it comes to scale and proportion simply happens though trial and error. To help (without forking out!), trawl through a few gardening magazines, nosy-in on what your neighbours are up to or why not pull out some containers and plants at your local garden centre and try out different combinations? Some will work straight away and some won't!

Part of the fun of container gardening is moving things around until the composition is pleasing – you can do this every day, if you want. Just remember that containers are the moveable garden feast, and as such they give you huge scope for different combinations.

GET TOGETHER!

For contemporary or minimalist designs, repetition is fundamental. Picture rows of identical plants in the same container – each one in harmony with the other. Personally, this isn't always my cup of tea, as I think it often looks a little stark and lifeless as an arrangement. My soft spot is for gardens with sporadic groupings because they look so right without trying too hard: relaxed and casual, just like the oil cans and pots arranged haphazardly in Mediterranean courtyards or on the street by the front door. When it comes to grouping different containers together, you don't need me to tell you where to put your pots. I'd be insulting your intelligence!

PERMANENT PLANTINGS

Traditionally, pots were a cheap way of bringing in temporary seasonal colour to windowsills or parts of the garden where flowers have come and gone. Not any more. Anything can be grown in a container as long as it's big enough – I've seen some that are so big they would dwarf the Harlem Globetrotters! Permanent displays of alpines, bulbs, herbs, perennials, conifers, shrubs and even small trees are perfect for beginners and lazy gardeners alike because, unlike temporary displays filled with spring or summer bedding, they don't need to be replaced every year. But it's important to emphasize that even permanent plantings will eventually need potting on. Look for signs of overcrowding, such as roots on the soil surface or peeking out through the drainage holes in the bottom. Perennials can be easily divided into smaller chunks and replanted back into the same tub, then you could pot up the extra clumps for yourself or give them to your neighbour – who knows what you'll get in return! Mature shrubs will also need a little attention every now and then. Either pot them on into a larger container or carefully trim the roots so they can go back into the original pot, just like a mature bonsai tree. Do make sure that you mostly trim the large thick roots; don't go crazy and

cut away all the thin fibrous or 'feeder' roots or the plant may die. And, lastly, always use fresh compost. In fact, even if you're not planning to re-pot mature displays you should replace the top inch or so of soil in the container with new compost each year.

ABOVE For permanent plantings nothing beats topiary in a pot, it has a sculptural quality and you can move it around to change the view.

BASKET CASE

When you think about growing plants in a basket hanging in mid-air with only a little compost it seems like a daft thing to do, but it works! The hanging basket, much like the window box, is a small garden on steroids – it needs lots of TLC because it's literally crammed full of plants. A typical 30cm (1ft) diameter basket may well contain more than fifteen plants! So feeding and watering needs have to be attended to daily and you can't slip up and forget this. If you go away for a weekend in the summer get a neighbour to water

your baskets, otherwise on your return you'll have miserable straw where you once had plants. Watch out where you hang them, too. Avoid places where people will bump their heads, or where they're tucked underneath a roof or suchlike so that they are deprived of natural light or additional rainwater, and don't put them anywhere that will make watering them tricky or a hassle.

BLENDING STYLE AND PRACTICALITY

Brackets and supports must be strong enough to bear the weight of the soil when it's wet, plus the weight of the plants themselves – which can be considerable. Always go for supports that seem chunkier than you'll need. If a gale blows and the fixings aren't secure, the basket will spin round and crash to the ground. If you live on the ground floor there won't be much damage, but if baskets are up high (like at first-floor level above a busy pavement), I'd be very nervous! If you think a hanging basket is a liability, the window box below a first-floor window and above a pavement can be a murder weapon.

ABOVE Compared to chunky terracotta or weighty terazzo, zinc containers are lightweight and easy to handle – ideal for gardening up high.

Think carefully when selecting your hanging container: plastic window boxes are naffness personified, whereas lead, terracotta or even a simple rectangular box of weatherproof plywood, painted (or not) won't detract from the plants. If you want a more rustic look, those old-fashioned hay troughs always look great on walls.

Apart from conventional boxes and baskets, plastic pouches are also available. Personally, I think these look utterly awful when first planted up, but they do the job quite well when the plants have finally covered the thing. I find them depressing to look at in their naked-plastic state, and can't bring myself to use them; that's just my prejudice (or is it laziness?). The container here is almost irrelevant as an element of design and is instead purely functional. If you really want to go down that path, though, Surfinia petunias and trailing *Lobelia* are suitable for these pouches, being very generous with flower and leaf.

You don't need fancy liners for your baskets, the cheapest solution is to get some moss, or hay from the pet shop, and line the basket with that, and it looks better, too. Once in place, lay part of a plastic bin liner on top, with holes punched in it, as a receptacle for the compost. Add a water-retaining polymer ('Swell Gel' is the most common) to the compost and, to make feeding a doddle, push in a couple of fertilizer sticks specially made for the job. If you have a lot of hanging baskets I'd buy a lance attachment for your hose, which lets you pump water into the baskets without having to teeter on stools with watering cans. Remember to position your empty window box before filling it with soil and plants; trying to cart a fully laden box up a steep flight of stairs is not a pleasant experience for your back, or the carpets!

FILL 'EM UP!

Once you've got all this sorted, so to the plants. Window boxes allow for some formality and obvious design. Miniature conifers live in quite small boxes perfectly well, as do evergreen herbs, small grasses like *Carex comans* and small ivies, and using a selection like this is the easiest way to achieve year-round interest. Just watch you don't pick too many evergreen shrubs like *Aucuba japonica* 'Crotonifoila' or *Skimmia japonica* 'Rubella', which are common in municipal displays, unless you're willing to plant them out after a year or so. You don't want your display looking like those outside the Red Lion round the corner – huge neglected outsized monsters looming out from teeny, tiny containers! To change the display, have small manageable boxes and grow seasonal bedding in a liner which you can drop into the box and, when the plants look tired, remove it and replace them with something different.

If there were only one rule for hanging baskets and boxes it would be this: cover the sides. The principal objective is to hide the container almost completely with massed planting that fluffs out, disguising what they're growing in. Only really nice verdigris baskets with curly feet look good if they're sparsely planted, nothing else does.

BOX CLEVER

For temporary displays in hanging baskets, window boxes and tubs, multipurpose compost is more than adequate, but for permanent displays you should go for a heavy loam-based compost like John Innes No. 3. Multipurpose compost soon becomes 'tired' and isn't substantial enough for long-term plantings. I like to mix my own; one-part John Innes, one-part peat-free multipurpose compost and one-part homemade compost. If you haven't got any homemade stuff (and you can't pinch any from your mum!), 50–50 multipurpose and John Innes will do fine. This way you get the best of both worlds: rich compost that drains well, doesn't compact and yet holds on to water and nutrients. It's weighty too, so there's less chance of plants falling over in the wind.

For plants like palms and phormiums which don't like the winter wet, you should substitute a quarter of the mix for some coarse horticultural grit.

If you want to grow acid-loving plants such as rhododendrons, azaleas or acers, you need to look out for 'ericaceous compost'. This is basically compost that is lime-free so that it is at the correct pH level for plants that need acid soils (between 1–6 on the pH scale). Alpine plants also need a special mix which contains a lot of grit so that they don't sit in too much water, and if you fancy growing bulbs, orchids, cacti or African violets there's a mix available at you local garden centre for them, too! The rule here is that if you're going for something that has special needs, make sure you attend to them.

POT PROWESS

Container plants are a bit like babies – they're totally dependent on you for their feeding and watering needs and, unless you've picked tough drought-tolerant plants, they'll soon sulk if you neglect them. Drying out is the biggest and most labour-intensive problem that affects container gardens – especially for baskets and window boxes because they have the least compost and they're also exposed to lots of sun and drying winds. So here are a few pointers to help keep your container displays at their best:

- Go for the biggest container possible: small pots and shallow bowls need watering copiously.
- Use water-retaining polymers. These are gels that swell up and hold on to valuable water, releasing it as and when the plants need it most.
- Leave a good-sized gap between the top of the pot and the surface of the compost so that you can fill it with water.
- Mulch the surface of the container with bark, cocoa shells, gravel, glass chippings: anything to prevent water evaporating in hot weather.
- Choose drought-resistant plants like lavender, houseleeks, dorothenthus and silver-leaved artemisia.
- Soak new terracotta pots in water before you plant them up. New terracotta will wick the water away from the compost leaving your new plantings parched, just when they need water most.
- In hot weather, place saucers under each container to trap irrigation water, but don't forget to remove them come winter or your plants may well have their roots sitting in water and they will rot.
- Group containers together in pleasing arrangements with taller planters at the back, not only because it makes it easier and more efficient to water them but because they provide protection for each other, too.
- Plant in non-porous, ceramic, glazed or metal containers, or line the sides of terracotta pots with plastic, leaving the drainage holes uncovered.
- Install a cheap irrigation system on a timer to help when you're busy or away on holiday.
- Put pots on castors so that in really hot weather you can move plants to a shadier part of the patio, or in cold weather you can move tender plants to a warmer, frost-free environment.
- Choose baskets with built-in reservoirs.
- To revive wilted planters and baskets, stand the container in a bath full of lukewarm water for at least thirty minutes. Permanent plantings stand more chance of recovery, so don't be surprised to find you can't breathe life into wilted bedding plants.

ABOVE To get gorgeous green leaves, you've got to feed them up!

KEEPING THEM HAPPY

As I've said, containers can be high maintenance and do require more attention than plants in beds or borders. With so many plants packed into a small space, food and water is at a premium and if you leave them to it, it's a case of survival of the fittest, or of none at all. So, a little water, food and protection from the nasties will make much happier plants.

FEEDING

Temporary displays of bedding plants compete voraciously for nutrients as the rules of spacing go out the window. Multipurpose composts contain a minor amount of nutrients which, for greedy feeders, is only enough for the first month or so and after that it's up to you to replenish stocks or your displays will soon flag and become susceptible to attacks by pests and diseases. To encourage flowering, I water my hanging baskets every week with a dilute solution of fast-acting tomato fertilizer, but controlled release fertilizers are the best option for peace of mind. Permanent plantings will usually need top-dressing with a slow-release fertilizer once in the spring, and possibly again in the summer. Do follow the application rate and don't be tempted to over-feed, thinking you'll get bigger and better plants with more flowers; you're likely to do more harm than good.

POT-SPECIFIC PESTS

The devil among pot plants has got to be the vine weevil. The adults, who only come out at night (that's helpful!) merely take irregular chunks out of the leaves, but it's the larvae that do the real damage. Look for horrid curled-up white grubs with a small tan-coloured head, lurking in the compost. They are insatiable feeders who love munching away on the roots of plants in pots. Kill them all on sight. No exceptions, no prisoners!

The most effective control is vigilance. Check any plants that you buy at the garden centre before you bring them home or, failing that, every year make a note on your calendar to buy vine-weevil nematodes: a natural and very effective way of clobbering the larvae. You simply take a sachet, mix it up with water and soak every pot you've got – indoors and out. For bad infestations, carefully remove the plant, shake off all the soil into the dustbin and re-pot the plant using fresh compost. The problem is just how many pots are infested!

The other common pests that hit containers are slugs and snails. Without a doubt the most effective things I've ever used to stop them munching my pot plants (even my hostas!) are the copper rings that you put round each plant, or the sticky copper bands that you fasten to the sides of the pot. This gives these soft-bodied munchers an electric shock, which makes them curl up and drop off – unless they have masochistic tendencies. Trust me, this works, I've even trialled them on TV.

If you grow lilies in pots, watch out for lily beetle. Get the kids to look out for this one: they're bright scarlet and easy to spot. Again, pick them off and get rid of them – they squash underfoot with a satisfying crunch!

MORE SECRETS OF SUCCESS

- Deadhead regularly to encourage more flowers. Simply pick the dead flower heads off by hand.
- Pinch out the growing tips or cut back by half any unruly bedding plants like *Lobelia*, *Bidens* and *Verbena* 'Homestead Purple' to encourage bushiness and maintain a sense of balance with the other plants in the container.
- Mulch the top of winter displays with moss, bark, glass chippings or gravel to help keep them warm and snug when the temperature dips below freezing.
- Remove yellow leaves and sweep up debris to keep your displays looking neat and to help prevent pests and diseases.
- Choose certified disease-resistant plants.
- Remove weeds early on before they take hold and swamp your lovelies. Established weeds are difficult to remove from containers without ripping out all the other plants too!

CHAPTER SEVEN
LOOKING AFTER YOUR GARDEN

ABOVE **Unfortunately, wonderful gardens like this never take care of themselves, but that's half the fun. Gardening is all about being 'dirty-hands creative'.**

This is where the real fun begins. The garden is done and at long last you've got the complete product: a garden of your specification and making which is now overflowing with plants. That outdoor seating area is beckoning, and after all the hard work, it's time to sit back and enjoy.

Trouble is, I'm the type of person who can't sit still for long. So it's just as well there's no such thing as a 'finished' garden. By definition, gardens are alive; they're ongoing, evolving things. Whether it's a total re-design or just a new dining area, the work doesn't end; there is always something to be done to keep your mini-estate looking good. We call it gardening!

Garden maintenance is what most people regard as gardening-proper: deadheading annuals to encourage fresh blooms, arching rose stems down to the ground to encourage a heavy crop of flowers, hoeing between shrubs to cull the first annual weeds in spring, watering when the weather's dry and trimming hedges to stop them barging out over the pavement. All this is good for the soul; it's soothing and it's a great way to cast your cares and troubles aside.

IT'S ALL IN THE DESIGN

The test of getting your design right for you is if it demands the amount of work you want to put in to keep it looking at its best. Whether you want a high- or low-maintenance garden, though, a successful design should require nothing more than a gentle tinkering, the opportunity to shape your design, add seasonal touches, and nurture it to its full potential. If your garden design was well thought through and properly executed, then maintenance work should be relaxing and fun. If you find your garden is proving to be hard work and stressful, then your design – or execution of it – was flawed.

Recognizing what you can do and what you can't is all a part of the design process, so never feel that keeping maintenance down is a bad thing, there's no shame in going for the low-maintenance option. Not all of us want to be gardening day in, day out, and many of us don't actually want to be gardeners in the first place. Just remember, though, that low maintenance doesn't mean *no* maintenance!

'I'm not a Buddhist, but gardening is where a practical adage of theirs comes in really handy: see the job, do the job. The sooner you tackle a potential problem the easier it will be in the long run. Don't let molehills become mountains!'

PLANTS

Plants will probably account for a fair chunk of your workload and your choice of plant will determine the amount of maintenance you will have to do. Every type of plant has different needs and demands. If you are going for any specialist plants, then it is worth reading up on them or getting some advice from nurseries on what specific care they require, but here are a few general pointers which cover most popular planting schemes.

HIGH- TO MEDIUM-MAINTENANCE PLANTINGS

If a bit of pottering and nurturing is what you fancy from your garden, these are the sort of jobs you should be thinking about doing.

ABOVE **Colourful like no other, annuals and biennials are unfortunately not for the low-maintenance gardener – they need replacing once, even twice, a year.**

Temporary window boxes, hanging baskets

Daily watering in summer (perhaps even twice a day in really hot weather), plus weekly feeding if you're not using a slow-release fertilizer (more on that later). Plants will need deadheading regularly to encourage more flowers, plus those like *Lobelia*, which can soon swamp a display, may need trimming occasionally to keep them in proportion to the rest of the plants. Plants will usually need replacing, once maybe twice a year, too.

Permanent container displays

Again, regular watering is essential, sometimes daily in hot, dry summers. Mulch and top-dress with a slow release fertilizer in spring, plus remove the top inch of soil and replace with fresh compost. Pot on a size every one to two years or so. Bring any tender plants under cover in autumn. Check the condition of the container regularly.

Roses

Modern bush roses usually need lots of attention right through the growing season. To avoid regular spraying with fungicides, etc, buy resistant varieties or species or old roses which aren't so susceptible. Prune modern bush roses in early spring (pruning heavily to within three or four buds off the ground for all but climbers and ramblers). As always, remember to remove the 'three ds' – dead, diseased and damaged wood – and tug away any suckers, too. You can spot these unwanted stems easily because they arise from below the soil and are usually a different colour and perhaps more vigorous than the plant itself.

Roses need feeding in spring to give the plant a boost and help it to produce flowering shoots after it's been cut back so hard. Climbers and ramblers will need regular tying in. All roses benefit from deadheading to help the plant produce more blooms (unless, of course, you are growing the rose for its brilliant hips in winter). Mulch deeply around each plant in spring and be sure to clean up and chuck away old leaves to prevent black spot and mildew from attacking the new foliage.

Annuals

Although you get a good colourful display, annuals are lots of work and are best planted in containers or little areas of mixed borders devoted specifically to them, which you can replace or re-sow every year. Producing half-hardy and hardy annuals also needs a fair bit of toil, unless you buy them as plugs from the garden centre. Half-hardies will need to be grown under cover and planted out when the danger of frost has passed (usually in mid May, although this does vary depending upon where you are in the country). Judicious and regular weeding is especially important, otherwise your pretties will quickly get swamped. Taller annuals, such as sunflowers and *Nicotiana*, will need regular staking. Deadhead (or not, as the case may be) to stop the plants going to seed.

ABOVE Veg needs lots of work, unless you have mini pot-gardens and stick to a few of your architectural favourites.

Fruit and vegetables

Again, like annuals, most veggies need lots of work. Regular watering, weeding, composting, etc, must be done to get the best crop from your plants. Raspberries, blackcurrants, beans, tomatoes, cucumbers and squash will need regular tying in to sturdy supports, and top and soft fruit need similar care and may also need training and tying in, depending upon the plant. Soft fruit will probably need netting to protect it from birds.

Tender plants

Tree ferns, bananas, tender palms and other plants which need protection from frost should be wrapped in horticultural fleece or have their crowns stuffed with straw. Lift the rootstock of cannas and dahlias, and store frost-free in dry compost over winter, or cover plants with a heavy mulch of straw, bark chips or compost in warmer areas to see them through.

ABOVE **If colourful annuals are your thing but looking after them isn't, mix them up with perennials to lessen the workload.**

MEDIUM- TO LOW-MAINTENANCE PLANTINGS

Established trees and shrubs

These plants need little maintenance, perhaps only an annual prune in spring or after flowering to keep their shape and encourage further flowering. Again, watch for the 'three ds' and cut out any areas where a variegated cultivar is showing signs of reverting to type (i.e, the original version where leaves are one colour). Check young trees for crossing branches and competing central leaders – if branches are fighting in a small space, it is a magnet for disease.

A general top dressing of Growmore is usually necessary in spring, plus a healthy mulch around the base, which will also control weeds. Some, like *Buddleja davidii*, *Cornus alba*, *Salix*, *Hydrangea paniculata* cultivars, *Prunus triloba*, *Caryopteris*, *Perovskia* and *Sambucus* require what often appears to be overly drastic pruning. This should be done in early spring and will encourage flowers or vivid coloured shoots to be produced on growth formed that year. Massed plantings of azaleas, rhododendrons, camellias, conifers, etc, generally look after themselves.

Climbers and ramblers

Maintaining these plants is as per above, but you should also prune as necessary to keep windows and gutters clear of stems. Tie in new growth in spring and expand the climbing framework when needed. Of course, free climbers need no tying at all, except perhaps when they're very young, and are perfect if you are veering towards the lower-maintenance end of the scale. Remember when pruning that you should avoid disturbing any nesting birds.

Perennials

Lift and divide perennials in early spring, separating the plants into smaller clumps every couple of years. This helps to reinvigorate the parent plant and allows you to discard the unproductive centre, which often forms as the clump swells out. Of course, it's also gives you a whole load more plants to fill gaps or give away to friends! As with other plants, top-dress in spring with a slow-release fertilizer and water them regularly.

Support any taller plants before they collapse under their own weight early in the season. It's a good idea to position the support before the plant flops over. I like using ring stakes, link stakes or flexible netting because they're almost invisible and provide support without detracting from the plant itself. Remove and compost dead and undiseased foliage in autumn/winter (but leave any striking or dramatic seed heads for winter interest).

Bulbs

Plant bulbs in spring or autumn; mark where you plant them so as not to over-plant with something else once the foliage has died down. Generally speaking, bulbs are planted nose up and double the depth of the bulb in a flat-bottomed hole. Specialist bulb planters are available but I much prefer a good old trowel – unless I'm planting them in drifts and then it's time for some spade action! Lift and divide the bulbs every few years when they become overcrowded. If you're growing bulbs in pots, re-pot every year in fresh compost, or plant out after flowering. Lift tender varieties to store in a frost-free position over winter. Above all else, resist the urge to cut back the foliage once the bulb has finished flowering – and that includes those bulbs which are naturalized in grass. This is when the bulbs are actively growing and bulking up for next year. Don't cut them back for at least two months, or until the foliage turns brown and floppy.

Heathers, alpines and rock gardens

These plants are generally slow-growing. Most are well-behaved and generally not bothered by pests and diseases. Some plants may need a little protection from rain in winter.

Ornamental grasses

Grasses are real toughies and are ideal plants for the novice gardener. They are surprisingly drought-tolerant, thrive in all but the wettest soil and require little maintenance. Only a few, such as *Poa chaixii* (spear grass), *Miscanthus*,

BELOW Most grasses tolerate serious neglect and positively thrive if you treat 'em mean to keep 'em keen!

Koeleria glauca (glaucous hair grass) and *Deschampsia* (hair grass) need cutting back in spring, most other evergreen grasses, such as *Carex conica* 'Snowline' and *Festuca glauca* 'Blaufuchs', can be left untouched all year round. Just comb them through with your hand to remove any dead leaves. Don't be tempted to feed or water evergreen and deciduous ornamental grasses too often; they'll only put on masses of leaf growth and usually to the detriment of the flowers. Taller varieties may also collapse by the end of the year, just when you'll want them looking their best, so treat 'em mean to keep 'em keen!

BOUNDARIES

Maintenance work on your boundaries is likely to be the type of job you always put off. Not because it's difficult or overly time-consuming, but because we live in constant hope that we can get away without doing it. So, we delay and delay until eventually it becomes a mammoth job. As I said earlier, when you see something that needs attention, do it straight away rather than letting the problem get bigger. It's much easier to re-point a stretch of wall that has been frost-damaged than wait until it's fallen into the road and needs rebuilding.

The best way to keep maintenance to a minimum is to erect the boundaries properly in the first place. If you inherit them, give them a thorough check over. Replace any damaged sections where necessary, or do a proper repair job if that's all that's required. Don't skimp on this – a slacker's job at the start means loads more work later on, especially as you'll inevitably end up trampling on mature borders in front of the boundary as you try and reach it.

HIGH- TO MEDIUM-MAINTENANCE

Formal hedges

The amount of trimming that a hedge needs very much depends on the plant itself. x *Cupressocyparis leylandii* is the classic, instant-hedge favourite, and my all-time nightmare. This plant is a big maintenance job, as it needs cutting back four or five times a year to keep it under control. Generally speaking, most formal hedges (those clipped into geometric shapes) need trimming at least three times as much as informal hedges (those where the shape of individual plants is often just visible). If a formal hedge is for you (and where space is a premium, it's often the best option), choose beech, yew, hawthorn or golden shrubby honeysuckle instead.

If you have painted walls, they will need to be repainted every two or three years if the crisp, clean approach is your thing. Depending upon the style of the rest of the garden, however, I prefer the elderly painted distressed-look.

MEDIUM- TO LOW-MAINTENANCE

Woven bamboo and heather screens

These screens only have a short-life of about five to ten years, depending on the product. However, apart from that, if they are erected properly they will need no maintenance at all.

Traditional fences

Traditional wooden fences last longer than you expect, but never as long as you want. So if you want them to survive for as long as possible, an annual dose of preservative will help. Use a clear one if you don't want the weathered colour to change. Check any capping strips and repair/replace if they are split or rotten. Reinforced concrete uprights don't look as good as timber, but they do provide longer-lasting support.

Panels

Maintenance for wooden trellis panels is as fences, but remember to choose the right weight of trellis for the job. Expanding trellis might be more decorative, but it won't support heavy climbers. Replace any broken bits with off-cuts from old trellis screens and if necessary strengthen them

ABOVE Hedges don't just surround your garden, topiary boxes like these are just mini hedges and need similar maintenance.

with pre-treated roofing battens or tree stakes, which will soon disappear under a clothing of plants. Mirrors and metal panels need zero maintenance, apart from an occasional scrub with water.

SURFACES

If they've been laid properly in the first place, most surfaces need little maintenance to keep them looking tiptop. Obviously, lawns are the exception to this rule.

HIGH MAINTENANCE

Lawns

Lawns might be a very children-friendly option but, oh dear, do they need regular mowing, spiking, scarifying and feeding. My mother hated the weekly tyranny of mowing so much that she dug up all the turf and replanted with a mix of flowering shrubs, fruit trees and perennials, interspersed with decorative bark paths leading to sheltered rose-bowers. She reserved a larger terraced area for a gravelled-over seating/dining space. Even with all that it's proving far less work than two lawns. It also looks far prettier and is much nicer to sit out in.

ABOVE Lawns in small city gardens – cut out or keep?

Mow lawns regularly in summer (two or three times a week for a top-class finish). Water them in dry spells and give them a good soaking, a short sprinkle will do them more harm than good. Scarify, spike, and feed in spring/early summer and spot-weed any invading dandelions, thistles, etc.

Water

If you have a pond with animal- and plant-life in it, scoop out annual waterweed in autumn and lay the tangled mass next to the pond to allow the wee pond beasties to crawl or drip back in. Compost all this 'orrible gloop. Do the same to blanket weed if it starts to take a hold, rolling it up round a stick to hoik it out. If lea- fall is a problem in autumn, string netting over the top of the pond to stop it sinking under the water and rotting in the bottom and poisoning the pond. In winter, float a tennis ball or inflated rubber ring on the water before the water freezes to stop ice breaking the pond or preventing air from reaching any wildlife below the surface. (Ponds using liners, made from flexible materials or with gently sloping sides, shouldn't have this problem.) If algal bloom is taking over, float pads of barley straw in the water. Check and clean filtration systems (necessary for fish in smaller ponds) at least twice a year – once in spring and again in summer.

Admittedly, this sounds like a lot of work, but pools, rills and ponds repay it all handsomely. A well-balanced pond (one without too many fish, situated away from trees, large enough to manage itself, and getting about eight hours

ABOVE **In a city garden, water makes the perfect focal point – but site it carefully or it may well become a real headache.**

sunlight a day in high summer) requires very little work; it's small ponds in less than ideal situations which can prove a handful.

Ornamental water features that do not have any resident pond-life simply need an annual scrub with diluted bleach or a pressure sprayer to clear off algae. You might also want to occasionally use a net to clean the water of leaves and grass clippings.

LOW MAINTENANCE

Areas of hard standing

Under this bracket come patios and paths. These surfaces simply need brushing regularly to remove leaves or winter muck. If they get really dirty it might be worth hosing them down with a pressure washer – just be careful not to blow out any pointing or that will lead to another maintenance job!

Decking

Widely viewed as one of the ultimate low-maintenance options if, of course, you use tanalized, pre-treated softwood, western red cedar or hardwoods like

Balau or Iroko. In those instances, all that's needed is an annual application of deck preservative to maintain the colour. In shady areas, use a pressure washer to clean off dirt and algae to prevent it become slippery.

Loose paths

Maintain and replace raised edges to paths that are made from loose aggregates, or else the surface material will only spill out over beds and borders (unless that's the look you are going for!). Try and encourage plants to flop over and soften the edges, but be prepared to cut back any greenery that encroaches too much. Bark paths simply need a replenishing top-up every year. Gravel paths and pebbled areas should merely need raking out every month or so. Weeds should never be a problem if you've laid a semi-permeable membrane before plonking your gravel on top.

ABOVE Paths or beds mulched with loose materials like slate look after themselves.

STRUCTURES

We consider it lucky if we inherit a garden with structures like swimming pools and glasshouses: someone's already done all the hard work of installing it for us. In many cases an existing structure is a welcome addition – except, of course, if it's decrepit and beyond repair.

HIGH- TO MEDIUM- MAINTENANCE

Hot tubs and swimming pools

For a swimming pool to look its best it needs regular maintenance. Check the filtration system regularly, hoover the bottom if sediment accumulates and scoop up wind-blown petals/leaves/muck from the surface. A roll-over cover will help to ease the amount of 'fishing!'

Greenhouses

Clean glass in spring and sterilize any nooks and crannies inside to kill algae or pests and diseases that might have over-wintered inside. To protect plants in high summer, paint the outside of the glass with thin whitewash, or use blinds to stop them getting scorched. Open windows and doors on hot summer days for increased ventilation (use heat-activated automatic openers to make it even easier). Fumigate if necessary at end of season and replace broken or cracked panes if needed. If you do not have a heating source in your greenhouse, hang bubble wrap inside the glass as a cheap way of keeping the temperature up a bit and insulating tender plants over winter.

ABOVE Low to the ground and low maintenance – and perfect for lazy gardeners in more ways than one!

LOW MAINTENANCE

Furniture

Most wooden garden furniture can be left outside over the winter, but it will benefit from a yearly dose of furniture oil or preservative, plus a furniture restorer if the colour has faded throughout the year. Protective covers also help, and although they are ugly to look at they will prolong the life of your furniture in the long run. Metal furniture needs little or no maintenance, except perhaps a touch-up with rust killer and a subtle respray where it's been chipped.

Features

Pergolas, arches, bowers and screens need little work. Simply check the structural framework in spring, and repair where necessary.

Buildings

Sheds, gazebos and summerhouses require only a splash of preservative every year or two. Do clear gutters and check the roof and repair or replace any broken shingles or roofing felt as necessary.

RIGHT PLANT, RIGHT PLACE

For trouble-free planting schemes, there is one simple rule: right plant, right place. Now don't misinterpret this, this doesn't always mean low maintenance. Some plants will always require more TLC than others: a vibrant hanging basket will need watering daily throughout the summer, whereas topiary might need nothing more than a light trim twice a year. But the wrong plant in the wrong place will always spell extra work. So before committing a plant to the soil, double check that you've selected the right one for your garden. Look to see if it requires full sun or shade, boggy conditions or dry, a climbing frame to scramble up or stakes to stop it flopping over.

Equally, a high-maintenance plant doesn't necessarily mean one that needs regular cosseting. Give a tender *Fremontodendron* a sunny south-facing wall, for example, and that might be all it needs, apart from an occasional clip now and then to maintain its shape. The right plant in the right place can be almost left alone to get on with it.

AILING PLANTS

In any garden a plant might ail away and ultimately die. You might have nurtured it, clobbered any pests, kept up with the feeding and watered it copiously, but all to no avail, and it will just give up the ghost. But unless you've actually neglected it, this shouldn't be seen as a failure – it's just gardening. Learning to live with successes and disappointments is partly what it's all about and it makes the whole thing exciting; ultimately you're not the one in control! So, there comes a point when you have to decide, is it worth carrying on or is it time to give up hope? To be honest, in most instances, it's worth chucking very sick plants as quickly as possible, simply because it will inevitably be the first port of call for pests and diseases which waft over you garden. These sickly plants may well in turn affect your healthy plants, too.

If you do decide to keep a sulky specimen and replant it elsewhere in the garden, give it a head start by double checking if you put it in the right place to start with. If the answer is yes, position it within easy reach so that you can tend it regularly. To help it re-establish well, sprinkle some food in the planting hole (bone meal and another slow-release fertilizer), and water it regularly for the first few months at least.

If it was in the wrong place, learn from your mistakes wherever possible. However, life is never that simple, and some plants are over-fussy madams, anyway! So even when you do everything right by a plant, it might still give up on you.

WATERING

Without a doubt the single biggest factor that affects the success of our plants is the amount of water they receive. But it's a funny old business; Nature gives us either too much or not enough of the stuff, so what we do is never going to be a precise science as we are always working with the weather. Learning exactly how to water is best learned by observation, practice, plus a certain amount of intuition, which you will pick up along the way.

WHO, WHEN, WHY?

If you have established shrubs and trees planted in the ground, you won't need to water them too often; their roots go deep and, even in a drought, most will survive. But what about the rest? Seedlings and baby annuals need priority care. The soil around them should always be moist. The same applies when transplanting them out into the garden. Transplanting shocks the young plant and it takes time for it to settle in. Always water new transplants well, and in dry weather check them twice daily for a couple of weeks at least.

Newly planted purchases also need regular watering while they are establishing themselves, perhaps every day for a month or so. This applies to all containerized plants: conifers, shrubs, herbaceous perennials, as well as bare-root shrubs and trees – in short, the lot! Do keep an eye on all of these plants for at least two summers, especially bare-root trees and root-balled conifers. Bedding plants in particular are susceptible to dying in just a few hours of July sun, so give them plenty of water and check them daily.

The most vulnerable plants are those grown in containers: window boxes, hanging baskets, pots, urns and troughs. All of these are dependent on you for their water. Unless you have an automatic watering system, you'll need to water every day in summer and sometimes (in the case of hanging baskets) two or three times a day. If you have winter hanging baskets under the eaves of your house, check them often, too – it's easy to forget in winter. Bigger containers hold water better so they will need watering less often; small pots dry out fast, but a drip tray under each pot will help. Although it's more difficult to over-water plants in the garden, if you are too lavish when watering containers you can actually drown the plant, because its roots will suffocate. Make sure all your containers have drainage holes for excess water to run out through, however, and do check with your fingers that the water has soaked into the compost, and hasn't just run straight out of the bottom.

Plants grown in the shadow of walls, such as climbers, get less rain than the rest of the garden and are often forgotten. You'll find that the soil is very dry near a wall and although in normal conditions the roots will usually find enough water, a very hot summer can cause many to die. A couple of large watering-cans-full of water per plant each week will help.

If a plant has a naturally shallow root system it comes under the category of risk plants and, in hot weather, may need watering even though it might be well established. This little group includes rhododendrons and some conifers.

Watering levels can also change at certain periods of a plant's growth cycle, in spring and summer, as they get going after a dormant winter, and as they flower and fruit, plants will need more water. Vegetables are particularly greedy creatures; abandon them and you'll have measly crops – this is especially true with peas, beans and potatoes, whereas greens will become tough. In general the quality of all veggies will be poor if they're neglected.

EYES OPEN

So, when do you water? The short answer is, before the plants have wilted and flopped over – the visible signs of drought. Regular watering is the key, but often there aren't any obvious signs that your plants are getting a little thirsty until it's almost too late, so you must look at the soil, too. Plunge a couple of fingers in to check. If the soil is dry to the touch it means that the plants are almost certainly parched, but if your fingers come out covered in traces of soil and feel slightly damp, you're probably ok for now. Sometimes the soil surface can look dry on the top but underneath it will be quite moist, so don't merely go by appearance – get your hands in there!

FEED ME, FEED ME NOW!

Plants get many nutrients such as carbon (C), hydrogen (H) and oxygen (O) from the air and water during the photosynthetic process, but many others that are essential to maintain plant growth come from the soil. Numerous essential nutrients are available in organic matter – the lifeblood of any soil – so much so that many gardeners rely on composts and green manures to feed soil life, condition the soil and release nutrients in a slow, balanced way. However, while there is no substitute for organic matter, sometimes a supplement or tonic may be required. (Which you can buy at your local garden centre.) Think of these concentrated fertilizers as tonics or pick-me-ups, merely replacing those nutrients that the plants have used.

Although they are good for bumping up nutritional levels, supplements do not improve the structure of the soil, nor prevent nutrients from being washed out, so they are not a substitute for organic matter. Plants that grow in poor soils with no humus will still perform badly, even when fed with supplements.

WATERING DOS AND DON'TS

Generally we only need to water regularly throughout spring and summer when temperatures are high and plants are actively growing, so an occasional dousing in winter should only be necessary in freakish dry spells.

Water in the early morning and/or in the evening to avoid scorching the foliage. Scorch occurs when water globules sitting on leaves and young stems intensify the suns rays, just like a magnifying glass, which in turn causes the foliage underneath to turn brown and die. Plants also get scorched depending on where they are in the garden: those situated against east-facing boundaries often get clobbered after rainfall early in the morning when the sun comes up.

Don't neglect those roots! It's the roots that need the water, not the leaves, so always soak the earth at the base of the main stem first before spraying water high into the air in a vain attempt to create rainbows. Admittedly, in heavily polluted areas you may need to ritually wash down your plants to cleanse them of dirt and dust – just don't neglect the roots. I've found that slowly counting to ten whilst holding the hose or watering can over each plant ensures each one gets enough. It's not based on any scientific fact, it's just that when I check afterwards the soil around the plant is usually nice and moist.

Always use clean water. If you have a water butt make sure you replenish it periodically to remove fungal pathogens.

Avoid blanket-watering mature plants. Spot-watering using a hose or watering can is the most suitable method for large plants and trees – you can ensure the roots get a good drench. Seep hoses are a preferred alternative to sprinklers. Lay them on the ground around the roots of plants, and then attach the end to the tap. This is an environmentally-friendly approach because water doesn't get wasted on paths and patios, as it does with sprinklers.

Check automated systems regularly for damaged or broken pipes, and the batteries in sophisticated timers.

If you are blanket-watering with a sprinkler, ensure that you wet the soil to the depth of the roots. Place a container under any plants in pots to measure how much water is being applied.

If you have a water meter, collect rainfall from your gutters into water butts to keep the cost down. Or grow plants like lavender, *Cistus* and *Ceanothus*, which originate from hotter climates and therefore usually tolerate dry spells.

Regularly mulch sandy soils or around shallow-rooted plants such as rhododendrons.

If you're using a sprinkler, watch for dry patches and move it to avoid over-watering (water literally running or puddling on the soil surface).

TO GET THE MOST OUT OF BULKY ORGANIC MATERIALS AND FERTILISERS YOU NEED:

- A good soil structure.
- A warm soil. (Soil works best above 6°C.)
- The right pH. Too acid or too alkaline can cause nutrients to be 'locked up' (unable to be released) in the soil.
- Plenty of organic matter/humus or clay to hold on to soil nutrients and prevent them being washed or 'leached' out.

SUPPLEMENTS ARE VERY USEFUL WHEN:

- Several crops a year are being grown from one area, i.e. vegetables, especially leafy greens.
- Plants are showing signs of a nutrient deficiency.
- You can't get hold of any composted organic matter.
- You've just moved into a new garden and haven't made any compost yet. Getting good results will inspire you to start making your own!

TRACE ELEMENTS

Iron (Fe), copper (Cu), zinc (Zn), boron (B), manganese (Mn) and molybdenum (Mo) make up the minor nutrients or 'trace elements'. Sulphur (Su), calcium (Ca) and magnesium (Mg) are often grouped here too, but are undoubtedly needed in higher quantities. So much so that they are often included in the major nutrients category below. You'll find this lot on the side of many fertilizer boxes in a baffling range of complex chemical symbols and formulas.

THE MAJOR NUTRIENTS

Without a doubt the three nutrients that plants need in the largest quantities are nitrogen, phosphorus (phosphate) and potassium (potash), or NPK for short. Plants need nitrogen the most as it helps leaves and shoots to grow. Phosphorus looks after a plant's roots and helps seeds to germinate and grow away strongly, and potassium is needed for flower and fruit development. Potash also keeps plants tough and able to resist frost and pests and diseases. Think of it like this if it'll help: NPK – shoots, roots, fruits. Nitrogen (N) is 'shoots'; phosphorus (P) is 'roots' and potassium (K) is 'fruits'. Fertilizers like Tomorite contain lots of potassium and are used to encourage plenty of fruits and flowers. Lawn fertilizers intended for use in spring usually contain more nitrogen than anything else.

HUNGRY PLANTS

If a plant looks unhappy, chances are it might be short of a specific nutrient, but how do you know which one? Look for these telltale signs:

- Plants needing a fix of nitrogen will have stunted, sickly, pale green leaves, with perhaps a pink or yellow tinge. Hanging-basket plants and veggies grown in small containers often suffer because they use up all the available nitrogen quickly.
- Plants hungry for phosphate will struggle to establish well and will have a dull blue/green hue on older leaves.
- Plants short of potassium will flower and fruit poorly and have leaves with a yellow/ brown edge. Fruit trees such as apples, pears and currants are particularly affected.
- Plants with mottled yellow, brown or purple leaves need a hit of magnesium.
- Plants with yellowing between the veins on new leaves will often be suffering from a shortage of iron and manganese. This is commonly found on acid-loving plants, such as rhododendrons and camellias, that are grown in alkaline soils. In this situation these two nutrients get 'locked up' and become unavailable to the plant.

SLOW RELEASE, QUICK RELEASE OR CONTROLLED RELEASE?

Supplements are commonly available as soluble or liquid feeds, in tiny plugs you poke into the soil or in granular or powdered form – which you sprinkle on the surface and 'work' into the soil. The nutrients are released in a form that's available to the plant in one of the following three ways.

SLOW-RELEASE FERTILIZERS, E.G. BONE MEAL

The idea is to feed plants gradually, not give them a huge amount of nutrients all at once; in this situation slow-release fertilizers are the answer. Some of these slowly degrade in the soil, while others absorb water until they swell and burst open. Because of their gradual application of nutrients, they do not cause weak, rapid growth and are not easily leached (washed out) from a soil by irrigation and rain.

The only downsides to this form of feed is that there is no control over nutrient release and it's not easy to predict the release of nutrients as it depends on the pH, temperature, etc.

QUICK-RELEASE OR FAST-ACTING, E.G. DRIED BLOOD

This form is ideal if certain nutrients are required by the plant straight away – look at it as a plant tonic. Because of the instant nature of this feed, it can cause rapid and weak growth, which is often therefore susceptible to pests and diseases, so don't use it too often. The other negative is that these fertilizers are often easily leached out of free-draining soils.

CONTROLLED-RELEASE FERTILIZERS, E.G. 'OSMOCOTE'

As the name suggests, these are ideal for controlling nutrient release over a selected period of time, and the speed at which they do this is determined by the thickness of the shell and soil temperature.

The pros to these fertilizers are that they don't cause weak, rapid growth as nutrient release is controlled over a specified time, and that nutrients are not easily leached out of a soil by excess irrigation and rain. The downside is that they are expensive, therefore they are only typically used for containers and baskets. As they don't have to be applied too frequently, however, you could make a saving in the long term, both in terms of cash and time.

WHEN TO FEED

The best time to feed established beds and borders is in spring, just before they come into leaf. Feeding once is usually enough, although some greedy feeders, such as roses, may need another 'top dressing' in midsummer. Pots, baskets, troughs and all containers need feeding each week during the growing season using a weak liquid or soluble fertilizer mixed into your watering can – unless, of course, you use a controlled-release fertilizer stick or plug which you should insert in spring and perhaps once again in mid-summer. Vegetable plots need more feed applications, and something like a slow-release fertilizer two or three times a year should replenish stocks used up by previous crops.

The worst time to apply fertilizers – especially those high in nitrogen – is late summer/ early autumn. This will only encourage a sudden burst of lush, sappy growth that will get burnt by the first autumn frost. Autumn 'feed and weed' turf fertilizers therefore have little or no nitrogen. Don't worry about feeding in winter, either, because most plants are dormant and not actively growing. This means that any application would be a waste of money, as winter rains would wash it away before the plant could use it.

HOW TO . . . APPLY A TOP DRESSING AROUND EXISTING PLANTING

The most common method of applying fertilizers by hand is by 'broadcasting', i.e, simply scattering the fertilizer by hand.

- Ensure that the area is free from both perennial and annual weeds – you don't want to feed those as well!
- Gently cultivate the soil.
- Rake to a fine 'tilth' – aim for a finish which resembles a mixture of marbles and breadcrumbs.
- Calculate the application rate and use an old set of scales to measure the fertilizer out correctly. I like to use metre-long bamboo canes to mark out the area.
- Apply fertilizer evenly over the designated area and avoid overlapping.
- Gently rake or hoe it in, avoiding damaging the roots of existing plants.
- Water if rain seems unlikely.

RULES TO REMEMBER

- Never apply fertilizer directly from the packet/ bag/ box – it's difficult to control.
- Always follow the application rate exactly and never over-apply – you'll do more harm than good.
- Be aware of any previous treatments, i.e, the addition of bulky organic matter, lime or other fertilizers which may have already been added.
- Always wear gloves and if necessary a face mask – some fertilizers are irritants and/ or poisonous.
- The method, or time you apply it, is essential, so always follow the manufacturer's instructions on the packet.

WEED 'EM AND REAP!

Like many gardeners I hate weeding, but it is a necessity. Don't just concentrate on the creative jobs, stay on top of your weeds throughout the year or you might end up with a real nightmare. Perennial weeds are the gardener's bugbear – strangling plants and competing with your lovelies for space, water, light and nutrients. Dandelions, climbing white-flowered bindweed, perennial stinging nettle, prickly creeping thistle, couch grass and horsetail (identifiable by its stiff, lime-green bottlebrush appearance) should be tackled immediately. Merely knocking them off at ground level or digging them in isn't usually sufficient; you've got to get the potentially invasive roots. But do you do this by hand or do you resort to chemicals?

If you're a beginner, or you are concerned about the environment, play safe and dig them out by hand. Use chemicals sparingly and only if you have a severe problem and you're tackling a virgin garden. Translocated weedkillers such as 'Round Up' (glyphosate) travel through the plant and kill the roots, and are therefore ideal to control real toughies. Take care around plants that you want to keep, though – contact weedkillers like 'Weedol' (diquat and paraquat) kill everything that they touch, so only control annuals with non-invasive roots such as fat hen, bitter-cress, chickweed, willow herb and groundsel with weedkillers like these. But, sometimes, what's the point?

However you do not *have* to use herbicides at all in the garden and, if you do, only apply them to the worst cases of perennial thuggery. Alternatives to chemicals involve more work and can be time-consuming, but they are 100 per cent safe. Digging weeds out by hand does work, but it is laborious, boring and takes ages – if only because you have to carefully distinguish which roots belong to the weed and which don't! Allotmenteers with ghastly perennial-infested plots can cover the whole ground with thick carpet and all the nasties will die off – in a couple of years – but you're less likely to want to do that in an

ornamental garden. Before you reach for the chemicals, however, try this: hire a flame gun and go over the whole area a few times. Choose a dry day, when the weeds are low to the ground (hack back any tall ones in advance), and scorch the new growth. This won't kill the roots, but it does severely weaken the plant and if done often enough will eventually kill it.

Annuals weeds should die in a second under any flaming, but you could, of course, simply reach for your trusty hoe. The best time to hoe out annual weeds is when it's very dry, because you can leave them on the soil surface to shrivel in the sun. The secret to controlling annual weeds is to not let them go to seed – hit them diligently for ten minutes, two or three times a week and your garden will soon be weed-free. If you've been away and your annual weeds are no longer merely tiny seedlings, the best time to pull them out is after the rain when plants come up easily, roots and all.

GOODIE OR BADDIE?

Forget-me-nots, comfrey, red dead nettle, cow parsley and field poppy are commonly mistaken as 'weeds.' Yet all are beautiful natives and will amass in little nooks and crannies where other plants are too chicken to grow. Gardeners often see them as an asset, so don't be too quick to douse them in Agent Orange! If you're at all unsure whether your 'weeds' are friend or foe, take a sample for identification to your local garden centre.

GOOD CULTURAL PRACTICES

Once the ground's free from weeds, a thick mulch or surface covering will help prevent them coming back. Mulching also helps to retain moisture in dry weather and keeps cold clay soils warmer for longer. If you use an organic mulch it will, in addition, 'feed' the soil and help maintain good soil structure. Whilst garden compost, horse manure, leaf mould, plastic and even old carpet will do, choose one that'll complement your design. Natural materials such as composted bark are cheap and give an inoffensive earthy look. Apply approximately 6cm (2in) every autumn and, if necessary, top it up in early spring before weeds have had a chance to germinate. Gravel can also make an attractive decorative mulch and is available in various sizes and colours, all of which will provide a foil for some well-thought-out planting. Lay a semi-permeable membrane (available at garden centres and DIY stores) and then put a 2.5cm (1in) deep layer of gravel on top.

My favourite way of dealing with weeds is to deny them space; a dense mix of trees, shrubs and perennials, without any visible bare soil, means that

most weeds don't even get a toehold! Dense, ground-hugging plants such as *Euonymus fortunei* 'Emerald Gaiety', *Pachysandra terminalis*, ivy, elephant's ears or European wild ginger (*Asarum europaeum*) are good, natural – and attractive – methods of preventing weeds taking over and, being evergreen, they are effective all year round.

HOW TO . . . 'MULCH'

- Clear the soil of perennial weeds.
- Irrigate copiously. Don't mulch bone-dry soil; it's difficult to re-wet as the mulch absorbs all the water.
- Apply the mulch the thicker the better. Spread it carefully and don't allow it to sit on foliage or right next to, or on top of, existing plants.
- Top up every year in either spring or autumn (if appropriate).

USING WEEDKILLERS

- Always read the label.
- Read the label again.
- Measure the quantities carefully – never over-apply.
- Wear appropriate personal protective equipment.
- Dispose of containers carefully.
- If appropriate, use one watering can for weedkiller and another for water to avoid accidents.
- Avoid drift, never spray in windy weather.
- Watch what you're spraying!

WEEDY TIPS

- Look before you buy plants – some weeds get a free ride from containerized plants to your garden.
- Be cautious of supposed 'ornamental' weeds, such as variegated ground elder, as you can never expect them to behave properly. If you really want to live dangerously, grow these anti-social mobsters in a container, never in the open ground.
- Learn to recognize what weeds you have *before* they start to flower. Once they seed you have a problem multiplied.
- Don't put the roots of pernicious perennial weeds on the compost heap. They belong in the bin!
- Always use clean compost in your pots.
- Store bags of organic matter like horse manure for a while so you can see if there are any perennials lurking in the bag.

PEST AND DISEASES

During the year most gardens appear to take care of themselves, but don't become complacent and let your guard down yet. Pests and diseases will inevitably create extra work, but if your plants are healthy they're less likely to get sick. Look at it this way, when us humans feel tired and stressed that's when we're most likely to get ill. The same applies for plants, too. So, ensuring you've chosen the right plant and kept them well watered and fed means they're less prone to attack by pests and diseases. To avoid splashing bug spray around, pre-empt any problems and use environmentally friendly cultural techniques or biological controls (see p263) to keep your plants healthy.

Fortunately, at the end of the summer many common bugs and beasties have done their worst, but you still need to be vigilant. The secret to controlling pests without the use of noxious chemicals is to hit 'em hard and hit 'em early. Regularly inspect your plants for caterpillars, slugs and snails, whitefly and blackfly and pick off or crush small infestations. If you're a little squeamish, a natural pest control containing fatty acids will also do the trick. It's easy to keep your plants healthy without chemicals, just continue to be diligent right to the end of the season.

Don't be too obsessive about tidiness. Leaf litter, fallen branches, piles of stones, etc, provide welcome hideaways for all those natural predators like ladybirds, lacewings, beetles, slow worms, frogs, toads and hedgehogs – helpers that make our gardening work that much lighter. My mum has a sage bush growing in a window box; it succumbs each spring to a hefty black fly infestation, but, before you know it, it's looking radiantly healthy again as masses of ladybirds and their larvae mop up the pests. She doesn't have to touch it or use insecticides; her garden has enough cubby-holes for natural predators to over-winter.

Don't forget to put out feeders to attract birds into the garden: thrushes and blackbirds will help keep the slug population under control, and blue tits will scour your roses for greenfly. Growing flowers which bees find attractive will help to ensure your fruiting bushes and trees crop well.

GOOD CULTURAL PRACTICES

- Only use plants suitable for your aspect, soil type etc.
- Buy pest and disease-resistant plants where available.
- Buy plants certified to be disease-free.
- Maintain a good level of hygiene and remove dead, diseased or damaged foliage or branches quickly.
- Take prompt action at the first sign of a problem.
- Maintain good soil structure with frequent applications of well-rotted organic matter.
- Remove and burn any affected debris.
- Keep your garden weed-free through diligent mulching and hand weeding.

CHAPTER EIGHT
PLANT DIRECTORIES

Plants suitable for polluted sites
Wind-tolerant plants
Plants for screening
Plants for security
Front-garden plants – easy maintenance
Front-garden plants – formal
Plants for dry shade
Plants for moist shade
Plants for hot exposed sites
Plants for thick clay soils
Plants for dry sandy soils
Plants for chalky soils
Acid-loving plants
Shallow marginals
Deep-water plants
Bog plants
Plants for jungly basements
Tough ground cover plants
Trees for small gardens
Powerful 'free' scents
'Up close and personal' scents/ 'Touchy-feely' scents
Night/evening scents
Topiary plants
Hedging plants

Plants to attract/for wildlife
Easy annuals and biennials
'Show-stopping' annuals and biennials
Herbs
Easy edibles
Architectural edibles
Climbers/ walls shrubs for North walls
Climbers/ wall shrubs for South walls
Climbers/ wall shrubs for East walls
Climbers/ wall shrubs for West walls
Architectural perennials and shrubs
Plants for containers
Plants for window boxes, hanging baskets, etc.
Indoor herbs & edibles
Easy houseplants
Huge houseplants
Houseplants for indirect light
Houseplants for brightly lit areas
Houseplants for humidity
Houseplants that like it hot and dry
Houseplants for a shady room
Scented houseplants
Houseplants you can't kill!
Conservatory plants

Plants suitable for polluted sites

Phyllostachys nigra (black bamboo)
Miscanthus 'Flamingo' (silver banner grass)
Eryngium giganteum (Miss Wilmott's Ghost'
Aucuba japonica 'Rozannie' (spotted laurel)
Mahonia aquifolium 'Smaragd' (Oregon grape)
Fatsia japonica 'Variegata' (false aralia)
Buxus microphylla 'Faulkner' (box)
Ilex aquifolium 'Silver Queen' (holly)
Thuja plicata 'Atrovirens' (western red cedar)
Potentilla 'Red Ace' (Cinquefoil)
Viburnum x burkwoodii 'Anne Russell'
Buddleja davidii 'White Profusion'
Prunus laurocerasus 'Otto Luyken'
Yucca filamentosa (Adam's needle)
Heuchera cylindrica 'Greenfinch'

Plants for screening

Parthenocissus tricuspidata (Boston ivy)
Yushania anceps
Clematis 'Elizabeth'
Solanum laxum 'Album' (potato vine)
Hedera helix 'Green Ripple'
Magnolia grandiflora (bull bay)
Carpenteria californica 'Elizabeth'
Ceanothus impressus (Californian lilac)
Viburnum x bodnantense 'Dawn'
Trachelospermum jasminoides (star jasmine)
Eucalyptus pauciflora subsp. niphophila (weeping gum)
Garrya elliptica 'James Roof' (silk tassel bush)
Camellia japonica 'Lady Vansittart'
Hydrangea anomala subsp. petiolaris (climbing hydrangea)
Itea illicifolia (sweet spire)

Wind-tolerant plants

Carex pendula (drooping sedge)
Festuca glauca 'Elijah Blue' (blue fescue)
Pyrus salicifolia 'Pendula' (weeping silver pear)
Alnus incana 'Aurea' (alder)
Crataegus laevigata 'Paul's Scarlet' (hawthorn)
Laburnum x watereri 'Vossii'
Forsythia 'Spring Glory'
Berberis x stenophylla
Deutzia x magnifica
Rosmarinus officinalis Prostratus Group (rosemary)
Pennisetum alopecuroides 'Hameln' (fountain grass)
Geranium 'Kashmir Purple'
Centranthus ruber (valerian)
Lonicera nitida 'Maigrün' (shrubby honey suckle)
Hebe pinguifolia 'Pagei'

Plants for security

Pyracantha 'Golden Charmer' (firethorn)
Crataegus monogyna (hawthorn)
Berberis thunbergii f. atropurpurea
Poncirus trifoliata (Japanese bitter orange)
Cotoneaster frigidus 'Cornubia'
Griselinia littoralis 'Variegata' (broadleaf)
Elaeagnus x ebbingei
Hippophae rhamnoides (sea buckthorn)
Rosa 'Roseraie de l'Haÿ'
Ulex europaeus (gorse)
Ilex aquifolium 'J. C van Tol' (holly)
Fagus sylvatica (beech)
Chamaecyparis lawsoniana (Lawson cypress)
Taxus baccata (yew)
Prunus spinosa (blackthorn)

Front-garden plants – easy maintenance

Anemanthele lessoniana (pheasant's tail grass)
Cotoneaster horizontalis (fishbone cotoneaster)
Lavandula 'Munstead' (lavender)
Crocosmia 'Lucifer'
Bergenia cordifolia 'Alba' (elephant's ears)
Panicum 'Heavy Metal'
Carex flagellifera (sedge)
Phormium tenax 'Atropurpureum' (New Zealand flax)
Agave americana 'Variegata'
Artemisia 'Powis Castle'
Kniphofia 'Fiery Fred' (red hot poker)
Convallaria majalis (lily-of-the-valley)
Lamium maculatum 'Beacon Silver'
Tellima grandiflora (fringe cups)
Hebe recurva

Front-garden plants – formal

Buxus sempervirens (box)
Laurus nobilis (sweet bay)
Juniperus scopulorum 'Skyrocket' (fastigiate juniper)
Cryptomeria japonica 'Pyramidata' (Japanese cedar)
Lonicera periclymenum 'Belgica' (Dutch honeysuckle) - clipped
Hedera helix 'Ivalace' – trained
Santolina chamaecyparissus (cotton lavender)
Viburnum tinus 'Gwenllian' (laurustinus) – clipped
Cupressus sempervirens (Italian cypress)
Tulipa 'Black Night (tulip) - en masse
Tillia 'Petiolaris' (lime – pleached)
Hebe 'Emerald Geme'
Pittosporum 'Tom Thumb'
Ligustrum delavayanum (small leaved privet)
Rosa Golden Wedding (rose) - standard

Plants for dry shade

Epimedium pubigerum
Dicentra 'Langtrees' (bleeding heart)
Convallaria majalis (lily-of-the-valley)
Symphytum 'Hidcote Pink'
Geranium phaeum 'Samobor'
Brunnera macrophylla 'Jack Frost'
Asarum europaeum (European wild ginger)
Lonicera nitida 'Maigrün' (shrubby honeysuckle)
Asplenium scolopendrium (harts-tongue fern)
Hydrangea anomala subsp. petiolaris (climbing hydrangea)
Liriope muscari
Mentha requienii (mint)
Blechnum spicant (hard fern)
Luzula nivea (snowy woodrush)
Helleborus foetidus (stinking hellebore)

Plants for moist shade

Caltha palustris 'Plena'
Hosta 'Sum and Substance'
Tricyrtis formosana (toad lily)
Polystichum setiferum Divisilobum Group (soft shield fern)
Iris foetidissima (roast beef iris)
Ligularia przewalskii
Geranium macrorrhizum (cransebill)
Anemone x hybrida 'Honorine Jobert' (Japanese anemone)
Rodgersia pinnata 'Superba'
Dicentra spectabilis 'Alba' (bleeding heart)
Primula beesiana
Scopolia carniolica
Trillium grandiflorum (wake robin)
Sanguinaria canadensis 'Plena' (blood root)
Persicaria bistorta 'Superba'

Plants for hot exposed sites

Perovskia 'Blue Spire' (Russian sage)
Anthemis tinctoria 'Sauce Hollandaise'
Helictotrichon sempervirens (blue oat grass)
Eryngium planum
Yucca gloriosa (Spanish dagger)
Stipa tenuissima (feather grass)
Eriobotrya japonica (loquat)
Achillea Summer Pastels Group (yarrow)
Agastache foeniculum 'Alabaster'
Artemisia 'Powis Castle'
Lavandula 'Hidcote' (lavender)
Echinops ritro (globe thistle)
Euphorbia mellifera (honey spurge)
Phlomis fruticosa (Jerusalem sage)
Agave americana

Plants for thick clay soils

Aster novi-belgii 'Jenny' (michaelmas daisy)
Malus 'John Downie' (crab apple)
Sambucus racemosa 'Sutherland Gold' (elderberry)
Weigela florida 'Foliis Purpureis'
Vitis coignetiae (grape vine)
Carex oshimensis 'Evergold' (sedge)
Hemerocallis 'Stella de Oro' (day lily)
Helenium 'Moerheim Beauty' (Helen's flower)
Hosta 'Gold Standard'
Polygonatum x hybridum (Solomon's seal)
Rodgersia pinnata
Solidago 'Golden Wings' (golden rod)
Spiraea nipponica 'Snowmound'
Skimmia japonica 'Rubella'
Kerria japonica 'Pleniflora'

Plants for dry sandy soils

Cistus x skanbergii
Ceratostigma willmottianum
Cytisus x praecox 'Allgold'
Helianthemum 'Wisley Primrose'
Lespedeza thunbergii
Hibiscus syriacus 'Oiseau Bleu'
Lavandula stoechas (French lavender)
Perovskia 'Blue Spire' (Russian sage)
Achillea filipendulina 'Cloth of Gold' (yarrow)
Nerine bowdenii
Potentilla 'Abbotswood'
Stachys byzantina 'Big Ears' (lambs ears)
Genista lydia
Cytisus 'Warminster' (broom)
Verbena bonariensis

Plants for chalky soils

Ceanothus 'Autumnal Blue' (Californian lilac)
Osmanthus x burkwoodii
Euonymus europaeus 'Red Cascade' (spindle)
Kolkwitzia amabilis 'Pink Cloud'
Buddleja globosa
Rosa rugosa 'Alba'
Cotinus coggygria 'Royal Purple' (smoke tree)
Philadelphus 'Lemoinei' (mock orange)
Dicentra spectabilis (bleeding heart)
Hypericum calycinum (rose of Sharon)
Deutzia x magnifica
Daphne pontica
Pittosporum tenuifolium 'Irene Paterson'
Spiraea 'Little Princess'
Paeonia lactiflora

Acid-loving plants

Magnolia delavayi
Clethra delavayi
Cornus canadensis
Erica arborea (tree heather)
Hamamelis x intermedia 'Diane' (witch hazel)
Enkianthus campanulatus
Pieris 'Wakehurst Flame'
Corylopsis spicata
Camellia japonica 'Adolphe Audusson'
Skimmia japonica 'Rubella'
Rhododendron luteum
Cydonia oblonga (quince)
Stachyurus praecox
Liquidambar orientalis (sweet gum)
Cornus kousa var. chinensis (flowering dogwood)

Deep-water plants (30–100cm)

Fontinalis antipyretica
Stratiotes aloides (water solider)
Ceratophyllum demersum (hornwort)
Ranunculus aquatilis (water crowfoot)
Nymphaea alba (white water lily)
Nymphaea 'Gonnère'
Nymphaea 'Virginia'
Nelumbo lutea (lotus)
Nymphoides indica (water snowflake)
Nelumbo 'Empress'
Aponogeton distachyos (water hawthorn)
Nuphar lutea (yellow pond lily)
Orontium aquaticum (golden club)
Marsilea quadrifolia (water clover)
Hottonia palustris (water violet)

Shallow marginals (5cm–30cm water)

Iris laevigata var.alba (10cm)
Thalia dealbata (10-15cm)
Pontederia cordata (pickerel weed) (10-15cm)
Schoenoplectus lacustris subsp. tabernaemontani 'Zebrinus' (7-15cm)
Typha minima (bulrush) (15-25cm)
Cyperus papyrus (paper reed) (20-30cm)
Glyceria maxima (water grass) (15-20cm)
Eriophorum angustifolium (common cotton grass) (5cm)
Zantedeschia aethiopica 'Green Goddess' (15-25cm)
Narthecium ossifragum (bog asphodel) (2-5cm)
Mentha aquatica (watermint) (10cm)
Houttuynia cordata 'Chameleon' (2-5cm)
Butomus umbellatus (10-40cm)
Calla palustris (bog arum) (5cm)
Juncus effusus f. spiralis (corkscrew rush) (2-5cm)

Bog plants

Filipendula purpurea (meadow sweet)
Hosta 'Frances Williams' (plantain lily)
Kirengeshoma palmata
Rodgersia podophylla
Lobelia cardinalis 'Queen Victoria'
Leucojum aestivum (summer snowflake)
Primula denticulata (drumstick Primula)
Aruncus dioicus (goats beard)
Iris sibirica (Siberian flag iris)
Persicaria bistorta 'Superba'
Osmunda regalis (royal fern)
Primula florindae (giant cowslip)
Actaea simplex Atropurpurea group (bugbane)
Rheum palmatum 'Atrosanguineum'
Matteuccia struthiopteris (shuttlecock fern)

Plants for jungly basements

Dicksonia antarctica (tree fern)
Miscanthus sacchariflorus (feather grass)
Melianthus major (honey flower)
Fascicularia pitcairniifolia (hardy pineapple)
Ophipogon planiscapus 'Nigrescens' (black mondo grass)
Chamaerops humilis (European fan palm)
Beaucarnea recurvata (Pony tail palm)
Phoenix canariensis (Canary island palm)
Pittosporum tobira
Cynara cardunculus (cardoon)
Astilboides tabularis (dinner plate plant)
Tropaeolum speciosum (flame creeper)
Eccremocarpus scaber (Chilean glory vine)
Embothrium coccineum (Chilean fire bush)
Hydrangea paniculata 'Grandiflora'

Trees for small gardens

Pyrus salicifolia 'Pendula' (weeping silver pear)
Betula pendula 'Youngii' (Youngs weeping birch)
Acer griseum (paper bark maple)
Malus 'Profusion' (crab apple)
Prunus serrula
Acer davidii 'Serpentine' (snake bark maple)
Prunus x subhirtella 'Autumnalis Rosea' (autumn flowering cherry)
Amelanchier lamarckii (snowy mespilus)
Prunus 'Amanogawa' (fastigiate Japanese cherry)
Cercis siliquastrum (Judas tree)
Sorbus cashmiriana (rowan)
Laburnum x watereri 'Vossii' (Voss' laburnum)
Morus alba 'Pendula' (weeping mulberry)
Olea europaea (olive)
Albizia julibrissin f. rosea (silk tree)

Tough ground cover plants

Cotoneaster dammeri
Hebe pinguifolia 'Pagei'
Alchemilla mollis (lady's mantle)
Thymus serpyllum (thyme)
Stachys byzantina 'Silver Carpet' (lamb ears)
Hedera helix 'Buttercup' (ivy)
Vinca minor (lesser periwinkle)
Viburnum davidii
Cornus canadensis (creeping dogwood)
Sagina subulata 'Aurea' (scotch moss)
Juniperus procumbens 'Nana' (dwarf Japanese juniper'
Mitchella repens (partridge berry)
Vaccinium angustifolium
Gaultheria procumbens (wintergreen)
Euonymus fortunei 'Coloratus'

Powerful 'free' scents

Lilium regale (regal lily)
Sarcococca confusa (Christmas box)
Mirabilis jalapa
Jasminum x stephanense
Lonicera japonica 'Halliana' (Japanese honeysuckle)
Rosa 'Roseraie de l'Haÿ'
Clematis armandii 'Snowdrift'/ 'Apple Blossom'
Chimonanthus praecox 'Luteus' (wintersweet)
Wisteria sinensis
Eucryphia x nymansensis 'Nymansay'
Daphne odora 'Aureomarginata'
Viburnum x bodnantense 'Dawn'
Trachelospermum jasminoides (star jasmine)
Pittosporum tobira (Japanese mock orange)
Akebia quinata (chocolate vine)

'Up close and personal' scents/ 'Touchy-feely' scents

Lavandula dentata (lavender)
Helichrysum italicum (curry plant)
Hamamelis 'Pallida' (witch hazel)
Syringa 'Madame Lemoine' (liliac)
Cyclamen hederifolium
Galanthus 'S. Arnott'
Artemisia abrotanum (southernwood)
Narcissus 'Eystettensis'
Magnolia stellata 'Rubra'
Rosa gallica
Buddleja alternifoila (butterfly bush)
Laurus nobilis (sweet bay)
Cosmos atrosanguineus (chocolate cosmos)
Convallaria majalis (lily-of-the-valley)
Iris graminea (plum-tart iris)

Night/evening scents

Ipomoea alba (moon flower)
Lonicera japonica 'Halliana' (Japanese honeysuckle)
Jasminum officinale (jasmine)
Matthiola bicornis (night scented stocks)
Oenothera biennis (evening primrose)
Daphne odora 'Aureomarginata'
Lilium regale (regal lily)
Lilium longiflorum
Lilium candidum (Madonna lily)
Zaluzianskya capensis (night phlox)
Brugmansia arborea (angels' trumpet)
Lonicera periclymenum 'Belgica' (Dutch honeysuckle)
Trachelospermum asiaticum (star jasmine)

Topiary plants

Buxus microphylla 'Faulkner' (box)
Chaenomeles x superba 'Nicoline' (Flowering quince) – wall trained
Pyracantha 'Mohave' (firethorn) – wall trained
Taxus baccata 'Fastigiata' (Irish yew)
Ilex aquifolium 'Silver Queen' (holly)
Viburnum tinus 'Eve Price' (laurustinus)
Fuchsia 'Riccartonii' - standard
Malus 'Gala' – espalier/ cordon
Quercus ilex (holm oak)
Myrtus communis subsp. tarentina (Tarentin myrtle)
Ilex crenata 'Convexa' (holly)
Fagus sylvatica 'Riversii' (beech)
Chamaecyparis lawsoniana 'Green Hedger' (Lawson cypress)
Cupressus macrocarpa 'Goldcrest' (cypress)
Prunus cerasus 'Morello' (cherry) – fan/ espalier

Hedging plants

Acca sellowiana (pineapple guava)
Aucuba japonica 'Variegata' (spotted laurel)
Euonymus alatus (winged spindle)
Ribes sanguineum 'Pulborough Scarlet' (flowering current)
Tamarix tetantra
Acer campestre (field maple)
Fuschia magellanica
Euonymus japonicus (Japanese spindle)
Osmanthus delavayi
Olearia macrodonta
Escallonia 'Apple Blossom'
Prunus laurocerasus 'Otto Lukyen'
Leptospermum scoparium (New Zealand tea tree)
Forsythia x intermedia
Abelia 'Edward Goucher'

Plants to attract/for wildlife

Buddleja davidii 'Royal Red' (butterfly bush)
Malus 'John Downie' (crab apple)
Crataegus laevigata 'Paul's Scarlet' (hawthorn)
Sorbus reducta (rowan)
Allium 'Globemaster'
Viburnum opulus (guelder rose)
Daphne mezereum
Thymus vulgaris
Rubus cockburnianus
Syringa pubescens subsp. microphylla (lilac)
Leycesteria formosa (Himalayan honeysuckle)
Sambucus nigra 'Black Beauty'
Pyracantha 'Golden Charmer' (firethorn)
Escallonia 'Donard Seedling'
Lavandula 'Kew Red' (lavender)

Easy annuals and biennials

Angelica gigas
Dianthus barbatus
Papaver somniferum (opium poppy)
Consolida ajacis (larkspur)
Agrostemma githago 'Milas' (corn cockle)
Ipomoea tricolor
Cerinthe major 'Purpurascens'
Nigella damascena 'Persian Jewels' (love-in-a-mist)
Lathyrus odoratus (sweet pea)
Eschscholzia californica (Californian poppy)
Iberis amara (candytuft)
Gypsophila elegans
Briza maxima
Centaurea cyanus (cornflower)
Myosotis alpestris (forget-me-not)

'Show-stopping' annuals and biennials

Amaranthus caudatus (love-lies-bleeding)
Ricinus communis
Cleome hassleriana (spider flower)
Digitalis purpurea (foxglove)
Alcea rosea (hollyhock)
Malope trifida
Helianthus annuus (sunflower)
Lunaria annua 'Variegata' (variegated honesty)
Salvia sclarea var. turkestanica (clary)
Verbascum bombyciferum
Zea mays 'Japonica Multicolour'
Echium pininana
Phaseolus coccineus 'Desiree' (runner bean)
Tropaeolum majus (nasturtium)
Eryngium giganteum 'Silver Ghost' (Miss Wilmott's Ghost)

Herbs

Mentha (mint)
Petroselinum crispum (parsley)
Salvia officinalis (sage)
Rosmarinus officinalis (rosemary)
Thymus vulgaris (thyme)
Allium schoenoprsaum (chives)
Melissa officinalis (lemon balm)
Thymus x citriodorus (lemon thyme)
Anethum graveolens (dill)
Laurus nobilis (sweet bay)
Origanum marjorana (sweet marjoram)
Melissa officinalis (lemon balm)
Helichrysum italicum (curry plant)
Ocimum minimum (dwarf Greek basil)
Tropaeolum majus (Nasturtium)

Easy edibles

Redcurrant 'Versailles Blanche'
Tomato 'Gardeners' Delight'
Ficus 'Brown Turkey' (fig)
Eruca vesicaria subsp. sativa (rocket)
Carrot 'Fly Away F1'
Spinach 'Bloomsdale'
Lettuce 'All year Round'
Rhubarb 'Valentine'
Radish 'Cherry Belle'
Mespilus germanica 'Nottingham' (medlar)
Cydonia oblonga (quince)
Blackcurrant 'Ben Lomond'
Gooseberry 'London'
Cherry 'Stella'
Runner bean 'Red Rum'

Architectural edibles

Cynara cardunculus (cardoon)
Chives (Allium schoenoprsuam)
Foeniculum vulgare 'Zefa Fino' (Fennel)
Helianthus tuberosus 'Boston Red' (Jerusalem artichoke)
Zea mays 'Silver Queen' (super-sweet corn)
Cynara cardunculusus 'Purple Globe' (globe artichoke)
Pyrus communis 'Beurré Hardy' - espalier
Cucurbita maxima 'Buttercup' (pumpkin)
Solanum tuberosum 'Wilja' (potato)
Phaseolus vulgaris 'Romano' (French bean)
Passiflora edulis 'Crackerjack' (passion flower
Actinidia deliciosa 'Jenny' (kiwi fruit)
Prunus dulcis (almond)
Arbutus unedo (strawberry tree)
Corylus avellana 'Cosford Cob' (filbert)

Climbers/walls shrubs for North walls

Hydrangea anomala subsp. petiolaris (climbing hydrangea)
Clematis 'Elizabeth'
Lapageria rosea (Chilean bellflower)
Camellia x williamsii 'Donation'
Chaenomeles speciosa 'Moerloosei' (flowering quince)
Crinodendron hookerianum
Drimys winteri (winterbark)
Garrya elliptica 'Evie' (silk tassel bush)
Hedera colchica 'Sulphur Heart' (Persian ivy)
Berberidopsis corallina (coral plant)
Hedera helix (English ivy)
Jasminum nudiflorum (winter jasmine)
Ribes laurifolium
Parthenocissus tricuspidata (Boston ivy)
Euonymus fortunei 'Silver Queen'

Climbers/wall shrubs for South walls

Solanum crispum 'Glasnevin' (potato vine)
Abutilon 'Kentish Belle'
Chimonanthus praecox 'Luteus' (wintersweet)
Clianthus puniceus 'Albus'
Fremontodendron 'California Glory'
Actinidia kolomikta
Itea ilicifolia (sweetspire)
Ceanothus 'Puget Blue' (Californian lilac)
Callistemon pallidus (bottlebrush)
Cytisus battandieri (pineapple broom)
Passiflora caerulea 'Constance Elliott' (passion flower)
Rosa 'Climbing Ena Harkness'
Jasminum officinale 'Argenteovariegatum'
Trachelospermum jasminoides (star jasmine)
Vitis vinifera 'Purpurea' (grape vine)

Climbers/wall shrubs for East walls

Vitis coignetiae
Clematis montana 'Pink Perfection'
Tropaeolum speciosum
Eucryphia milliganii
Jasminum humile
Humulus lupulus 'Aureus' (golden hop)
Rosa 'Danse du Feu'
Pileostegia viburnoides
Rosa 'Zéphirine Drouhin'
Akebia quinata (chocolate vine)
Clematis 'Nelly Moser'
Rosa 'Climbing Iceberg'
Hydrangea anomala subsp. petiolaris
Lonicera japonica 'Halliana' (Japanese honeysuckle)
Schizophragma integrifolium

Climbers/wall shrubs for West walls

Clematis armandii 'Snowdrift'
Cydonia oblonga (quince)
Lonicera fragrantissima (winter flowering honeysuckle)
Clematis 'Etoile Violette'
Eccremocarpus scaber (Chilean glory flower)
Lathyrus odoratus 'Annabelle' (sweet pea)
Clematis 'Niobe'
Clematis 'Bill MacKenzie'
Jasminum officinale (jasmine)
Wisteria sinensis (Chinese wisteria)
Rhodochiton atrosanguineus (purple bell vine)
Rosa 'Constance Spry'
Ipomoea 'Heavenly Blue' (morning glory)
Solanum laxum 'Album' (potato vine)
Rosa banksiae 'Lutea'

Architectural perennials and shrubs

Agave americana 'Variegata'
Fargesia murelae (bamboo)
Phormium 'Sundowner' (New Zealand flax)
Paulownia tomentosa (foxglove tree)
Euphorbia characias subsp. wulfenii (spurge)
Phyllostachys aureosulcata (bamboo)
Trachycarpus fortunei (chusan palm)
Corylus avellana 'Contorta' (twisted hazel)
Fatsia japonica 'Variegata'
Aralia elata (Japanese angelica)
Lupinus arboreus (tree lupin)
Cordyline australis (cabbage palm)
Sambucus racemosa 'Sutherland Gold' (golden elderberry)
Juniperus scopulorum 'Skyrocket'
Cornus controversa 'Variegata' (wedding cake tree)

Plants for containers

Agapanthus 'Snowy Owl' (African lily)
Buxus sempervirens (box)
Imperata cylindrica 'Rubra' (blood grass)
Tradescantia pallida 'Purple Heart'
Aeonium 'Zwartkop'
Lavandula stoechas (French lavender)
Calopsis paniculata
Allium 'Purple Sensation'
Cordyline australis 'Atropurpurea' (cabbage palm)
Hosta 'Wide Brim' (plantain lily)
Canna 'Wyoming' (Indian shot)
Tulipa 'Queen of Night' (tulip)
Dahlia 'Roxy'
Carex buchananii (sedge)
Convolvulus cneorum

Plants for window boxes, hanging baskets, etc.

Hedera helix 'Oro di Bogliasco' (ivy)
Narcissus 'Tête à Tête' (jonquil)
Iris reticulata
Helichrysum petiolare
Pelargonium 'Bushfire' (geranium)
Solenostemon 'Black Prince'
Osteospermum 'Whirlygig'
Silene uniflora 'Swan Lake'
Celosia argentea Kimono Series
Nicotiana x sanderae Havana Series
Lobelia erinus Fountain Series
Isotoma axillaris
Lagurus ovatus
Fuchsia 'Annabel'
Scaevola aemula 'Blue Wonder'

Indoor herbs & edibles

Watercress
Mustard cress
Navel Orange 'Washington'
Lemon 'Gareys Eureka'
Basil
Mint
Cucumber 'Fembaby'
Tomato 'Tumbler'
Wheat grass
Root ginger
Chilli pepper 'Jalapeno'
Mung beans
Basil
Cut-and-come-again salads 'Saladisi'
Coriander

Easy houseplants

Chamaedorea elegans (Parlour palm)
Sansevieria trifasciata var. laurentii (mother-in-law's tongue)
Yucca elephantipes
Echeveria 'Perle von Nurnberg'
Ficus benjamina (weeping fig)
Aspidistra elatior (cast iron plant)
Veitchia merrillii (adonidia palm)
Aloe vera
Anthurium scherzerianum 'Blondo'
Spathiphyllum 'Mauna Loa' (peace lily)
Zamioculcas zamiifolia (devils root)
Tradescantia pallida 'Purple Heart'
Ficus pumila (creeping fig)
Philodendron scandens (sweetheart plant)
Cissus rhombifolia (grape ivy)

Huge houseplants

Adonidia merrillir (Christmas palm)
Hyophorbe verschaffeltii (Spindle palm)
Ficus 'Audrey' (fig)
Schefflera actinophylla (umbrella tree)
Cocos nucifera (coconut palm)
Araucaria heterophylla (Norfolk Island palm)
Schefflera arboricola (umbrella plant)
Strelitzia reginae (bird of paradise)
Howea forsteriana (kentia palm)
Ficus barteri (narrow-leaved fig)
Beaucarnea recurvata (pony tail palm)
Schefflera elegantissima (false aralia)
Jacaranda mimosifolia
Cyperus alternifolius (umbrella plant)
Aeonium arboreum 'Schwarzkopf'

Houseplants for lots of indirect light/a warm windowsill

Hibiscus rosa-sinensis
Pachystachys lutea
Aeschynanthus speciosus
Campanula isophylla (Italian bell flower)
Clivia miniata
Cyclamen
Schefflera elegantissima (false aralia)
Eucharis amazonica
Medinilla magnifica
Jacaranda mimosifolia

Houseplants for warm, brightly lit areas with some direct sun

Gerbera jamesonii
Gloriosa superba (glory lily)
Cryptanthus acaulis (Green earth star)
Heliconia illustris 'Aureostriata'
Jasminum officinale
Codiaeum variegatum var. pictum (croton)
Ceropegia linearis subsp. woodii (rosary vine)
Nertera granadensis (bead plant)
Zamioculcas zamiifolia (devils root)
Saxifraga stolonifera (mother of thousands)

Houseplants for good humidity

Adiantum raddianum (maidenhair fern)
Maranta (prayer plant)
Cyrtomium falcatum 'Rochfordianum' (holly fern)
Soleirolia soleirolii (mind-your-own-business)
Lantana camara
Manettia luteorubra
Pteris cretica (table fern)
Cyperus alternifolius (umbrella plant)
Asplenium nidus (birds nest fern)
Nephrolepis exaltata 'Bostoniensis' (Boston fern)

Houseplants that like it hot and dry

Cacti
Agave americana
Aeonium arboreum 'Schwarzkopf'
Haworthia margaritifera (pearl plant)
Kalanchoe blossfeldiana
Echeveria secunda var. glauca
Crassula ovata (money tree)
Aloe vera
Sempervivum (houseleek)
Ceropegia linearis woodii (rosary vine)

Houseplants for shady rooms

Chamaedorea elegans (parlour palm)
Philodendron scandens
Spathiphyllum wallisii (peace lily)
Dracaena marginata
Dypsis lutescens
Howea forsteriana
Sansevieria hahnii (mother-in-laws-tongue)
Tolmiea menziesii (piggyback plant)
Syngonium podophyllum (goosefoot plant)
Cissus rhombifolia (grape ivy)

Scented houseplants

Hoya lanceolata bella (wax plant)
Exacum affine (Persian violet)
Gardenia jasminoides
Jasminum polyanthum (jasmine)
Pelargonium (scented geranium)
Heliotropium arborescens
Citrus x meyeri 'Meyer' (Meyer's lemon)
Spathiphyllum 'Mauna Loa' (peace lily)
Brunfelsia pauciflora
x Citrofortunella microcarpa (Calomondin orange)

Houseplants you can't kill!

Spathiphyllum wallisii (peace lily)
Ficus benjamina (Weeping fig)
Pilea cadierei (aluminium plant)
Sansevieria trifasciata (mother-in-law's tongue)
Schefflera arboricola (umbrella plant)
Yucca elephantipes
Aspidistra (cast iron plant)
Dracaena marginata (dragon tree)
Kalanchoe blossfeldiana (flaming Katy)
Tradescantia pallida 'Purpurea' (purple heart)

Conservatory plants

Bougainvillea glabra (paper flower)
Alocasia sanderiana (Kris plant)
Musa acuminata 'Dwarf Cavendish' (banana)
Aristolochia gigantea (Dutchman's pipe)
Brugmansia candida (angel's trumpet)
Stephanotis floribunda (Madagascar Jasmine)
Nerium oleander (oleander)
Ixora coccinea (jungle flame)
Gloriosa superba (glory lily)
Cuphea ignea (cigar plant)

Index

Acknowledgements

This book is the result of some long hours and sleepless nights by a great many people. Mucho thanks.

Special thanks to: Helena Caldon for her tireless hard graft. All at Transworld Publishers, especially Sarah Emsley, Doug Young and Philip Lord. Emily Hedges and everyone at Smith & Gilmour. Ali Gunn and Jacquie Drewe at Curtis Brown – thanks for helping to keep me sane. Channel 4 and TwoFour for *The City Gardener*. My family, especially Rachel King for her relentless support. And Ellie.

The publishers would like to thank:
Capel Manor, Bullsmoor Lane, Enfield, Middlesex, EN1 4RQ
Clifton Nurseries, 5a Clifton Villas, Little Venice, London W9 2PH
Fulham Palace Road Garden Centre, Bishops Avenue, London, SW6
Petersham Nurseries, Church Lane, Petersham, Surrey TW10 7AG
Planet Pots, Robin Wood Farm, Kingston Vale, London, SW15 3FQ
for allowing us to take photographs at their fantastic locations.

The publishers would like to thank the following sources for permission to reproduce their photographs in this book:

Page 1–14 Noel Murphy; 16 Andrew Lawson; 18 GPL/Pernilla Bergdahl; 19 Marianne Majerus; 20 Noel Murphy; 22 GPL/Friederich Strauss; 23 Noel Murphy; 25 GPL/Clive Boursenell; 26 Marianne Majerus/Alain Provost; 27 GPL/Juliette Wade; 28–2CG endmatter9 Noel Murphy; 31 Marianne Majerus; 32 GPL/Suzie Gibbons; 33 Matt James; 35 Noel Murphy; 36 Marianne Majerus/Gardens and Beyond; 38 Noel Murphy; 41 Clive Nichols/Trevyn McDowell; 42 Jonathan Buckley/James Fraser; 43 Clive Nichols/Amir Schlezinger/My Landscapes; 45 GPL/Steven Wooster; 46 Jonathan Buckley/Diarmuid Gavin; 49 Marianne Majerus/Simon Steele; 50–51 Noel Murphy; 53 GPL/Clive Nichols; 55 Noel Murphy; 56 Clive Nichols/Stephen Woodhams; 58–59 Noel Murphy; 61 Marianne Majerus/Paul Gazerwitz; 62 Jonathan Buckley; 65 GPL/Suzie Gibbons; 66–69 Noel Murphy; 73 Clive Nichols/Wynniat-Husey Clarke; 74–79 Noel Murphy; 80–81 Tim Sandall/The Garden; 83–84 Noel Murphy; 85 Marianne Majerus/Stephen Hall; 86–87 Noel Murphy; 88 GPL/Juliette Wade; 90–91 Noel Murphy; 93 GPL/Marianne Majerus; 94 Clive Nichols/Cartier, Chelsea '98; 96 Marianne Majerus; 97 Jonathan Buckley/James Fraser; 98 Jonathan Buckley; 100 Garden Exposures/Andrea Jones/Dan Curtis; 102 GPL/Howard Rice; 103 Marianne Majerus/Jinny Blom; 104–10 Noel Murphy; 106 Clive Nichols/Lisette Pleasance; 107 Marianne Majerus; 108 GPL/Linda Burgess; 109 Clive Nichols/Jonathan Bailie; 110 Marianne Majerus/Henrietta Courtauld; 111 Noel Murphy; 113 Matt James; 114 Clive Nichols; 116 GPL/Ron Sutherland; 118–119 Noel Murphy; 120 Garden Exposures/Andrea Jones/Joe Swift; 121 GPL/Jacqui Hurst; 122 Marianne Majerus/Susanne Blair; 124 Garden Exposures/Andrea Jones/Jason Payne; 125 Clive Nichols/Charlotte Sanderson; 126 Noel Murphy; 128 GPL/Steven Wooster; 130–131 Noel Murphy; 132 Garden Exposures/Andrea Jones; 133–135 Noel Murphy; 136 Clive Nichols/Alison Weir Associates; 137 GPL/Ron Sutherland/Ann Mollo; 139 Clive Nichols/Sarah Leyton; 140 Jonathan Buckley/Penny Smith; 142 GPL/Ron Sutherland; 143 GPL/John Glover; 144 GPL/Brigitte Thomas; 146–147 Noel Murphy; 148 Marianne Majerus/Declan Buckley; 150 Noel Murphy; 152 Matt James; 155–158 Noel Murphy; 161 GPL; 162 Clive Nichols/Joe Swift; 163 Noel Murphy; 166 Matt James; 167 Marianne Majerus; 169 Matt James; 171 GPL/Steven Wooster; 173 Garden Exposures/Andrea Jones/Dale Loth; 174 Clive Nichols/Lisette Pleasance; 175 Garden Exposures/Andrea Jones/Dale Loth; 177 Clive Nichols/Robin Green & Ralph Cade; 178–183 Noel Murphy; 184 GPL/Nigel Francis; 187 left Marianne Majerus/Michele Osborne; 187 right GPL/Geoff Dann; 188 Noel Murphy; 189 Garden Exposures/Andrea Jones; 190–191 Noel Murphy; 192 Clive Nichols//Trevyn McDowell; 193 Clive Nichols/Wyniatt-Husey Clarke; 194 Marianne Majerus/Declan Buckley; 195 Marianne Majerus/Paul Gazerwitz; 197 GPL/John Glover; 198 Noel Murphy; 199 Garden Exposures/Andrea Jones/Graham West; 200 Marianne Majerus/Stephen Crisp; 202–204 Noel Murphy; 205 Marianne Majerus/Jill Billington; 207 Noel Murphy; 208 GPL/Juliette Wade; 209 GPL/Leigh Clapp; 211 GPL/Gary Rogers; 212 Garden Exposures/Andrea Jones, 215–218 Noel Murphy; 223 Clive Nichols/Joe Swift; 225 Marianne Majerus/Peter Aldington; 227–236 Noel Murphy; 238 GPL/John Glover; 241–247 Noel Murphy; 248GPL/John Glover; 249–252 Noel Murphy; 254 Jonathan Buckley/Anthony Goff; 255 GPL/Marie O'Hara; 257 GPL/Friedrich Strauss; 258 Noel Murphy; 259 Marianne Majerus/Susanne Blair; 262–265 Noel Murphy; 266 GPL/Clive Nichols; 268 GPL/Gary Rogers; 269 Clive Nichols/Sir Terence Conran; 270 GPL/Mark Bolton; 271 GPL/Howard Rice; 273 GPL/Ron Sutherland; 274 Noel Murphy; 275 Clive Nichols/Anthony Joel; 276 GPL/Suzie Gibbons; 277 Garden Exposures/Andrea Jones/Joe Swift; 278–279 Noel Murphy; 280 Clive Nichols/Alison Weir Associates; 286–312 Noel Murphy.

GPL = Garden Picture Library